PRAISE FOR *SYSTEMS THINKING FOR BUSINESS AND MANAGEMENT*

'A tour de force which manages to explain the theory in simple terms while remaining rooted in the practice. An ideal introduction to our modern world of systems'
Sir Iain Vallance, former CEO and Chairman of British Telecom

'Ideal for students learning about and using systems thinking. It is well-written, easy to understand and provides a solid foundation for those interested in modelling systems. Providing a comprehensive overview of systems thinking, this textbook includes discussions of basic concepts, methods and models, as well as applications of systems thinking in various industrial business case studies and future systems thinking.'
Joniarto Parung, Professor of Supply Chain Management and Rector, University of Surabaya, Indonesia

'Invaluable for both practitioners and students of business and operations. There is no other book that covers these topics in such a useful way.'
Kathryn E Stecke, Professor of Operations Management, University of Texas, USA

'The authors' ability to apply systems thinking to practical problems is an indispensable resource for students and for those of us managing a business in today's complex, interconnected and volatile world.'
Gilad Tiefenbrun, CEO, Linn products

Systems Thinking for Business and Management

Principles and practice

Umit S Bititci
Agnessa Spanellis

KoganPage

First published in Great Britain and the United States in 2024 by Kogan Page Limited

2nd Floor, 45 Gee Street
London
EC1V 3RS
United Kingdom

8 W 38th Street, Suite 902
New York, NY 10018
USA

4737/23 Ansari Road
Daryaganj
New Delhi 110002
India

www.koganpage.com

Kogan Page books are printed on paper from sustainable forests.

ISBNs
Hardback 978 1 3986 1168 9
Paperback 978 1 3986 1166 5
Ebook 978 1 3986 1167 2

British Library Cataloguing-in-Publication Data
A CIP record for this book is available from the British Library.

Library of Congress Control Number
2023944541

Typeset by Integra Software Services, Pondicherry
Print production managed by Jellyfish

Printed and bound by Henry Ling Limited at the Dorset Press, Dorchester DT1 1HD

CONTENTS

Introduction 1

Everything in this world, and indeed the universe, is connected to something else and is part of something bigger. Our actions have wide consequences that affect people, organizations and society around us. These consequences may be negligible or significant; they may be immediate or several years down the line. Have you ever made a decision or done something expecting one outcome, but the result was quite different and quite unexpected? Most of us have had this experience. It might have happened in the school playground, in a sports team, on a social network with family and friends, or at work. In fact, the world's history is full of examples of unintended consequences. Two such examples include:

- In Borneo in the 1950s, to eliminate the problem of malaria, the World Health Organization recommended spraying DDT pesticide to kill the carrier mosquitos; it had two unrelated consequences. First, DDT also killed a species of wasp that controlled the population of caterpillars. Most roofs of Borneo houses are made of thatch, and with natural pest control gone the roofs started to collapse. Second, DDT affected other insects which were a food source for geckos. Although geckos could tolerate the DDT in their bodies it stayed in their system for long enough to kill the population of cats that ate them. With the cats gone the island's population of rats exploded, resulting in the destruction of grain stores and a dramatic increase in the plague. They ended up parachuting cats back into Borneo to address the problem (O'Shaughnessy, 2008).
- The global financial crisis of 2008 was caused by a downturn in the US housing market and a rising number of borrowers unable to repay their loans, and it spread throughout the world. The underlying cause of the crisis was the confidence that the strong economic growth throughout the preceding years would continue. This, together with increasing competition between lenders and weak or lax regulations for sub-prime lending, resulted in lenders taking excessive risks by giving mortgages to high-risk homeowners and home builders. To be able to lend more, the lenders borrowed more money. The spark that started the crisis was the rising number of lenders not able to repay their loans coinciding with oversupply

of homes, resulting in house prices falling and institutions not being able to meet their short-term loan repayment commitments, thus stressing the US financial systems. With a number of foreign banks participating in the US financial markets, it was inevitable that financial systems and economies of other countries were affected. These financial stresses resulted in the failure of several financial institutions across the globe, starting with Lehman Brothers in the United States (Crotty, 2009)

In both examples we can clearly observe that everything is connected to something else, and it is part of something bigger. Sometimes these connections are obvious, but in most cases, they are not so obvious and only become visible retrospectively after we have observed the implications of actions and decisions. In short, systems thinking offers us a way to see the world, communicate and work together more productively by understanding and managing these interconnections. It enables us to look at the world more holistically, see things we have not seen before, ask better questions before jumping to conclusions, and make better sense of the complexity that surrounds us.

The purpose of this book is to help you, the reader, to understand what systems thinking is, and put this understanding into practical use in your life.

The book will not only introduce you to the theories, principles and methods behind systems thinking, it will also give you insights into the tools and techniques for modelling, analysing, improving and designing complex systems in organizations and beyond. It will help you to conceptualize and better understand complex problems, communicate and investigate potential solutions, and design interventions to address complex organizational issues.

1.1 Origins and development of systems thinking

The origins of systems thinking can be traced as far back as antiquity with some evidence emerging from Sumerian cuneiform, Mayan numerals and engineering of the Egyptian pyramids. However, the origins of systems thinking as a discipline are attributable to Macy conferences that took place between 1942 and 1960 with the purpose of bringing scholars from different disciplines to promote meaningful conversations between scientific disciplines and develop unity in science. One outcome of this series of conferences was the emergence of the science of Cybernetics, i.e. the science of communications and automatic control systems in both machines and living things, which underpinned the development of complex systems and systems thinking as a discipline (Ashby, 1957; Wiener, 2019).

Before that, with the work of scientists such as James Joule[1] and Nicolas Sadi Carnot,[2] the 19th century saw the emergence of systems in the rationalist hard sciences, which in turn led to the development of the **system reference model** (an abstract framework consisting of an interlinked set of clearly defined concepts to encourage clear communication) as a formal scientific object. Fuelled by these ideas and seeing the opportunity in understanding things as a connected whole, similar ideas emerged from scientists in different disciplines, such as biology, psychology, education, management, sociology and anthropology. In 1956, several such scientists came together to form a society for the exploration and development of general systems theory, which was subsequently renamed The International Society for Systems Science in 1988 and continues working to this date (see www.isss.org).

These developments resulted in Bertalanffy's[3] general system theory (Bertalanffy, 1968). However, in the literature there is a debate around how Alexander Bogdanov's earlier works on Tectology, a new science unifying all social, biological and physical sciences by considering them as systems of relationships and by seeking the organizational principles that underlie all systems, may have provided the conceptual base for Bertalanffy's general systems theory (Zelený, 1988; Jackson, 2022).

The ideas behind General Systems Theory and preceding works were adopted by others, to study concepts such as chaos, complexity, self-organization, connectionism[4] and adaptive systems. In fields like cybernetics, researchers examined complex systems discovering self-managing and self-reproducing systems (discussed later in the book). In addition, the 20th century saw the development of systems thinking and systems theory in sociology, leading to the development of action theory (Parsons, 1937) and social systems theory (Luhmann, 1995).

In this book we will refrain from delving deeply into these works. We will, however, borrow from them, focusing on those we think are more useful to help you develop a working understanding of systems thinking and its application in business and management.

1.2 Background to the book

We both discovered systems thinking early in our careers whilst undertaking our master's degrees: 1983 in Umit's case and 2011 in Agnessa's case. We both found that it helped us immensely in our work, our social network and our relationships with family, friends and colleagues.

Umit is an engineer who designed products and then the manufacturing systems to make these products, before moving on to developing advanced manufacturing systems, manufacturing consultancy and then to academia where he specializes in understanding how companies measure and manage performance and what makes high-performing organizations different. His earlier engineering and management consultancy experience enabled him to practise systems thinking and observe the consequences of not thinking in systems. His academic work on performance measurement and management is grounded in systems thinking and more specifically in cybernetics and organizational control systems. In this context he sees organizations, supply chains and wider value-creating networks as complex systems that can be understood and improved through systems thinking.

Agnessa is an engineer who worked on the intersection of operations management, logistics and supply chain management as well as marketing and sales of fast-moving consumer products in a large multinational enterprise. From her experience she could see how different functions come with different perspectives and have different goals in a wider system, and how many problems and disruptions were often the result of a certain function not understanding the processes and goals of another function. In other words, they lacked a systemic view of how the organization operated. She then moved to academia and initially became interested in how knowledge flows through organizations through interpersonal relations. She then developed an interest in gamification and observed how introducing simple game elements in organizational processes can have a profound impact on how people interact with each other, enabling learning, knowledge sharing and, ultimately, improving organizational performance. Systems thinking underpins the design of interventions in her research, with systems thinking principles and methods applied throughout the design process. Many examples included in this book are based on this work.

Umit develop the first master's-level course on Systems Thinking and Analysis in 2008 whilst he was at the University of Strathclyde, which was taken by a wide range of students with backgrounds in engineering, business, social sciences, arts and humanities. In all cases he received feedback suggesting that this was one of the most eye-opening courses and that it should be mandatory for students from all disciplines, be it undergraduate, postgraduate or post-experience level. One student even commented that the course made her realize why her relationships with her family, particularly with her sister, were tenuous at best, and helped her improve these relationships. When

Umit moved to Edinburgh Business School, he further developed the course, bringing forward the lessons from his previous experiences, and launched a new course in 2014. Since then, this course has been further developed in collaboration with Agnessa, resulting in the structure we have today.

Throughout this period, we have tried to find a book that covers systems thinking in the way we have been covering it in these courses. Whereas there are a number of books on the subject, we found that they either cover only parts of what we cover in this book or they are written from one particular perspective and do not effectively bring together different ways of thinking about systems, or they are too technical and difficult for a non-specialist to follow. Thus, our purpose in writing this book is to bring this knowledge to a non-specialist reader in an accessible way to encourage more managers in business and the public sector to think in systems. Of course, we also envisage that this book will provide the basis for postgraduate and post-experience courses aimed at people working and studying business and management.

1.3 Motivation and principals

We live in an increasingly uncertain, volatile and interconnected modern world facing wicked problems, as summarized in Figure 1.1. While living, playing and working in these challenging times we make decisions about our lives, our families and our organizations almost on a daily basis. Understanding this complex world and facing such challenges requires a new way of thinking; we need to think in systems, rather than look at problems in isolation. For example, instead of focusing on the downside of Big Tech and seeing it as a problem, we should be looking at this as a whole system and ask questions such as *how do we enjoy the upsides of Big Tech whilst controlling the downsides?*

Having personally experienced the benefits of systems thinking in our personal lives and in our professional work in business, management and education, we strongly feel that we need to encourage more people, particularly more managers, organizations and businesses to think in systems.

The advantage of looking at organizations, people and societies as a system is that one can begin to understand and predict their emergent behaviour under given conditions. Without systems thinking and accompanying tools and techniques, it would be almost impossible to predict the behaviour of complex systems, particularly human activity systems such as organizations.

Figure 1.1 Challenges of the world we live in

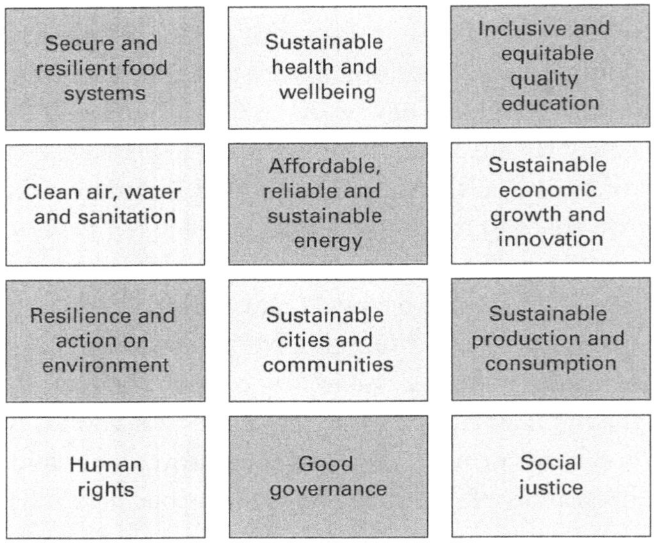

Systems thinking can enhance the problem analysis and solution capability of people from all walks of life, whatever level of seniority they work and live in. It is a life skill that is important for working and living.

The main principle behind this book is to make the subject accessible to people from a broad range of backgrounds by using simple language and developing the subject in layers, from underlying concepts and their definitions to models and frameworks that provide different perspectives on systems, giving practical insights into different techniques for modelling, analysing and improving systems with different characteristics.

1.4 Who is this book for?

Primarily the book is aimed at practising managers and students of business and management. However, as we believe systems thinking is a life skill, this book will speak to everyone with an interest in making the world a better place for themselves, their families, colleagues and society.

A manager's ultimate responsibility is to manage their part of an organization. If you are a chief executive of a multinational, you are responsible for effective management of the whole organization. If you are a manager of a function or a team leader you are responsible for effective management of your part of the organization, while contributing to the goals of the wider organization. Even if you are an individual with no management responsibility, you are still responsible for doing your bit and making a contribution to the overall goals of the organization where you belong. In this context, it does not matter what your organization is. It could be anything – a large multinational, a small enterprise, a large public sector organization, a small charity or even a one-person micro-enterprise, a sports or art club – you and your organization exist as part of an interconnected system, and thinking in systems will help you and your organization to better understand your position in the wider system and why the organization and the wider system behave the way they do.

In management education we all too often focus on disciplines of management, such as strategic management, financial management, human resource management, operations management and so on, and leave the individuals to work out for themselves how to knit these bits together to effectively manage the organization. But we rarely teach people how to see themselves, their organizations and the world as a connected whole. We believe what is in this book will help you to knit some of these bits together towards forming a better understanding of how your organization and its wider environment work and what you may be able to do to improve things.

1.5 How to get the best out of this book

The book is designed to start by introducing the basic concepts that underpin systems thinking in the first part. It also introduces different perspectives to help you think in systems before discussing the tools and techniques that will enable you to model, understand and improve systems. For this reason, we would recommend that you read the book from the beginning.

However, if you are already familiar with basic principles of systems thinking and interested in particular aspects, such as different models and perspectives or different ways of modelling, analysing and improving systems, then you can go straight to the relevant chapter or even the relevant section of each chapter. Be mindful that if you are going to adopt this approach, as the book develops from Chapter 2 onwards it introduces the concepts and their definitions that we use in later chapters. With systems thinking being a diverse and rather fragmented field, during our journey we have come across different terminologies describing the same things, and we have also seen the same terminology describing different things. To help sort out this confusion, we have introduced formal definitions for the concepts we use throughout the book, which are collected in the Glossary.

To support you in the systems thinking journey, at the end of each chapter we have included some reflective questions and exercises. The more time you take in reflecting on these questions and working through these exercises, the deeper your understanding of the subject will develop. In fact, systems thinking is a skill just like riding a bicycle. You cannot learn systems thinking just by reading a book; you need to practise, make a few mistakes and learn to think in systems. However, once you have learnt to think in systems you will always think in systems, and life will be better for it.

1.6 Structure of the book

The book is divided into four parts, comprising 11 chapters. In the current chapter we have given you an overview of what this book is about, the origins and development of systems thinking, who the book is for and how to get the best out of it.

The first part of the book (Part One) focuses on the fundamentals of systems thinking. In Chapter 2 we develop the concept of 'a system' and answer the question 'What is a system?' as well as introduce some core concepts. We finish this chapter by discussing the value of systems thinking, and provide systems thinking examples. In Chapter 3 we develop a deeper understanding of systems and systems thinking by introducing and defining more advanced concepts.

Part Two focuses on models and methods. In Chapter 4 we explore some of the common systems models and frameworks. This is not an exhaustive list of all systems models and frameworks. Indeed, there are too many and the field can get confusing. In this chapter we have focused on systems thinking models and frameworks that provide different perspectives and those we have found useful in our work. In Chapters 5 and 6 we cover two different approaches to systems thinking and modelling. In Chapter 5 we introduce hard systems thinking as an approach to thinking in systems and alternative methods for modelling hard systems; in Chapter 6 we introduce soft systems thinking and a set of complementary methods that enable us to understand, model, analyse and improve complex systems. One of the techniques we introduce in Chapter 6 for modelling soft systems is causal loop diagrams, which we further develop in Chapter 7 to demonstrate how they may be used in an inclusive way for open strategizing and group decision making.

In Part Three we explore systems complexity in greater detail. In Chapter 8 we use the En-ROADS climate simulator as the backbone to introducing systems dynamics as a method for modelling and understanding complex systems. It focuses on highlighting the behavioural dynamics within a system, including unintended consequences of decisions and interventions. In the penultimate section, using the knowledge from previous sections, you are guided to use the En-ROADS simulator to understand the climate change problem and develop your own solution. In Chapter 9 we explore the ever-changing nature of complex systems by exploring the levers or leverage points in complex systems that can influence and change the behaviour of the entire system. We introduce different types of levers, specifically structural levers, temporal levers, conceptual levers and boundary levers, and give examples of how they can be used in practice.

The final part of the book, Part Four, looks into the future and considers systems that do not yet exist. In Chapter 10 we start with discussing creativity and innovation and barriers to thinking about the future creatively and innovatively. We then discuss why thinking about alternative futures is more useful than trying to predict the future, and guide you through various aspects of trying to imagine systems that do not yet exist, specifically by identifying signals and drivers, and then creating different alternative scenarios of a future system. In this chapter we also discuss how ideas about future systems can be elicited using roleplay or alternate reality games.

In the final chapter we summarize the four parts of the book and the key lessons and takeaways you should have gained from this book.

Notes

1 James Prescott Joule (1818–1889) was an English physicist and mathematician who developed the first law of thermodynamics on the conservation of energy. The unit of energy, the *joule*, is named after him.

2 Nicolas Léonard Sadi Carnot (1796–1832) was a French mechanical engineer, often described as the 'father of thermodynamics'. He established the second law of thermodynamics and defined the concept of entropy.

3 Karl Ludwig von Bertalanffy (1901–1972) was an Austrian biologist known as one of the founders of general systems theory (GST).

4 An approach in the field of cognitive science that tries to explain mental phenomena using artificial neural networks.

References

Ashby, WR (1957) *An Introduction to Cybernetics*, Chapman and Hall

Bertalanffy LV (1968) *General System Theory: Foundations, development, applications*, G. Braziller

Crotty, J (2009) Structural causes of the global financial crisis: a critical assessment of the 'new financial architecture', *Cambridge Journal of Economics*, **33** (4), pp 563–80

Jackson, MC (2022) Alexander Bogdanov, Stafford Beer and intimations of a post-capitalist future, *Systems Research and Behavioral Science,* **40** (2)

Luhmann N (1995) *Social Systems*, Stanford University Press

O'Shaughnessy, PT (2008) Parachuting cats and crushed eggs the controversy over the use of DDT to control malaria, *American Journal of Public Health*, **98** (11), pp 1940–48

Parsons, T (1937) *The Structure of Social Interaction*, McGraw Hill Book Company, New York and London

Wiener, N (2019) *Cybernetics or Control and Communication in the Animal and the Machine*, MIT press.

Zelený, M (1988) Tectology, *International Journal of General System*, **14** (4), pp 331–42

PART ONE
Fundamentals of systems thinking

In this part of the book, which consists of Chapters 2 and 3, we focus on developing the fundamental concepts and definitions that underpin systems thinking. In Chapter 2 we develop the concept of 'a system' and answer the question 'What is a system?' as well as introduce some of the core concepts. We finish this chapter by discussing the value of systems thinking and providing systems thinking examples. In Chapter 3 we develop a deeper understanding of systems and systems thinking by introducing systems components and their definitions. Throughout the rest of the book, we use these concepts and definitions to explore the theory and practice of systems thinking.

Introduction to systems 2

The objective of this chapter is to introduce the reader to what a system is, its core definitions and the value of systems thinking, and to provide some examples of how systems thinking could facilitate problem solving and innovation through real-life practical examples.

LEARNING OUTCOMES

- Understand what a system is
- Understand the core concepts of systems thinking, including:
  - open and closed systems
  - hard and soft systems
  - worldviews
  - complexity
  - emergence
  - self-organizing systems and organizational models
  - different kinds of systems problems
  - value of systems thinking
- Understand how to think and talk about organizations using core systems concepts

2.1 What is a system?

All of us have come across the term *system* at some point in our lives and this term might create different associations for different people depending on their cultural and professional background. For instance, if you work in a manufacturing company, you might think about a system as a production system or a supply chain system. The company itself is a system, comprising a group of people united by a common business goal. If you went to study abroad, you might start thinking about the educational system in your home country and how it compares with that of the host country, and this will be a very different type of system. While living in a new country, you might also pay closer attention to the cultural or political system of that country without necessarily realizing that these are also types of systems. What is a system then?

> A system is a collection of interacting parts/components/actors, in which the interactions result in system-level properties and behaviours not attributable to the sum of individual parts.

This idea is not new – it comes from ancient Greek philosophy, specifically that the whole is more than the sum of the parts. A car, a school, a city, a factory or a tree are all systems. These systems are very different but they also have something in common, and that is a purpose. For instance, the car serves a purpose – the purpose of the users. The set of behaviours that a system performs is known as a function of the system. You may be wondering if there is anything that is not a system. The answer is yes. A conglomeration without any particular interconnections or any function is not a system. For example, sand scattered by the road is not a system because you can add or take away sand and it will remain the sand by the road, nothing more.

Let us think of four examples: a car, a human, a company and a society. Take a moment to think about what is important about each of these systems. What are the first things that come to your mind?

If you start with the car, perhaps the first thing that comes to your mind is car parts, such as an engine, a battery, tyres, steering wheel, windscreen, etc. But you might also think about travel safety, road rules and regulations, the driver or other aspects of the system in which the car can operate. All these aspects indicate that you already start thinking in systems. Or perhaps you will think about travel, which is the purpose of the car as a system.

If you think about a human, perhaps the first things that comes to your mind will be body parts and internal organs, such as legs, arms, a heart, a brain or kidneys. Perhaps you might also think about systems that comprise the human body, like the respiratory system or immune system. Or perhaps you might consider human qualities, such as attitudes or character, or parts of the surrounding system in which the human exists, for instance a family.

A company is a more complex system than a human, and you will probably immediately consider a lot of aspects, such as products, services, customers, employees, managers, processes, business units, profits, equipment, buildings and so on. Perhaps you will also consider its structure and the aspects that govern the company, such as its strategy, policies, value and culture, or corporate image.

When thinking about a society, you will probably start with people, communities, culture, social norms, laws and regulations. As a system that is even more complex than a company, it will have a lot of aspects with complex relationships connecting them.

Obviously, these systems are very different from each other. However, even the same system can be seen differently by various people because they see different subsystems and have different viewpoints. For example, if several students are asked to draw an image of a university, some might draw a building in which they study. However, if they study online, their learning experience will be very different, and they might draw a laptop or an online environment instead. Figure 2.1 shows images of a university drawn by four different students during the first (the upper row) and the second (the lower row) year of the Covid-19 pandemic. We can see as the students started returning to campus, their image of the university also changed.

Figure 2.1 Images of a university drawn by different students

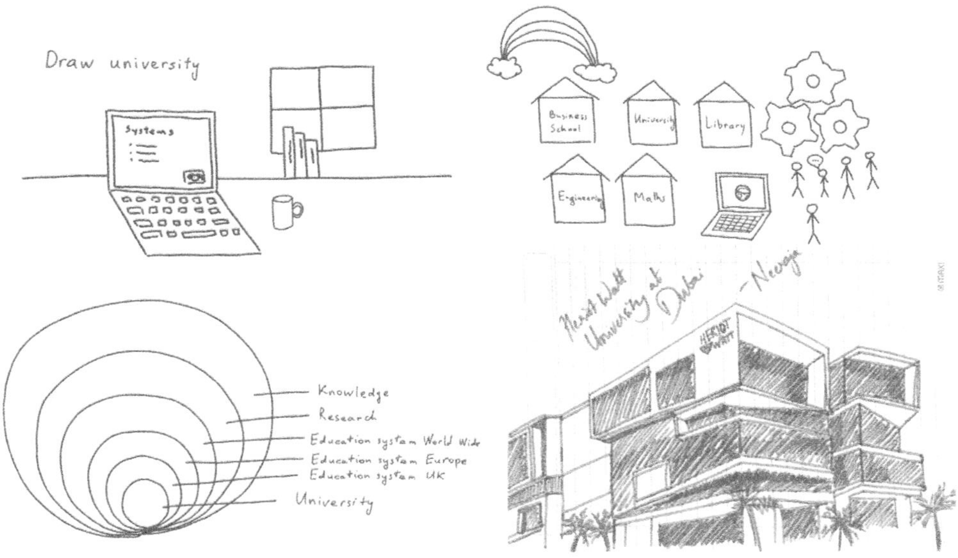

Others might focus on people and draw their peers, teachers and other staff they interact with. From this viewpoint, a university is not so much a physical system, rather it is a system of people exchanging ideas. Others yet might think about a university as consisting of subsystems, such as schools, departments and research institutes, and existing in a wider system, the system of higher education, as well as interacting with other systems, such as industry and government.

Based on the above discussion we offer three different definitions of systems thinking as summarized in Table 2.1, none of which are perfect. Instead, they highlight complementary facets of systems thinking. One of the objectives of systems thinking then might be helping to create a shared image – a shared language and view of the system.

Table 2.1 Definitions of systems thinking

Source	Definition
Checkland (1999: p. 3)	The use of systems ideas in trying to understand the world's complexity.
Randle and Stroink (2018: p. 646)	A cognitive paradigm with which people come to perceive themselves and the world to be dynamic entities that display continually emerging patterns arising from the interactions among many interdependent connecting components.
Monat and Gannon (2015)	A perspective (i.e. holistic as opposed to analytical thinking), a language (system's terminology and core concepts), and a set of tools (methods and frameworks for modelling and analysing systems).

2.2 Core concepts

In the previous section, we discussed that the same system can be seen in different ways depending on a viewpoint. Systems can be classified in different ways, and sometimes drawing such distinctions can be useful in helping to understand a system. In this section, we are going to discuss some of the core concepts that underpin systems thinking.

Open and closed systems

Systems can be open or closed. Open systems interact with the environment. They can change the environment and they can be changed by the environment. If we take the ocean as an example, it is a system comprising different elements, such as water and its chemical composition, marine flora and fauna, as well as products of human activities (such as plastic pollution). It interacts freely with the surrounding environment. On the surface it interacts with the atmosphere through chemical reactions and exchange of matter, such as evaporation of water from the surface that is then returned back to the ocean in the form of rain. Ocean currents signify the patterns of system behaviour and impact atmospheric temperature in different parts of the planet. The ocean also interacts with outer space through the atmosphere; in particular, sunlight can reach its surface and change its temperature, which will impact interactions between different parts of the marine ecosystem below the surface.

Closed systems, on the other hand, do not interact with the environment (Figure 2.2) and therefore they do not have any reaction behaviour to the environment. In fact, closed vs open system is not a binary state, rather systems exist in a spectrum that ranges from fully open systems at one end to fully closed systems at the other end. Most systems are open, but although closed systems are rare, they do exist. A good example of a closed system is a controlled experiment in a laboratory, such as virus research. In such a system, the virus cultured and grown in the lab must be part of a closed system. If it is open, even a little bit, the virus might escape into the environment.

In some cases, North Korea is used as an example of a closed system, which is not strictly true. You could argue North Korea is actually an open

Figure 2.2 The spectrum of open and closed systems

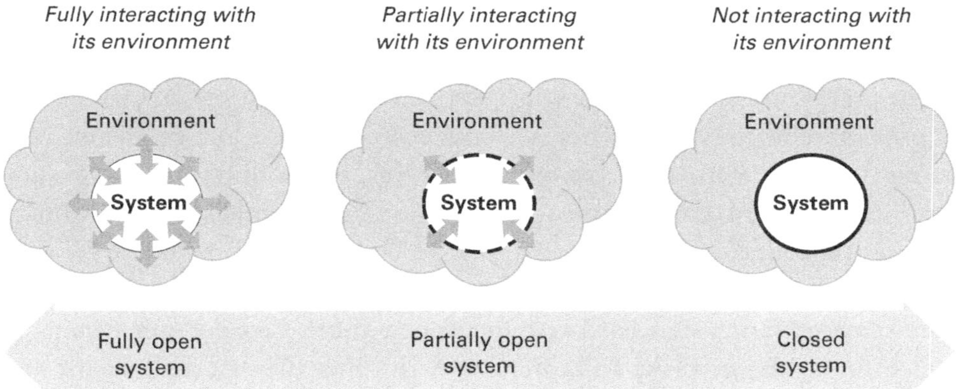

system because it has some interactions with its environment, that is some of the neighbouring countries, and has limited trade with the world outside its boundaries – it's just that its economic and political systems are not as open as other countries.

From a business and management perspective all organizations are open systems, although the degree of their openness may vary significantly. For instance, a local grocery store is a more closed system than a large chain like Tesco, because it only interacts with a few suppliers and caters to the needs of the local community. Its key advantage is convenience. While Tesco has to be integrated into large international supply networks to procure a large variety of products and satisfy the needs of a diverse range of customers and understand the heterogeneous customer groups well to survive competition from other large chains.

Hard and soft systems

Some systems, for example machines, are engineered. They have high-integrity components and predictable behaviours. Their parts are connected through well-understood interaction patterns, and feedback is used to compensate for deviation by adjusting technical control parameters. These systems stem from an engineering paradigm and are hard systems. A car in itself is an example of a hard system.

Engineers naturally develop an ability to think in systems when studying and imagining hard systems, how different components in such systems behave, and how they interact with each other. However, they tend to find it difficult to replicate this experience with other types of systems. Other types of systems are composed of autonomous agents (normally people or animals). These are known as soft systems. For example, a school or a society is a soft system. These systems stem from a social paradigm. Soft system parts, autonomous agents, are characterized by high variety of change and unpredictable behaviours. They are connected through loosely defined dynamic webs of relationships, power structures, shared interests and values. Feedback is used to compensate for deviation through influence, motivations and persuasion.

In a way, all hard systems are embedded into soft systems. If we look at the car example, the car as a hard system exists within a broader soft system, in which the driver drives it and interacts with other drivers, pedestrians and local ecosystems (e.g. by emitting pollutants into the atmosphere). These interactions are governed by rules formalized to a varying degree. When designing a car, engineers will ensure that it complies with formalized regulations as well as study the conditions of its use, but they cannot always anticipate the ways in which the car might be used, and what kinds of new behaviours it might produce. For instance, when designing an autonomous vehicle, the designers might not be able to foresee the new behaviours from the pedestrians and other drivers who might want to try and test it to its limits or 'play' the system.

If we build upon the car example, the car as a hard system is very predictable. If you drive 100 Mini Coopers in the same day you will feel that they are all the same. This is because the components that make these cars are highly engineered with tight tolerances. Thus, engineers can predict, within certain parameters, how various components and subsystems interact with each other and how the cars they produce will drive. However, once you put the human component, i.e. the driver, into the car the system becomes a lot more unpredictable, because we cannot predict how the human component will interact with the car and how the car will behave in response to these interactions. Control systems, such as the highway code (rules of the road), have been produced to make these systems more predictable and increase road safety, but we still cannot predict how somebody who has had a restless night or an argument with their partner in the morning will behave when driving to work that morning. This is why insurance companies when insuring our cars place greater emphasis on the driver than they do on the cars.

From a business and management perspective, all organizations are soft systems that contain subsystems, some of which may be hard systems. For example, in a manufacturing company there are several different subsystems, such as human resource management, manufacturing and planning systems. The planning system will knit together a number of people from different functions such as sales, manufacturing, purchasing and finance who will use enterprise requirements planning (ERP) software to develop business, sales, manufacturing or procurement plans. In this example, the planning system is a soft system as it comprises autonomous human agents, but it also contains a hard subsystem, i.e. the ERP software.

Worldviews

In systems thinking, different people can look at or study the same system but see different things. In other words, they conceptualize the system differently.

To some extent this is exemplified in the students' sketches of the university (Figure 2.1). Usually people's worldview, i.e. the way they see and interpret the things around them, is influenced by parameters such as their background, culture, upbringing, education, profession and life experiences. Usually, people develop mental models and assumptions about life, work, relationships and so on that shape their worldview over the course of their lives. For instance, often what we read in the news is only one side of the story understood through the filters of our own upbringing. The *Guardian*'s 1986 'Points of view' video, which you can find online (see video link 2.1 in the online resources on the Koganpage.com product page) is illustrative of how the same event can have diverse interpretations when seen from three different points of view.

If you ask a finance manager, an operations manager and a marketing manager about how their business works, they will probably give you different stories about the same business, although the three stories will most probably have a degree of consistency and overlap between them. That is because they are looking at the same business or system from different angles and have different worldviews that shape their viewpoint. A lot of soft systems are influenced by different viewpoints and mental models, and this is probably one of the main differences between hard and soft systems.

The worldview of someone also influences how the systems are conceptualized, modelled and analysed. Organizational routines or processes can be modelled as a flow chart, and this approach will be in line with the hard systems paradigm. At the same time, we can tell a story about what happens in the process, and this approach will be consistent with the soft systems paradigm. The flow chart will show the nuts and bolts of the process, but it will probably fail to capture what goes on in meetings, discussions over a water cooler, in emails and so on – i.e. human activities behind the flow-charted process. In the meantime, the story will capture much richer information about what really happens in the process. It reflects human activities that bring the process to life and make things happen.

Complexity and systems

When talking about complexity, we can think of it in terms of technical and perceived complexity. **Technical complexity** is an intrinsic property of a system. What makes systems complex are:

- the number of parts
- the number of connections

- dynamic relationships between parts
- non-linear interactions
- varying responses (predictability of response)

Perceived complexity is all about how stakeholders see a system. They may perceive a system to be more or less complex because they do not understand all the parts and/or the connections.

Systems can be complicated or complex. When we talk about the complexity of systems, we really need to understand the difference between the two concepts. The term *complicated* comes from the Latin words *com* and *plic*, meaning folded together. If we take an example of a car, we can deconstruct it, study each component and understand it, and then put it back together – the car will work in the same way and by studying each component and subsystem we can understand how it works as a whole. Hard systems are normally complicated. Although they may have multiple parts, hard systems can be understood in parts, and the behaviour of these parts interacting with each other will be predictable based on the behaviour of each part.

In contrast, complex systems cannot be understood simply by studying individual parts of the system. If you think about a pianist, an office manager and a burglar, they are all composed of the same parts (such as heart, lungs, kidneys, brain) and subsystems (such as circulatory system, respiratory system, nervous system) but their behaviours are very different and so much more complicated than the sum of their body parts. There is the whole range of external factors such as education, upbringing, the environment they work in and so on that influence the behaviour of a human as a system. All these factors create unpredictable behaviour of how the components of a human being come together and create complex behavioural patterns.

The term complex comes from the Latin word *complexus*, which means plaited or woven together. In other words, the parts of a complex system are woven together. Therefore, the system can only be understood as a whole. Human beings, teams, organizations, supply chains, value-creating ecosystems are complex systems. There is a lot more to complexity than what we have said in this short section; however, the theme of complexity builds up throughout the book as you advance through the chapters.

Emergence

Emergence is one of the most fascinating features of our universe and it is a key concept of systems. **Emergence** refers to the properties of the system that are caused by the interactions and relationships between elements rather than by the elements themselves. We may observe these as simple things forming bigger, more complex things that have different properties than the sum of their parts. In other words, emergence is complexity arising from simplicity and it can be observed everywhere in the world around us. At some point you must have seen a flock of birds or shoal of fish making patterns in the sky or water. Flocks of birds are bound together by some very simple rules, such as being within a wing's length of each other, which results in the emergence of the patterns we observe in the sky. If you search the internet for *flock of birds* videos you can see some examples of these emergent behaviours. In these systems there is no predetermined pattern, there is no emperor bird or fish that says let's create this or that shape. The shapes emerge as a result of the individual actions of each bird/fish and the interactions between the birds/fish within a flock/shoal.

In a similar vein, if you have never seen geese in flight, you would never guess that they would form a 'V' shape. This pattern emerges because of the relationships between each bird, i.e. the components of the system. When a goose moves its wings through the air, the wing tips create vortices that make it easier for another goose to fly behind, because these vortices create additional lift. A trailing goose naturally moves to fly behind the wingtip of the leading goose, where it finds the greatest lift. When several birds are together, this results in that classic 'V' shape. A group of birds flying together in this way can fly 70 per cent further than a single bird.

Scientists also talk about emergence when they study the behaviour of physical things. For example, the shape of each snowflake is unique and it emerges as a result of the interaction of different water molecules experiencing different temperatures under different atmospheric conditions. Similarly, we can also observe emergent behaviour in wider society. The traffic in our cities or the culture of a particular tribe or country emerges as a result of the individual beliefs and behaviours of each driver and person, i.e. component of the system, and their interactions – and often these are difficult to predict. For example, if we think of slums in some of our large cities, no one in the city planning office said, 'let's create a slum here'. These slums emerge through complex interactions between a number of forces that include large numbers of people living in dense spaces, local leaders competing for power, the economy of the country, poverty, traffic, pollution, health services, education, conflicts with the police, neglect by the state and so on all resulting in a unique sense of community, culture, music, expressions, sometimes even architectural beauty and currency, which feels very different to other parts of the same city or country. In these situations the outcome is unpredictable – it can generate corruption and violence as well as relative peace and a tourism economy.

We can find similar examples of emergent behaviour in organizational systems. For instance, in the absence of a clear mission or goals an organization's strategy emerges over time because of actions taken and the pattern these actions create over time. At any point in time, we may be able to look back at various decisions and actions the organization followed to see the pattern that defines the organization's journey. Emergence is also true even if an organization has a specific mission and goals. In many cases organizations define their goals and how they are going to achieve these, but as they exist as part of a larger economic system, things happen around them that make them respond to the changes in their operating environment. As a result, what they realize is often not the same as what they set out to do. In the strategy literature this is known as the intended strategy, i.e. what they set out to do, and the emergent or realized strategy, i.e. what they actually ended up doing.

Based on the above discussion the level of emergence can vary between weak and strong. **Weak emergence** means that the behaviour of the system can be explained, modelled or predicted (for example, engineered systems). **Strong emergence** means that the behaviour of the system is more difficult to explain, model or predict as is the case in soft systems. Again, these concepts of emergence will develop further as we progress through this book.

Self-organization systems and organizational models

When we think about organizations, we automatically think about hierarchy, although the degree of hierarchy can vary. In nature, whilst some species, such as apes, are organized hierarchically, other species resemble much more a network demonstrating emergent behaviours through simple rules. For example, when we look at a flock of birds, we can see order emerging from apparent chaos.

Such order is an example of a self-organizing system, whereby organization is decentralized and distributed over all the elements of the system, i.e. individual birds in the flock. In this system no single bird sets the pattern or pre-defines the behaviour of the flock, nor is their behaviour managed by external forces, although it can be altered in response to external events, such as an approaching bird of prey. Instead, the system is self-managed or self-organized. This type of system is therefore significantly different from a centrally managed or indeed a hierarchical system; it is essentially a network that self-organizes (Figure 2.3). We can describe **self-organization** in decentralized systems as a process where some form of overall order arises from local interactions between parts of an initially disordered system. The system somehow develops simple rules that each element obeys. As a consequence, complex and unpredictable behaviours emerge.

Hierarchies and central control systems are generally associated with higher levels of intelligence, but in nature, networks can function equally well. In fact, from the organizational perspective, the more self-organized the system is, the more resilient it is. If in a centralized system something happens to the central unit, the whole organization can stop functioning. Similarly, hierarchies, although a little bit more resilient, have multiple points of failure. If one of the nodes in one of the branches fails it would take out the whole of that branch, affecting the performance of the system. In networks there are no concentrations of points of failure, and therefore failure of any single unit will not have a significant impact on the overall functioning of the system; consequently, as a system a network is far more resilient.

From a business and management perspective the degree of self-organization or self-management in a system has become an important

Figure 2.3 Alternative organizational structures

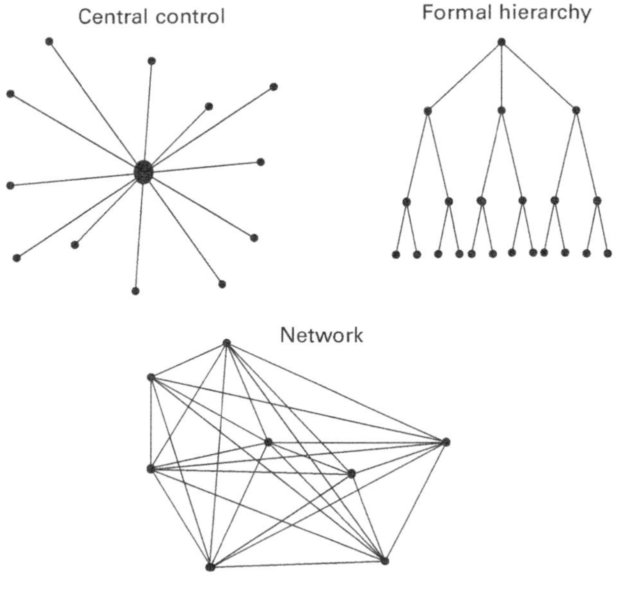

consideration, as it helps us to better understand the system and its behaviour. In most economies, industry sectors (such as textiles, engineering, food and drink, pharmaceutical) are not managed by a central organization. Each company is an autonomous part of the wider system (i.e. a sector) which operates within a given set of rules (legal, regulatory, moral). Thus we can consider these as self-organizing systems. If we wish to change the behaviour of a self-organizing system, we usually have to change the governing rules of the system. For example, in the transport sector if we wish to increase the uptake of electric vehicles, we create new rules that incentivize the supply and use of electric vehicles and disincentivize the supply and use of vehicles burning fossil fuels.

At an organizational level, however, most organizations have a defined management structure, and thus they are not considered as self-organizing systems. However, we do occasionally see elements of self-organization within organizations. Conceptually, a self-managing work team is an example of a self-organizing system, but in practice they are rarely completely autonomous and often they have internal management structures.

Continuing in this vein, **holacracy** is a form of organization that distributes authority and decision making through a network of self-organized teams that are bound together with a shared purpose and common set of goals and rules. The term has been derived from the word *holos*, which means 'whole' in Greek, and describes autonomous, self-organizing units that are dependent on the greater whole of which they are part, essentially a bit like a shoal of fish, a flock of birds or a company in an ecosystem. In this book we do not intend to go into lengthy debates about organizational structures and governance models, but it would suffice to say that in terms of organizational structure, holacracy is a form of self-organizing network.

In the literature it is also common to come across terminologies such as **autocracy** (central control or command and control), **bureaucracy** (hierarchical control) and **netocracy** (network-based self-management) that describe different governance philosophies and models.

Systems problems

The key value of systems thinking is in helping us see complex systems as a whole, and understand their behaviour and the underlying problems so that we can develop effective solutions to systems problems. Systems problems can be broadly classified into tame, messy and wicked problems.

Tame problems can be defined and solved. They have a correct solution, and it can be optimized. Most engineering problems are tame problems. An example of such problems is a location problem in logistics that requires an organization to identify the most optimal location for a warehouse to minimize transportation costs for delivery operations. To solve this problem scientists and engineers can develop optimization algorithms that can work out the optimal location for a warehouse.

Messy problems are the most common type of problem. They are poorly defined and do not have a single correct solution. Instead, often we are looking for a 'good enough' solution. This happens in most real-world problems, whereby the solutions require compromises. An example can be building a wind farm that might blend in with the natural landscape that local residents value. In such a situation, the proposed problem, building a wind farm, might benefit some stakeholders, e.g. the energy supplier and residents with renewable energy, but disadvantage others, e.g. the tourism industry. Solving this problem requires negotiations and compromises, which might eventually benefit everyone to an extent.

Wicked problems always involve a loser and a winner. These are problems that cannot be solved but must nevertheless be managed. Climate change is an example of such a wicked problem. For instance, we know that if we want to continue supporting economic growth, it will have a more significant environmental impact, but reducing economic growth will have a significant negative impact on many groups of people. There is no ideal solution; instead, both impacts will have to be managed. In relation to climate change, a company might be faced with a wicked problem of understanding its impact on operations and deciding how to prepare for its adverse effects. This might require decisions that might prove unpopular in the short term but will ensure long-term sustainability and survival of the business.

2.3 Value of systems thinking

To understand the real value of systems thinking, we need to recognize that nothing in this world exists in isolation and that everything is connected to something else. Everything is affected by something and potentially affects something else. With systems thinking, one can begin to understand, explain and predict why complex systems such as organizations, people and societies behave the way they do.

We saw this with the financial crisis in 2008–2009, when one policy in one sector of the economy had a huge impact on the economies of most countries around the world. We have also seen it happening during the Covid-19 pandemic. Disruptions in specific parts of supply chains had a cascading effect of disruption along the whole supply chain. As a result, people's lives were disrupted in all sorts of ways; for example the UK ran short of toilet paper due to panic buying, and housebuilders ran out of construction materials and were not able to complete homes for as long as nine months. These disruptions were not predicted and the supply chain was not prepared to quickly adjust to these changes. These examples demonstrate the connectedness and unpredictability of the world we live in today. Therefore, when we make changes to our organizations or to our life, we need to think about how that might impact other parts of the organization or the wider system.

With systems thinking, we can begin to understand and explain why organizations behave the way they do and start predicting how they might behave in the future. The models and methods covered in Part 2 of this book will equip you with tools to help you understand the systems and start modelling them to explain their patterns of behaviour. Parts 3 and 4 of the book will discuss further how we can predict the behaviour of a system by simulating system models, particularly when dealing with complex systems, and how we can start modelling systems that do not yet exist. These tools will help us to gain answers to various strategic questions. For example, how will supply chains perform in 5, 10 or 40 years with the impact of climate change? Or what could a new industrial system look like in response to future trends and constraints? Then we can start thinking about the interventions that allow us to change the system's behaviour.

Systems thinking and analysis is a life skill. It will enhance the problem analysis and solutions capability of people from all walks of life irrespective of where they live, their level of seniority and the sector they work in. It is a skill that is important for working and living. Without systems thinking and accompanying tools and techniques it would be near impossible to predict the behaviour of complex systems, particularly human activity and societal systems such as organizations, supply chains, the education system, innovation systems, healthcare systems and so on.

CASE STUDY A systems thinking case study

This case study focuses on the supply system between an international chemical manufacturing company producing dynamite, and quarries who buy sticks of dynamite to blast rockfaces to make gravel.

The manufacturing company produces dynamite from two inert liquids by mixing them together to create an explosive. The explosive liquid has to be stored somewhere safely before it is plasticized by adding plasticizers. The plasticizing process resembles that of making a dough. The plasticized explosive liquid becomes dynamite. The dynamite needs to be stored somewhere safely until it is transported and delivered to the customers, i.e. the quarries.

Naturally, when we look at business processes, we ask ourselves a question: how do we improve performance? The most obvious solutions would be to improve the on-time delivery performance, reduce the cost, or perhaps improve productivity in different steps of the process. However, these solutions will only result in incremental improvements to this system. If, on the other hand, we take a wider view of the system, we may be able to see other kinds of improvement opportunities.

The first step in this journey might be asking the question of what the customer does with this dynamite. This question expands the boundaries of the system. If we look at the wider picture, then we will see that the dynamite is transported to a quarry, the quarry receives the dynamite and stores it, then they employ qualified people to administer the dynamite on the rock face. They drill holes on the rock face, then they place correct amounts of dynamite inside the holes, wire it together, and finally press a button to perform the explosion. The explosion turns the rockface to large pieces of rock, i.e. rock on the ground. After the explosion, the quarry takes large pieces of rock scattered on the ground and processes this rock into smaller pieces of gravel using crushing machines. This gravel is later used in construction to make roads, aggregate for concrete, gardens, etc. In this supply system the quarry creates value by processing the rock using the crushing machines, and this is where the quarry has the majority of its investment.

When we look at this extended system, we can recognize a lot of non-value-adding activities. A lot of the steps in the process involve storing and transporting hazardous compounds, which requires a lot of attention to safety and security, where explosives might attract unwanted criminal attention. The safety and security requirements not only increase costs, they also slow the system down. Thinking about it, plasticizing is only there to make the explosive transportable, so how can we remove the unessential steps, simplify the supply system, and improve its performance?

The only steps that add value are rock-processing activities. When we come to this realization, the question that should be asking instead is: how do we get the explosive to the rock face to get 'the rock on the ground?'. When the manufacturing company asked themselves this question and recognized the objective of the wider system, they came up with the Mobile Manufacturing Unit (MMU) solution, which eventually replaced all other manufacturing facilities. The MMU is a truck with two tanks for storing the two inert liquids separately and safely. With this approach all the steps between storing the two inert liquids and providing rock on the ground are replaced with the MMU.

For the customer, the process has also changed. Now all they need to do is call the company and say how many tonnes of rock they need and how they want the rock distributed. Then the MMU will do the calculations, drill the holes, pump the two liquids into the holes, and therefore make the explosive right inside the holes. They will then wire it up, perform the explosion, and finally deliver the 'rock on the ground' for the customer to process it. This change, which is illustrated in Figure 2.4, means that the quarries just need to focus on their core business, i.e. processing the rock on the ground.

What this example demonstrates is that if we look at only one part of a system, and ask how to improve the system, we get one set of answers. But this part does not exist in isolation. It is connected to the wider world through its customers, suppliers and other stakeholders. When we expand the boundaries of the system and when we look at the wider system, e.g. by including the customer in these boundaries and looking at what the customer does with our product, we get a different solution.

For the manufacturing company, this was a significant change in the business model. They changed their business model from manufacturing dynamite to providing rock on the ground service. In other words, they transformed from a manufacturing company to a service provider.

Figure 2.4 Before and after scenarios in the case study system

Previous system		New system	
Manufacturer	• Store inert liquid • Mix inert liquid to make explosive • Store explosive liquid • Plasticize explosive liquid to make dynamite • Store dynamite • Transport/deliver dynamite	Manufacturer	• Store inert liquid  • Mobile Manufacturing Unit goes to the quarry • Employ qualified staff to administer dynamite
Quarry	• Store dynamite • Employ qualified staff to administer dynamite • Rock on the ground • Use crushing machines to crush rock into gravel • Sell gravel to customers	Quarry	• Rock on the ground • Use crushing machines to crush rock into gravel • Sell gravel to customers

This is an example of the power of systems thinking; it helps us think about the wider system and develop more meaningful ways of changing the system, for the benefit of everyone.

Reflective questions

- In the above case study, we have demonstrated how by changing the boundaries and taking a wider systems perspective the company was able to find a different solution that made the whole system significantly more effective for both organizations. Try to reflect on other types of stakeholders that might be involved in the system. Can you think of any emergent behaviour that this new type of relationship might lead to?
- If you were to describe the viewpoint of the company before and after the change, how would you do it? In your opinion, has the viewpoint of the gravel manufacturers changed with the introduction of the new business model by their supplier?
- Reflect on the type of problem that the new business model has helped to solve. What other types of problems might it have created?

2.4 Summary

In this chapter we have introduced the definition and characteristics of a system, discussed different types of system classifications, e.g. open vs closed systems or hard vs soft systems, and introduced some of the key concepts such as emergence and self-organization. We then discussed the types of problems that systems thinking addresses, the value of systems thinking, and provided an example of how systems thinking can help facilitate problem solving and innovation.

REFLECTIVE EXERCISE

Emergence – In this chapter we defined emergence as the behavioural properties of the system that are caused by the interactions and relationships between elements rather than by the elements themselves. Reflecting on your experiences, think of situations where you experienced emergence. For example, have you ever been in a situation where before you went into a meeting you had talked to a few people and you had a good idea as to how the meeting was going to go, but it did not go quite as you expected? Think about what caused this unexpected outcome: was it just one person saying something unexpected that ended up changing the course of the discussion? It is often small, unexpected occurrences or interventions that create unexpected outcomes. Reflecting on your experiences, can you think about what these small, unexpected interventions may have been that resulted in the unexpected outcomes?

Management structure – Think about what management structures you have experienced. As a student you may have worked for a small corner shop stacking shelves where the owner/manager was the central controller who told everyone what to do. Did you work in an organization that had a bureaucratic hierarchical structure? Have you experienced a self-organizing netocratic organization, even such as a group of friends with a common interest where you all decide to do something fun at the weekends? Think about these different experiences and what worked well and what did not work so well in different contexts. Could self-organization work as well or better in the organization where you may have experienced central control? What would be the challenges?

TEAM EXERCISE: REFLECTIONS ON AN ORGANIZATION

The purpose of this exercise is to demonstrate that when different people conceptualize the same organization everyone's conceptualization may be different. Before you start the exercise, you should identify an organization everyone is familiar with. This could be a well-known local fast-food restaurant or even the participants' university or school. If everyone is from the same organization then ask each member to draw an image of their organization.

Ask the participants to draw a quick sketch/image of the organization in no more than three minutes. It is important that they do not overthink this; they should draw the first image that comes to their mind. Then ask each participant to explain the image to others. For larger groups, to save time, this can be done in smaller groups of three or four people.

While explaining their pictures encourage the participants to tell a story behind the image rather than simply describe different components. Note the differences between the stories. You might notice that different people tell the same story using different images and words. Some will take a much more hard systems approach (e.g. products, manufacturing equipment, information systems) and others will focus more on the people side of the organization. Reflect on the worldviews emerging from these stories.

If the exercise has been conducted with people working in the same organization this exercise should also help participants see each other's worldviews, which may help to explain some of the differences and even tensions in the organization.

References

Checkland PB (1999) *Systems Thinking, Systems Practice*, Wiley

Monat, JP and Gannon, TF (2015) What is systems thinking? A review of selected literature plus recommendations, *American Journal of Systems Science*, **4** (1), pp 11–26

Randle, JM and Stroink, ML (2018) The development and initial validation of the paradigm of systems thinking, *Systems Research and Behavioral Science*, **35** (6), pp 645–57

Further reading

Bernstein, E, Bunch, J, Canner, N and Lee, M (2016) Beyond the Holacracy Hype, *Harvard Business Review*, Jul–Aug, https://hbr.org/2016/07/beyond-the-holacracy-hype (archived at https://perma.cc/RB2F-LZLC)

Understanding systems 3

In the previous chapter we asked the question 'What is a system?' and defined it as a collection of interacting parts, components or actors in which the interactions result in system-level properties and behaviours not attributable to the sum of individual parts. With this definition we also introduced several concepts that underpin systems thinking, including hard and soft systems; open and closed systems; complex vs complicated systems; systems behaviour and emergence; systems problems (tame, messy and wicked); worldview; and self-organization. In this chapter we will build upon these concepts and definitions to provide you with a deeper and more complete understanding of systems, their structure and properties.

LEARNING OUTCOMES

- Understand
  - the function and purpose of a system
  - systems inputs and outputs
  - system performance
  - stocks, flows and forces
  - system structure and boundary
  - interconnections and feedback loops
  - processes in the context of systems
  - entropy and homeostasis
- Able to conceptualize relatively complex systems visually and verbally
- Identify and discuss the factors that explain behaviours of simple systems

3.1 Function and purpose

Based on our discussions in the previous chapter we could surmise that all systems have properties. The **purpose** and **function** of a system are two important properties that help us to understand systems. The purpose of the system is what it does, and the function is how it delivers this purpose. This is best explained through the following example. The purposes of a car, an aeroplane and a horse and cart are all to transport people from A to B, so their purposes are the same. But the ways in which they transport people from A to B are quite different – this is the function of the system. Other examples include a digestive system which processes food (function) to produce energy for the body (purpose) or an irrigation system which directs water through canals (function) to irrigate land (purpose).

Although there is general agreement that all systems, however complex or simple, have a function, there is some debate as to whether all systems have a purpose. What is the purpose of the solar system? We know what its function is (to keep the planets within the system balanced), but for what purpose? From these simple examples we can observe that in some systems, such as the solar system, we are not sure of its purpose, i.e. why it exists, even though we can scientifically explain how it functions. In systems thinking some argue that whilst all systems have a function, they do not need to have a purpose. Others argue that all systems have a function and a purpose, it's just that we may not know or understand the purpose of the system; the solar system may have a purpose but at this stage we do not know or understand what this purpose may be.

In business and management most of the systems we deal with usually have a function and a purpose, thus this tension between function and purpose may be a moot point but it is an important one to bear in mind as not everyone who is involved with the system may understand its function or its purpose. In fact, in many cases, in complex organizations a system may have multiple purposes depending on the viewpoints/worldviews of its stakeholders. For example, what is the purpose of a university? Students and their parents may say that it is to provide them with a good education that enables them to get good jobs. Industry may say that the purpose of a university is to create new knowledge and technologies through research and development that allows them to improve their business. The local government may say it is to fuel economic development by creating spinouts and supporting enterprises. The central government may say it is to create revenues from foreign students paying fees. Although these views appear radically different, there are some overlaps amongst them and in our experience they are valid views, which we have encountered in the past.

In this context it is worth thinking about the function and purpose of a system using the following structure. ***A system does something (function) for a particular purpose*** and even though its function may be known and understood, its purpose may not be so clear.

3.2 Inputs and outputs

Unless a system is completely closed it interacts with its environment through inputs and outputs. Even in completely closed systems, its subsystems will interact with each other through inputs and outputs. In short, it would be safe to say that all systems have inputs and outputs. Following from our earlier examples an information processing system takes one form of information as an input, it processes the input and outputs it in a different form. For instance, a digestive system takes food as an input and produces energy and waste as outputs. In a similar vein, the primary input to the solar system is energy from the big bang, which arguably is still continuing, and its output is the motion of the planets, moons, etc. that serve to keep that solar system in balance.

Examining this in further detail we will observe that there are different kinds of inputs and outputs to a system. We could categorize and define these as follows:

- **Inputs** are processed through the system and leave the system in a changed state. For example, a management information system receives raw data (input) and produces management reports (output).
- **Resources** (also a form of input) are consumed by the function of the system. They include energy, time of people and other resources and assets; for example, when a machine is used for a time, it consumes part of its useful life.
- **Controls** (also a form of input) set the expectations, standards or requirements a system should fulfil. In effect these define the parameters within which the system needs to function.
- **Outputs** are produced by the system in line with its function and, where known, its purpose. Outputs may be useful when they are consistent with

the purpose of the system; other outputs may be unintended due to the emergent behaviour of the system. They can also be waste produced as a result of the function of the system.

3.3 System performance

In simple terms performance has two dimensions: **efficiency** and **effectiveness**. Thus, performance of a system is broadly defined as *the effectiveness and efficiency of a system*. In this context, *effectiveness* is defined as the extent to which the output fulfils the specification, requirements or expectations defined by the controls. Whereas *efficiency* is defined as the recourses consumed to produce the outputs.

Of course, if the other unintended outputs and/or waste are being produced along with the intended useful outputs, we would also need to consider the resources that are consumed to produce these outputs when we are thinking about efficiency. However, we must bear in mind that not all unintended outputs are waste; in some cases an unintended output from a system may be quite useful.

At this point it would also be useful to discuss the term *efficacy*, which is commonly used in systems thinking. Efficacy is similar to effectiveness and they are often used interchangeably. However, there is a difference between the two. For example, in understanding effectiveness of vaccines the term efficacy is used to measure the effectiveness of the vaccine in a laboratory setting, whereas the term effectiveness is used to measure its performance in the real world. Thus, a vaccine may have 90 per cent efficacy in the laboratory but be only 60 per cent effective in the real world, such as the influenza vaccine. When we apply the same thinking to systems, efficacy is concerned with the potential performance of the system, and arguably when we ask about the efficacy of the system we are interested in, i.e. 'is this the best performance?'.

3.4 Stocks, flows and forces

When discussing the inputs and outputs of a system we implied that things flow through a system. That is indeed the case. Let us look at different systems to understand what sort of things flows through the system.

- In a manufacturing system raw materials and components arrive as inputs and are processed through the system into products that leave the system as outputs. In this example materials are flowing through the system.
- In an information processing system, such as processing of mortgage applications, information arrives into the system as an input in the form of a mortgage application, the information is then processed, and the output is also information in the form of a decision. In this example information is what flows through the system.
- In a customer experience system, such as a cruise package, customers arrive as inputs to the system, they are processed throughout the cruise (entertainment, games, activities, dining, excursions, etc.), and then they become outputs of the system hopefully as healthier, more relaxed and tanned customers.
- In an electrical distribution system, energy, in the form of electricity, flows through the system.

Based on these rather simplistic examples we could surmise that a variety of things may flow through a system: materials, information, customers, people, energy and so on. In reality, many things flow through a system to enable the system to function effectively and efficiently. For example, in the manufacturing system example, apart from materials, there are many other things that flow through, including:

- information to make the products;
- energy to run the machines and the factory;
- money to finance inputs (raw materials, components, energy) and the resources (people, equipment, consumables);
- customers who may interact with the manufacturing system at different points (such as specification, design approval, testing, acceptance, etc.).

Clearly, these flows need to come from somewhere, they do not just materialize from nothing. They come from stocks. **Stocks** and **flows** are concepts commonly used in systems thinking but they are also prevalent in the disciplines of engineering, business, accounting and economics. A stock is defined as a quantity existing at a given point in time. For example, today you might have £100 in your bank account. It may have accumulated in your account over a period of time; you might have been receiving £10 every week for the past 10 weeks. In this case the flow is £10 per week resulting in the stock of

£100 that you have in your bank account today. Of course, if you start spending this money it creates a new flow, which may reduce the stock.

In short, stocks and flows are concepts used in systems thinking to understand the dynamics of a system over time. Stocks are measures of quantity at a given time (we have £100 today), whereas flows are measures of quantity over time (£10 per week over 10 weeks).

So far, the examples we have provided for stocks and flows have been for tangible things (money, materials, information, energy); however, in systems thinking intangible things (knowledge, goodwill, resentment, misunderstanding, etc.) can also be represented as stocks and flows. For example, several unpopular decisions taken by the management of an organization may result in the build-up of some resentment within the workforce that may in turn result in unexpected and/or unhelpful behaviours. In fact, often it is the tangible stocks and flows that help us to describe hard systems, and the intangible stocks and flows, sometimes referred to as forces, that help us understand soft systems (discussed later in this chapter).

Later in this book when we start discussing systems dynamics we will build upon the concept of stocks and flows. At this stage we will refrain from going into further detail and instead summarize what we have learned so far about the structure of a system.

3.5 System structure

In Figure 3.1 we have attempted to summarize the concepts introduced earlier in this chapter to define the structure of a typical system. According to this illustration the system has a purpose and a function. It has inputs and outputs. It has controls that govern the system and it uses resources to carry out its function and transform the inputs to outputs. While carrying out its function, things (materials, information, people, energy, etc.) flow through the system. These flows come from stocks which either exist within the system or come from outside the system. We can conceptualize and measure the performance of the system as effectiveness and efficiency of the system.

In the previous paragraph, when we say 'the flows come from stocks which either exist within the system or come from outside the system', it implies that the system has a *boundary* and that some flows come from within this boundary and some from outside the boundary. This has further structural implications that are not captured in Figure 3.1. If we consider the definition

Figure 3.1 The structure of a system

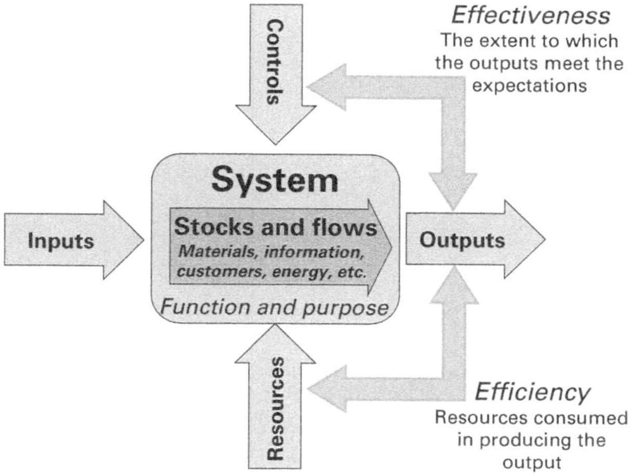

of a system as 'a collection of interacting parts, components or actors in which the interactions result in system-level properties and behaviours not attributable to the sum of individual parts', introduced earlier, and the notion that 'nothing in this world exists in isolation, everything is connected to something else and everything is part of something larger', discussed in in the previous chapter, it suggests that a system consists of interconnected parts, which are systems in their own right (i.e. subsystems) and that a system exists as part of a larger system as depicted in Figure 3.2. In this context the higher-level systems are **systems of systems**, and the lower-level systems are **sub-systems** or **systems within systems.**

Examples of this hierarchical system structure are illustrated in Figure 3.3 showing two perspectives. Figure 3.3a illustrates how individual components are parts of a car, which in turn are parts of an enterprise system, which in turn is part of an industry system, which in turn is part of an economic system and so on. In contrast, Figure 3.3b illustrates the administrative systems starting from business processes and moving on to business units as higher-level systems that in turn exist as part of the overall business, which in turn is part of the automotive industry. These examples provide just two of many ways we can conceptualize and structure the system we wish to understand. Clearly, organization structure (i.e. individuals, teams, departments, divisions) is an alternative systems perspective of the organization.

Figure 3.2 System of systems and systems within systems

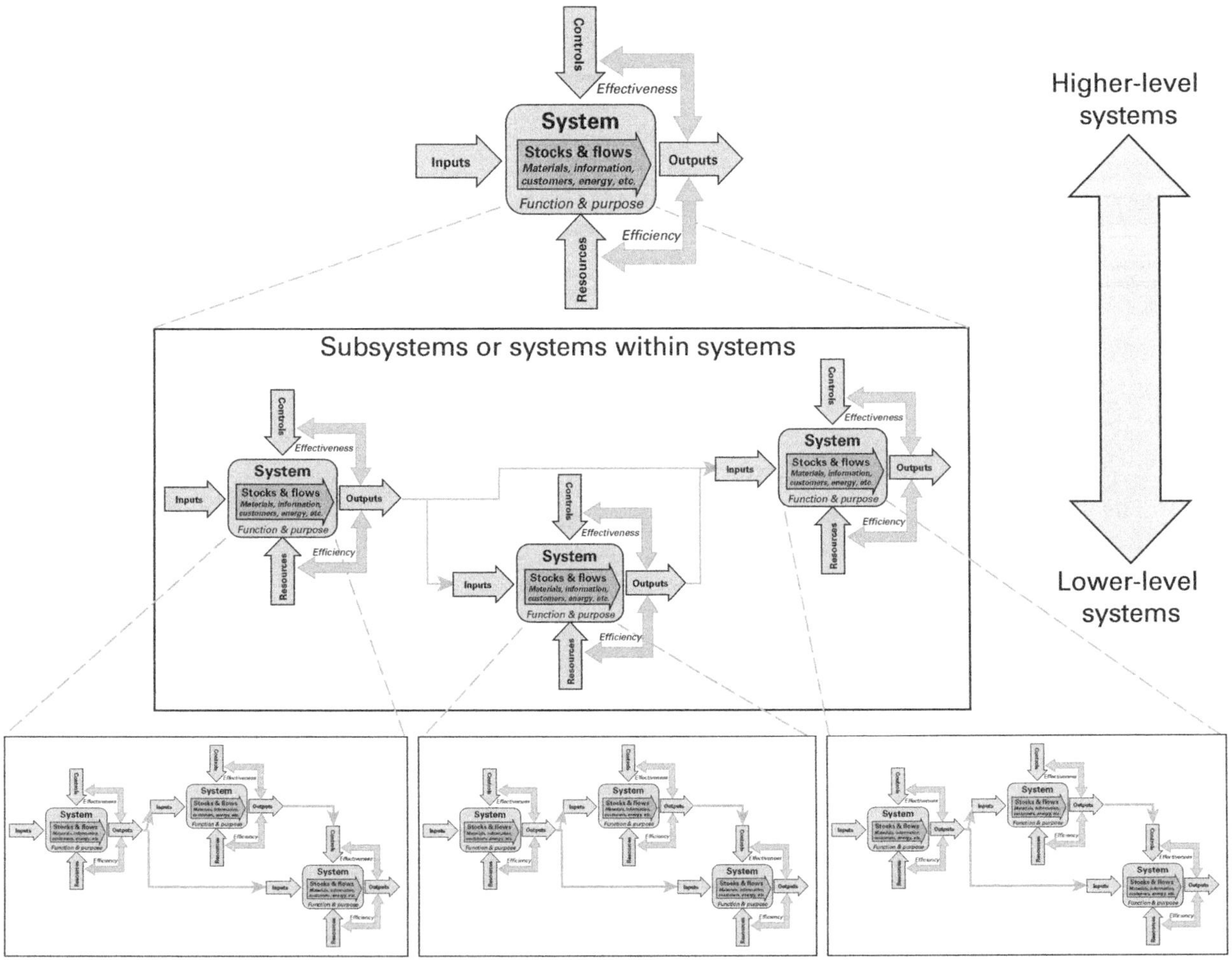

Figure 3.3 Examples of the hierarchical structures of systems from different perspectives

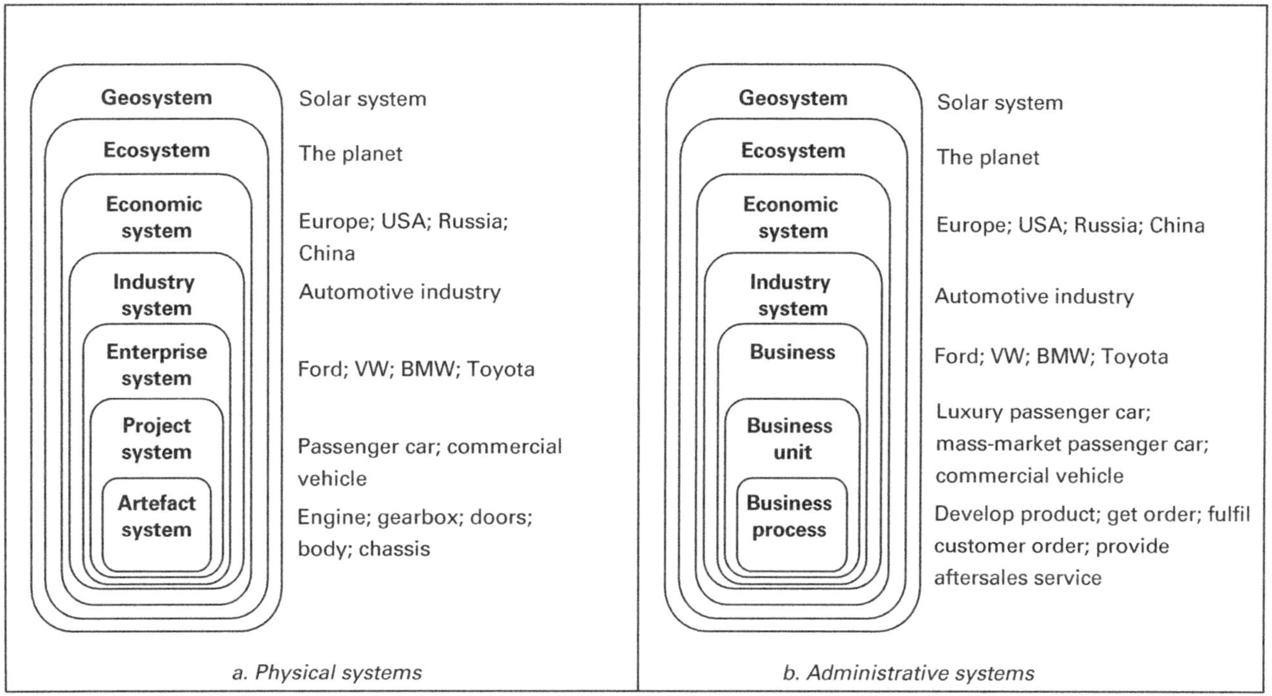

However, if we take a horizontal slice through any system in the hierarchies shown in Figure 3.3, we will see that there is an additional level of complexity. For example, if we consider the economic system of a region, it is not concerned with just one single industry system. The economic system of a region typically contains several industries and other systems as illustrated by the diagram in Figure 3.4. The size of each bubble on this diagram depicts the significance of the subsystem on the wider economic system, while the thickness of the lines connecting different subsystems depicts the interdependency between different subsystems.

Figure 3.4 Interdependency between different subsystems

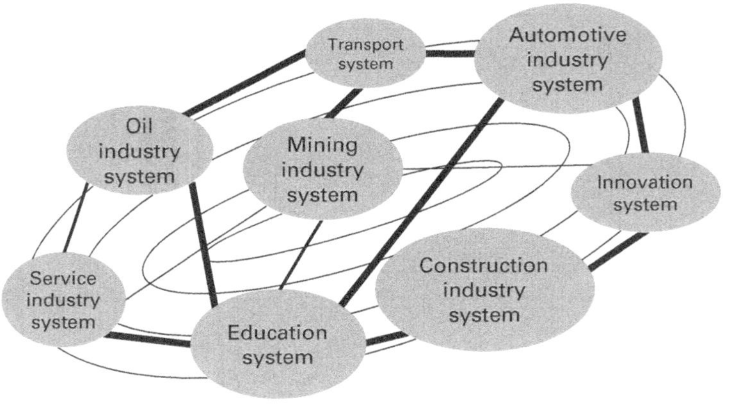

3.6 System boundary

The discussion above brings us to the point about the boundaries of a system. Indeed, all systems have boundaries and different components or subsystems are connected to one another within these boundaries. They can also be connected to components or subsystems of other systems through these boundaries. For instance, if we are an insurance company and interested in assessing the risk of a car, we set the system boundary around the car as a mechanical object. We assess its performance, track record, technical reliability, cost of repairs, age, etc. However, if expand the boundary of the system and include the driver then we are assessing a different system. We will pay equal if not more attention to the experience of the driver, track record of the driver and the driver's age and gender. According to insurance companies these parameters will play a much more dominant role in assessing the insurance risk of a particular car, when the driver is considered. We can extend the boundaries of a system even further and look at where the car is parked and used. In rural areas the traffic density is lower, and the risk of traffic accidents is also lower. In this context, postcode can have an impact on the insurance risk as different areas within the same city will have different crime rates, frequency of accidents, etc.

But the big question is 'how do we know where the boundary of a system lies?' Often the answer to this question is 'it depends'. In reality, the boundary of a system is an artificial concept because the components of a system are connected together, and they act in concert. Thus, the **system boundary** is an artificial concept to aid the analyst or the manager in conceptualizing and understanding the system. For instance, in Figure 3.4 we see that the regional economy is a function of several interacting subsystems. If we wish to understand the impact of our innovation system on the regional economy, where do we draw our boundaries? Particularly if we consider that the higher education system, through its research and development activities, could be a significant contributor to the innovation output, where do we draw our boundaries? Do we make higher education a subsystem within the innovation system? Or do we keep higher education as part of the wider education system and show the connections between the higher education subsystem and the innovation system? The answer to this question often is *it does not matter*; the important point is that we understand the connections between the higher education subsystem and other subsystems within the innovation system. Indeed, it is not just the connections between the innovation and higher education systems that are in question here. If we need to understand innovation as a system within our economy we need to understand how it is connected to other systems within the economy, otherwise we risk developing an incomplete understanding of the system.

In short, it is the systems analyst or the manager who needs to decide where the boundaries of the system should be as long as the pertinent connections between the system that is being studied and other systems that are important to its function are understood, and the connections are included in the analysis.

3.7 Interconnections and feedback loops

At the very start of this book, we said that in this world everything is connected to everything else, and that systems thinking enables us to see through this complexity and understand why complex systems behave the way they do. We also defined a system as *a collection of interacting parts, components or actors in which the interactions result in system-level properties and behaviours not attributable to the sum of individual parts.* Earlier in this section in describing the structure and properties of a system we demonstrated that whilst within itself the parts of a system interact with each other through stocks and flows, the system itself also interacts with other systems in its environment. Naturally, these interactions result in the system being influenced/changed by its environment as well as the system influencing/changing its environment. Indeed, these interactions take place at different levels.

Key to understanding these relationships are the connections between the parts of the system as well as the connections between the system and the other systems operating within the environment of the system. These connections are not just flows that describe the quantities of things flowing from one part of the system to another, they are also causal relations between the connected parts that may affect the behaviour of a part resulting in not just local but potentially system-wide behavioural changes. This idea of this *causality* may be demonstrated simply through the following example:

- At a given interest rate, the greater the bank balance (A), the greater the interest earned (B).

This is a very simple example of causality where A causes B. But of course, the causality in this example does not stop there because:

- At a given interest rate, the greater the interest earned (B) the greater the bank balance (A).

Here we can see that there is a similar causal relationship in the opposite direction. In systems thinking this phenomenon is known as reinforcing loops or feedback loops as depicted in Figure 3.5.

In systems, particularly in complex ones, we can observe many such loops with different characteristics. However, we will refrain from going into further detail about connections as we will develop these ideas further as we learn about different methods later in this book. At this point it will suffice to say that the connections and causal relationships are critical in helping us to understand and predict the behaviour of complex systems.

3.8 Processes and systems

A common question we get at this point is 'what is the difference between a process and a system?... is a system not just a process?' This is a fair question,

Figure 3.5 Causal relationships between two parts of a system resulting in a reinforcing/feedback loop

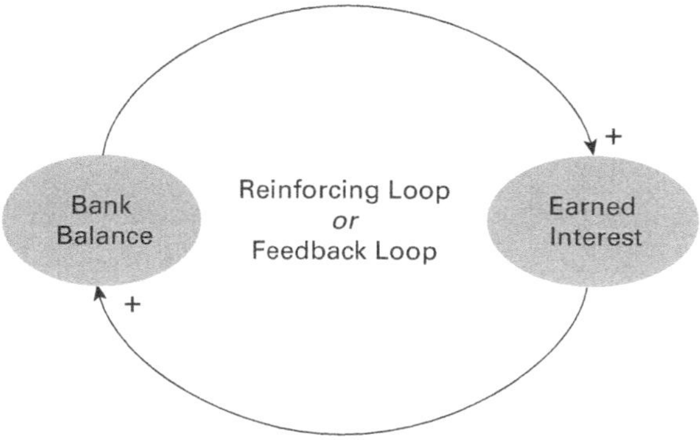

and it usually comes from people who have been trained in process management and improvement techniques such as Total Quality Management (TQM), Lean Management and Six-Sigma. In essence a process is a system, but a system can be much bigger than a process. In TQM, Lean and Six-Sigma the process focuses on very specific systems such as the manufacturing process, the order fulfilment process, the planning process and so on. We would argue that whilst all processes are systems not all systems are processes. For example, the national economic system discussed before is not a process, but comprises many subsystems and many processes within it. In short, process thinking is consistent with systems thinking, but in systems thinking we are concerned with systems of all sizes and their interconnections with other relevant systems.

3.9 Entropy and homeostasis

Finally, before we conclude this chapter, it would be pertinent to introduce two further concepts that help us explain the behaviour of systems. Earlier we defined a system as a collection of interacting parts that result in system-level behaviours. The individual parts of the system, whether they are technical components, individual people or organizations, do exhibit autonomous behaviours. In most cases the parts of a system are divergent and as a result, if left to their own devices they move towards disorder or disorganization.

This phenomenon is best explained through an example like those shown below:

- **Example 1.** Think about a garden that is well manicured and organized; it is quite nice to look at. But if you leave the garden unattended for a while the plants will start competing with each other as they try to take over the soil and after a while you end up with a mess. In this case the organizing force is the gardener who regularly maintains the garden to keep it nice and organized. Without this organizing force the orderly garden will gradually decline into disorder.
- **Example 2.** Thinking in similar lines about a car which is also made of many parts, each having a specific function. Over time, each part wears out and their interactions with other parts change. Gradually the nice shiny new car deteriorates into an old car that does not drive or perform as well as it used to. However, as we all know we can slow down and even prevent this gradual deterioration through regular servicing and maintenance. Without this intervention the orderly system will gradually decline to disorder.
- **Example 3.** Thinking back to the flock of birds we discussed in the previous chapter, you may ask: if systems deteriorate to disorder over time, what keeps these birds dancing in the sky and creating these unique patterns? What keeps these birds together is herd or swarm behaviour (i.e. the behaviour of individuals or animals in a group acting collectively without centralized direction) which comes about because of very simple rules that are genetically coded into these birds. This rule may be something as simple as *I will not be more than six inches apart from the other birds in my flock*. In this case, unlike the previous two cases where there was an external intervention or control, there is an intrinsic system in place that keeps the flock together. In fact, it is this intrinsic control system that defines self-organizing systems we discussed earlier in this chapter.
- **Example 4.** Let us think about a crossroads junction with no external controls such as a roundabout, traffic lights or even a policeman directing the traffic the old-fashioned way. In this case only one rule applies and that is self-preservation; in other words *do not hit anyone as it may injure me and/or it will cost money*. Watching such a crossroads from a distance is quite unsettling; often it looks like chaos, but accidents are rare, and life goes on. If you wish to see one of these traffic junctions just search for *crazy traffic junctions* in YouTube and look for the ones with no traffic

lights, roundabouts or a policeman directing the traffic (see video link 3.1 and 3.2 in the online resources on the Koganpage.com product page).

So far through these examples we have established that systems without an intrinsic or extrinsic control system tend to move from order to disorder. In systems thinking this phenomenon is known as **entropy**. The term entropy is borrowed from physics where it is used to describe how organized heat energy is lost into the random background energy of the surrounding environment (the Second Law of Thermodynamics). As such, in systems thinking entropy can be used as a metaphor for ageing, skill fade, obsolescence, or similar.

Entropy equally applies to organizations. In fact, from a systems thinking perspective a key purpose of management is to prevent entropy. This is typically achieved through continuous improvement change and renewal.

Homeostasis is another term used within systems thinking to describe a system that maintains its 'steady state' or a system that is in a 'dynamic equilibrium'. Examples include the human body's ability to remain at a steady temperature and an organization's ability to maintain its performance within its market. In the above examples, intrinsic and extrinsic controls or interventions prevent entropy and enable systems to achieve homeostasis.

In the next chapter we will explore common models and frameworks that underpin systems thinking, providing further insights into these intrinsic and extrinsic controls.

CASE STUDY A systems thinking case study

As we have seen in this section, there are different ways to conceptualize systems. When it comes to thinking about organizations, one of the first things that comes to most people's minds is the organization structure. Although this is a valid way of conceptualizing an organization in systems, there are other ways that are often more useful.

This case study is based around a whisky manufacturing company which distils whisky in its distilling plants and then stores the beverage for anything from 5 to 25 years. The older the whisky the more valuable it is. The company bottles the whisky in its bottling plants before the product is distributed to various customers and retailers around the world.

On the surface all the products appear the same; whisky is an output from a distillation process. It stays in stock for some time (5 to 25 years) and then in the bottling plant it is poured into a bottle, a cap or a cork is put on top, and then two or three labels are applied to the bottle identifying the product and telling its story. Sometimes the bottle is packed into a cardboard or a metal case and the bottle/case is then inserted into a cardboard box containing six bottles or cases. Boxes are palletized onto standard transport pallets and the product is ready for shipping to the customer. So far so good!

When we analyse how these products behave in the market and the customer buying behaviour, we see two distinctive groups emerging. One group of products, lower-value products, behave as commodities. They are sold throughout the year in reasonably high volumes. The customers are more interested in what is inside the bottle, i.e. the whisky, and they are less interested in the bottle or the packaging. The other group is high-value products that behave like fashion items or pieces of art. They are significantly more expensive, and are bought and used like trophies. Often, they are given as presents or corporate gifts. They have a brand value and a story behind the product. They are sold in much lower quantities and the sales volumes are much more seasonal and variable. The customers are more interested in the brand and the story. In some cases the bottles become collectors' items and increase in value with time. Some people treat these as investments; thus they do not open the bottle and drink its contents. The customers pay more attention to packaging, which must look elegant and be representative of high price.

If we examine how these products are made, the low-value products are made in fully automated high-speed production lines in high volumes. The quality and cost of the packaging (i.e. the bottle, label, cap/cork, etc.) are comparatively low. In contrast, the high-value product is made in smaller quantities in semi-automated and sometimes manual production lines using higher-quality/value components such as coated bottles, embossed labels, weighted bottle caps, metal cases, etc. The speed of production is much lower, and special care is taken to ensure that the bottles and labels are not scratched or damaged by rubbing against each other. The look and feel of the bottle must be right. In terms of finances, the margins from high-value products are significantly higher than those of the low-value products even though they cost more to produce.

When we analyse how the products behave from these perspectives we see two systems within this company: one system for high-value products and another one for low-value products, with each being produced differently and serving different markets. Although both of these systems may have the same purpose, i.e. to make money for the company, their functions are clearly different. The two systems would also have different performance measures, one emphasizing speed and efficiency, the other quality and image. If we were to improve the performance of this company we would need to understand how each one of these systems behaves before designing an intervention. The consequence of looking at just one of these systems and designing a performance improvement intervention without differentiating between the two subsystems would certainly be counterproductive and would result in negative outcomes.

Reflective questions

- In the above case study we have already identified how the two systems may differ from each other in terms of purpose, function and performance measures. Can you think about what may be the external forces that could influence the behaviour of each system? Think about how these forces may influence the behaviour of these systems.
- Think about the organizational structure of this company. How would the structure we identified above impact the design of the organizational structure? Would you have two different management teams, one for each system, or would you have just one management team managing both systems?

3.10 Summary

We started this chapter with the aim of building upon the key systems thinking concepts and definitions introduced in the previous chapter by giving, you, the reader, a deeper and more complete understanding of systems, their structure and properties. Based on the discussion so far, we can summarize that:

- A system has a purpose (usually) and a function.
- A variety of things (materials, people, information, knowledge, energy and so on) flow through the system as inputs and outputs.
- Stocks and flows are useful ways of thinking about a system, and they are not limited to tangible things like materials, people and energy, but they can also be intangible things such as knowledge, experience and goodwill.
- These stocks and flows create the forces that shape the emergent behaviour of systems.
- The performance of a system may be conceptualized as effectiveness and efficiency of a system.
- A system exists within a wider operating environment and is connected to other systems within this environment. Indeed, that wider system itself may be part of an even wider and bigger system.

- A system has a boundary, but these boundaries can be defined by the nature of the enquiry and/or the worldview of the manager/analyst studying the system.
- A system has a structure that comprises parts that are interconnected with one another within the system. These parts may also be connected to other systems in the wider environment through the system's boundary. Indeed, these parts may be subsystems in their own right with their own internal structures.
- A system interacts with other systems in its environment. This interaction results in the system being influenced/changed by its environment as well as the system influencing/changing its environment.
- Connections between parts of the system are critical in helping us to understand the causalities between these parts and how these interact in concert to define the behaviour of the system.

Understanding the structure, purpose, function and performance measures of the systems within organizations from different perspectives is critical first step for understanding why organizations behave the way they do. When we are managing an organization, making decisions without this understanding is likely to produce unexpected and unintended outcomes.

REFLECTIVE EXERCISE

At this early stage, as a new manager or a student of systems thinking, it may be quite challenging to conceptualize your own organization (or part of it) as a system. It usually helps to start thinking about a system in simple terms and then move on to building a more complex picture. Thus, in order to help you ground your learning we would encourage you to start thinking about your own organization or part of the organization by conceptualizing it as an image, illustrated in Figure 3.6. Here we have used just some of the systems concepts and properties we have introduced thus far. In your own exercise you do not have to use all of these or be limited to these, but it is a start.

You may start by drawing the boundary and then start putting in parts of the system that you think may belong to this system. If it is helpful, you may also put parts of other systems outside the boundary. Then start thinking about what flows between these parts but also about what happens during these flows and how they may influence each other. For example, sales forecasts may flow

Figure 3.6 A simple generic template to start thinking about your organization as a system

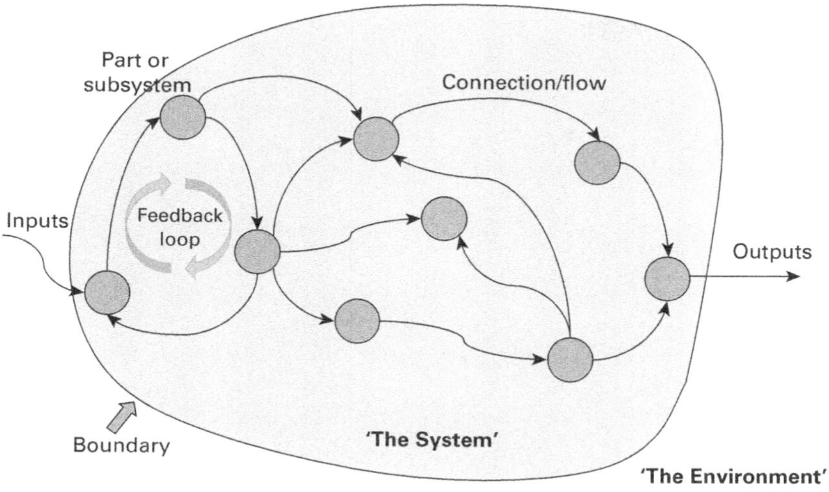

between two parts. You can also think about what happens when these forecasts are wrong or intentionally under-reported. Try to capture the feelings and perspectives of people or teams in the relevant parts of the system and try to explain the resultant behaviour.

In order to explain the picture, you will find it helpful to write a narrative of what is happening in the picture. Keep this short and to the point, but make an effort to capture the causalities behind various behaviours.

TEAM EXERCISE

As a facilitator, try to identify a system that is common to your group of managers or students. This may be their workplace or equally somewhere they all identify with, something like a local well-known fast-food restaurant, sports club, or even their place or programme of study. Ask each of them to do the above exercise individually. Then ask each member of the group to talk through their model. Try to draw attention to the similarities and differences between the models. Ask them to discuss why the differences may be there.

PART TWO
Models and methods

This part of the book focuses on models and methods commonly used for understanding and modelling systems. In Chapter 4 we explore some of the common systems models and frameworks that provide different perspectives and those we have found useful in our work. In Chapters 5 and 6 we cover different methods for modelling hard and soft systems respectively. The soft systems modelling methods we introduce in Chapter 6, particularly the causal loop diagrams, provide a segway to Part 3 of the book, which explores systems complexity in greater detail.

Common system models and frameworks 4

In the previous chapters we introduced what a system is and went on to develop various concepts and definitions that underpin systems thinking. By now you should be familiar with these concepts and their definitions, and you should be able to think about your organization, your job, programme of study and even your life from a systems perspective.

In this chapter we will build upon these concepts and definitions to introduce a number of systems models and frameworks that are commonly cited and used. Furthermore, the models and frameworks we have selected to include in this chapter take different complementary perspectives to systems which should further enhance your understanding and help you to start thinking in systems.

LEARNING OUTCOMES

- Understand
  - characteristics of living systems
  - the control and communication within viable systems
  - the importance of systems architecture
  - how variation and worldviews may interact with and shape the behaviour of systems
  - how constraints govern the performance of a system
- Able to conceptualize complex systems and explain their behaviours in terms of their control and communication systems, architecture, sources of variation, worldviews and constraints
- Identify basic improvement opportunities in these systems

4.1. Miller's Living Systems Theory

James Grier Miller (1916–2002) was an American psychologist, psychiatrist, an academic and a forerunner of systems thinking. He established and led the Mental Health Research Institute at the University of Michigan, United States. He is also the creator of the Living Systems Theory, which was intended to be a general theory about the existence of all living systems (Miller, 1978).

Miller first developed his theory of living systems in 1978 by focusing on concrete (in other words tangible) systems and then extended his theories to include conceptual and abstract systems. He organized living systems into eight nested hierarchical levels, each lower level a subsystem within the higher-level system as depicted in Figure 4.1.

According to Miller's theory, *cells* represent fundamental building blocks of life, which organize themselves into *organs*, which in turn organize themselves into *organisms*. Organisms organize themselves into *groups* and in turn groups organize themselves into *organizations*. *Communities* include both individual organisms and groups, with different functions within the community. *Societies* are associations of communities and *supranational* systems are organizations of societies.

Figure 4.1 Adapted from Miller's eight levels of nested systems

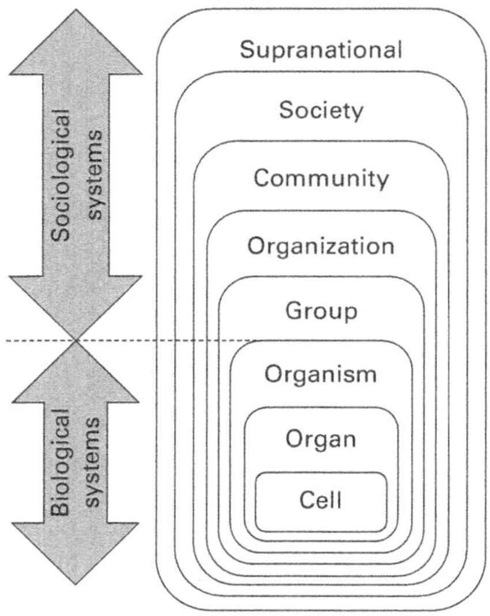

Core to his theory is that all nature is a continuum, and that the endless complexity of life can be organized into patterns that repeat themselves at each level of system. All eight levels of systems are considered open self-organizing systems that may be conceptualized using four dimensions – *matter/energy,*[1] *information*, *space* and *time* – because the living systems exist in a space-time continuum and they are made of matter and energy organized by information.

Miller's theory suggests that all eight levels of systems sustain themselves through 20 subsystems that *recur*[2] at each level. Some of these 20 subsystems process both matter/energy and information, others process matter/energy or information. These subsystems, which are arranged by input-throughput-output processes, are defined in Table 4.1.

Miller, having focused on concrete systems when developing his theory, also distinguishes between concrete, abstract and conceptual systems where:

- **A concrete system** is a system that exists in reality and is composed of tangible (physical) objects such as materials, information, plants and so on. In other words, they are hard systems.
- **A conceptual system** is a system that exists in reality and is composed of intangible (non-physical) objects (such as ideas, knowledge, feelings). Most existing soft systems are conceptual systems even though they may have some concrete elements as they deal with people's feelings, knowledge and thoughts.
- **An abstract system** is a system composed of tangible and/or intangible objects, but it does not exist in reality, it exists only in thought as an idea. For example, the Star Ship Enterprise and the race of Klingons from the *Star Trek* programmes do not exist in reality, they exist only in imagination.

Time is also a fundamental dimension of Miller's theory, which is captured in the definition of a living system. A **living system**, by itself, integrates divergent parts into a convergent whole in dynamic relationships internally and externally in an ongoing moment-by-moment process of self-organization and self-creation (Holliday and Jones, 2015), which captures several systems thinking concepts in the context of Miller's Living Systems Theory. These are:

- Systems consist of several parts or subsystems that are divergent. Thus, left alone these divergent systems would transition into a state of chaos, i.e. entropy.

- A living system integrates divergent parts into a convergent whole. Thus a control system exists creating this convergence.
- Internal and external relationships or connections that are dynamic. That is, the relationships change over time.
- Moment-by-moment process of self-organization and self-creation. That is, over time there is a continuous process of self-organization and self-creation.

In this context Miller's 20 subsystems summarized in Table 4.1 are his attempt at generalizing the subsystems and functions that enable a living system to integrate its divergent parts into a convergent whole through a continuous process of self-organization and self-creation.

In short, we can surmise that with the 20 subsystems that sustain living systems, Miller is identifying the subsystem that controls the behaviour of living systems that prevent entropy and promote homeostasis.

Table 4.1 Twenty subsystems that sustain each system

Stage	Subsystem	Function	Processes
Input Stage	Input Transducer	Brings information into the System Ingestor	• Information
	Ingestor	Brings matter/energy into the System Processes	• Matter/Energy
Throughput Stage *(Information processes)*	Internal Transducer	Receives and converts information brought into the system	• Information
	Channel and Net	Distributes information throughout the system decoder	• Information
	Decoder	Prepares information for use by the system timer	• Information
	Timer	Maintains the appropriate spatial/temporal relationships	• Information
	Associator	Maintains appropriate relationships between information sources	• Information
	Memory	Stores information for system use	• Information
	Decider	Makes decisions about various system operations	• Information
	Encoder	Converts information to needed and usable forms	• Information

(continued)

Table 4.1 (Continued)

Stage	Subsystem	Function	Processes
Throughput Stage (Matter/Energy processes)	Reproducer	Uses information to carry out reproductive functions	• Information • Matter/Energy
	Boundary	Uses information to protect the system from outside influences	• Information • Matter/Energy
	Distributor	Distributes matter/energy for use throughout the system	• Matter/Energy
	Converter	Converts matter/energy into a suitable form for use by the system	• Matter/Energy
	Producer	Synthesizes matter/energy for use within the system	• Matter/Energy
	M/E Storage	Stores matter/energy used by the system	• Matter/Energy
	Motor	Handles mobility of various parts of the system	• Matter/Energy
	Supporter	Provides physical support to the system	• Matter/Energy
Output Stage	Output Transducer	Handles information output of the system	• Information
	Extruder	Handles matter/energy discharged by the system	• Matter/Energy

4.2 Beer's Viable Systems Model

Anthony Stafford Beer (1962–2002) was a British consultant and an academic best known for his work in management cybernetics. **Cybernetics** is the study of control and communication systems in animals and machines. It is concerned with understanding complex systems behaviours such as learning, cognition and change. **Management cybernetics** is the application of cybernetics to management and organizations.

Stafford Beer's definition of a system is consistent with our earlier definition, that a system is a set of connected things or parts forming a complex whole. However, he also introduced the concept of viability to systems thinking (Beer, 1972, 1979 and 1985). So, what is a viable system?

Stafford Beer defines a **viable system** as a system that can *self-produce*. So, you may ask what is **self-production**? This concept is best explained through an example.

Example 1 – a human being. Think about how old you are. If you are reading this book your response may range anywhere between 20 and 90 and possibly more. Well, you would all be wrong! You may have been living in this world for 20 to 90 years but throughout this period your cells have been replacing themselves at very regular intervals. In fact, the average age of a human cell is eight years. So, we could argue that over a period of about 8–12 years most if not all of your cells have renewed themselves. But you, your friends, family and colleagues still recognize you for who you are, even though every cell in your body may be different.

Example 2 – IBM. International Business Machines (IBM) started life in 1911 producing punch-card tabulators and other office products. It moved on to producing electric typewriters (1933), then computers (1952) and later entered into the personal computers market (1981). Then it divested from manufacturing to work on supercomputers, computer services and software (2005). Throughout this 94-year period we can imagine that most parts of IBM (buildings, equipment, people) have been renewed. They were replaced by parts that were more relevant for the context within which the company was operating. In short, although every part of IBM has changed over the years, we still recognize it for what it is.

In the above two examples we have illustrated the concept of self-production. In other words, self-production is the ability of a system to renew its parts, in some cases with improved, enhanced parts appropriately adapting to the environment within which it operates. In the wider systems thinking literature self-production is also referred to as *self-creation* or **autopoiesis**. The term autopoiesis comes from the Greek words 'auto' and 'poiesis', meaning self-creation. It was borrowed from the field of cellular biology, where it refers to the capacity of living cells to reproduce and renew themselves. In a broader context of systems thinking it describes the ability of systems to reproduce certain behaviours by repeating their own operations. At this point, it is important to emphasize that self-production is not the same as self-organization, which we discussed in Chapter 2. Whilst self-organization is about a system's ability to organize and manage itself in the absence of a central or external organizing/managing authority (e.g. hierarchy), self-production is about the system's ability to renew its components. In other words, not all self-organizing systems can self-produce, and similarly not all self-producing systems are self-organizing systems. This is reflected in the IBM example above; whilst IBM is not a self-organizing system, as it has a management hierarchy, it has proven itself to be a self-producing system.

It was Stafford Beer's life's ambition to understand what makes a system viable, and as a result he came up with the Viable Systems Model (VSM) illustrated in Figure 4.2. VSM as illustrated in this figure may look complicated but is quite simple once it is explained. According to Beer, any viable system comprises five subsystems, which we will call systems for simplicity.

By definition, a system comprises a number of parts. In VSM each part is known as a System 1. A system may have as many parts or System 1s as necessary. In Figure 4.2. we have shown three Systems 1s. At this stage do not worry about what is inside these System 1s or parts, as we will come to them later.

System 2 provides the information and communication channels and mechanisms enabling different parts, that is Systems 1s, to communicate amongst each other. System 2 also enables System 3 to monitor and coordinate the activities within System 1s, providing a resource-sharing function for System 1s.

Systems 3, 4 and 5 together, shown on the left in Figure 4.2, represent the management function for the system. Within this management function, System 3 represents the controls that are put into place to establish the rules, resources, roles and responsibilities of System 1s. System 3 also provides an interface with Systems 4 and 5.

Figure 4.2 Adapted from the Viable Systems Model

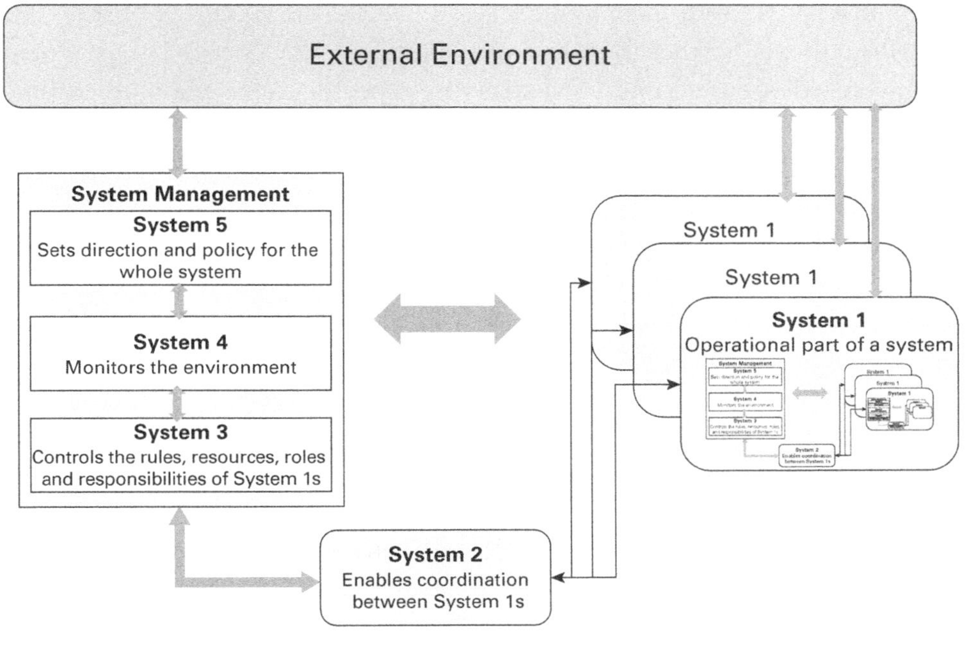

System 4 is responsible for looking outwards to the environment, monitoring what is happening around the system, providing essential information on how the system needs to change, and adapt to remain viable.

System 5 is responsible for setting direction and policy within the whole system, balancing demands from different parts of the system and directing the system as a whole.

It is worth spending a little more time discussing the differences between the functions of Systems 2 and 3. Whilst both are providing some form of coordination function between parts of the system, that is System 1s, System 3 works more as a planning and scheduling function whereas System 2 provides a more immediate, real-time, coordination function. For example, if you are playing tennis, imagine the ball is about to go to the left-hand corner of the court. You do not stop and say, *ah, the ball is about to go to the left corner, so I need to tell my legs to go that way and my right arm with the racket to turn and lift up this way.* Instead, you react immediately in real time. It is the purpose of System 2 to coordinate amongst System 1s to enable this real-time reaction. In this real-time scenario System 2 achieves such a response by enabling the individual management functions of System 1s to coordinate amongst each other without the need for instructions from System 3.

At this point, it would be appropriate to introduce the concept of *recursion,* which we have already intimated in previous chapters when we discussed systems of systems and systems within systems. In Figure 4.2, if you examine what is inside each System 1 you will see the recursion of the VSM described above. Further to this, if you investigate the System 1s in the next level, you will see the same VSM structure repeating once again. According to VSM, all viable systems are recursive. In other words, the structure (Systems 1, 2, 3, 4 and 5 described above) will repeat in subsystems, sub-subsystems and so on.

In describing this sort of control structure, what Beer does is describe the cybernetic control system, which exists within many systems. You can apply this to an amoeba, a shoal of fish, an organization or even the governance structure of a nation. Let us look at two examples:

EXAMPLE 1: A SHOAL OF FISH

A shoal comprises thousands of fish with each fish representing a system in its own right (System 1), but the whole shoal operates to some common, genetically coded rules such as staying within six inches of each other (System 5). This simple rule makes this collection of fish behave as a shoal. This shoal of fish has many eyes that enable it to monitor what is happening in the outside world (System 4). When one fish detects a threat, such as a dolphin coming towards them, it responds immediately (System 3) by breaking away from the shoal, which causes other fish to also break away because of the six-inch rule, even though they may have not detected the threat (System 2). So, the shoal splits in two, trying to avoid the dolphin. Once the threat is gone the shoal comes back together again because of the six-inch rule.

EXAMPLE 2: A MANUFACTURING ORGANIZATION

Let us assume that a manufacturing organization has two business units (System 1s). One business unit designs, manufactures and sells custom-made pumping solutions and the other one manufactures and sells standard industrial pumps that you can buy from a catalogue. The custom-made pumping solution business competes primarily on the company's reputation for engineering excellence and designing reliable pumping solutions that meet customers' expectations. The standard pumps business competes mainly on price. Essentially these are two different businesses founded on the same product, i.e. a pump, that are serving two completely different markets on a different competitive basis.

If we examine each business unit, we will see that both of them have the same processes, such as Develop Product, Get Order, Fulfil Order, Support Product. These are System 1s at the next level of recursion. We will also see that, although each business unit may comprise similar subsystems or processes, the functions of these subsystems will be significantly different. In one business the focus of the Get Order process (System 1) is to sell a standard product at a competitive price, while in the other business unit the focus of the Get Order process is to convince the customer that they offer the best engineering capability and solution.

Naturally, at the business unit level, these two different businesses compete differently in their respective markets (System 4); they would need to have different strategies and business plans (System 5), different management structures and rules (System 3) and different coordination mechanisms that would coordinate the processes or subsystems within each business unit (System 2). Of course, higher-level Systems 3, 4 and 5 would also exist to ensure cohesion and optimization of the overall business.

Having defined the five systems that underpin the capability of a system to self-produce and renew itself, Beer takes his model further and includes a system of performance measures. He characterizes performance as:

- **Actuality:** what the system is able to do now with existing resources and under existing constraints.
- **Capability:** what the system is able to do now with existing resources and under existing constraints, if it really worked at it.
- **Potentiality:** what system should be achieving if it developed its resources and removed its constraints.

An example of this could be that the manufacturing company is delivering 65 per cent of its orders on time (Actuality), but based on past performance, we know that with current resources and constraints, it can deliver 80 per cent of its orders on time (Capability). However, if we remove all the constraints and develop all the resources, its potential is 100 per cent on-time delivery (Potentiality).

In this context, Systems 4 and 5 are jointly responsible for realizing the potentiality of the system. To enable this, Beer offers three further performance measures based on the above concepts, which are somewhat different but complementary to our discussions on systems performance in the previous chapter:

- **Productivity:** the ratio of actuality to capability.
- **Latency:** the ratio of capability to potentiality.
- **Performance:** the ratio of actuality to potentiality.

A key feature of the VSM and the performance measures discussed so far is that the performance measures enable *algedonic signals* to be communicated throughout the system to interrupt conscious thought to provoke reflex action. In cybernetics an algedonic signal is a pre-emptive message concerning pleasure or pain that provides an important survival mechanism to a system by alerting it to an imminent threat. For example, when we are crossing a road, we might see a car coming towards us but the car is far enough away that our conscious thinking mechanism makes us walk faster to get across the road safely. This is conscious thought. In contrast, an algedonic signal is when we accidentally put our hands near a very hot surface and our reflex reaction kicks in and we immediately pull back our hand without conscious thought. In living systems, an algedonic signal is an essential component that enables the living system to respond to immediate threats, in effect avoiding disastrous consequences.

In fact, our earlier example of a tennis player's reflex reaction is also a response to an algedonic signal. In sports, training helps to develop the person's ability to recognize threats and opportunities and gain an ability to respond through reflex reaction rather than conscious thought. In organizations, the algedonic signal works the same way. When someone somewhere does something extraordinarily badly, an algedonic signal is sent, which may initiate immediate action with all relevant System 1s enabled by System 2 coordinating a response in a timely manner. In common terminology we may recognize this as a corrective action. However, the signal is also sent to management (Systems 3, 4 and 5), which may, after conscious thought, take a preventative action so that the same pain does not happen again.

From a business and management perspective, a good example of an algedonic signal is the *stop-the-line* or *stop-the-process* signal, which is akin to pulling the emergency handle to stop a bus or train. A stop-the-line/process signal is commonly used to enable people working in the production line or a business process to stop the line or process when they detect a significant problem. For example, in a manufacturing line, if a faulty part is detected but the manufacturing process continues using these faulty parts, all the products with the faulty parts would have to be reworked or thrown to waste. Thus, stopping the line/process and dealing with the problem immediately saves a lot of pain down the line.

Based on the discussion so far, we can surmise that Beer, like Miller, in developing the Viable Systems Model, identifies the subsystem, controls and signals that are essential for systems to respond to their external environment, govern their performance, see opportunities and threats, and respond to these in a timely manner. As a result, viable systems self-produce/self-create themselves, changing and adapting to new emerging conditions within their operating environment. In short, Beer provides insight into the mechanisms that govern the behaviour of systems that can sustain themselves, preventing entropy and promoting homeostasis.

4.3 Hitchens' Systems Architecture

Derek Hitchins (1935–) is a British systems engineer and a professor of engineering management. Having had a career in the Royal Air Force followed by systems engineering and senior management roles in various engineering organizations, he has worked all his life with complex systems. His academic work focuses on developing a better understanding of the architecture that underpins these complex systems (Hitchins, 2003 and 2008). In this context **systems architecture** is defined as the pattern made by all the subsystems and their interconnections to support the function, purpose and performance of the system. Hitchens' Systems Architecture, although developed from a perspective of technical or engineered systems, is equally relevant to living and soft systems such as organizations, as will be discussed in this section.

An architecture is not the same as the structure of the five systems in the viable systems model or the 20 subsystems identified in Miller's Living Systems Theory. Rather, an architecture assumed in this framework relates to how various parts of the system are organized in relation to each other. Unlike Miller's theory and Beer's VSM, Hitchins' Systems Architecture is not universal; it is specific to the purpose and function of a system. For example, if we look at different living systems such as an amoeba, a worm, a snake, a cheetah and a human, the architecture of each of them is quite different. An amoeba is a single-cell animal so its architecture is very simple: it is a single cell. A worm is a rather more complex system; its architecture is a tube with its vital parts (organs) organized within this tube. A snake, although similar to a worm, is bigger, so it needs a skeleton to support and organize its parts. A cheetah's architecture is different again. It has parts (arms and legs) that a snake does not have. In terms of parts, there is little difference between a cheetah and a human. If we assume that the purpose of both is to survive and reproduce, their functions are quite different. A cheetah's architecture is optimized to give it speed in short pursuits whereas a human's architecture is more upright, enabling them to walk long distances more efficiently.

At this point it would be worth reflecting on the whisky company case study presented at the end of the previous chapter, where we concluded that the whisky company comprises two systems – the high-value products business and the low-value products business. You may also recall that at the end of the case study we asked a reflective question about the organizational structure. In fact, this question is really about what the appropriate architecture would be to support the purpose and function of these two systems. Do we create two separate architectures, or do we create a single architecture that would support both systems? In practice there is no single answer to this question. Different companies have addressed this same issue in different ways. The important point here is to understand that there are different systems that we are trying to manage, and that they may require different architectures to support their purpose and function.

Further to this, considering the evolution of humans as systems we will observe that their architecture has evolved over time, and it is continuing to do so, to support the changes in the function of the system. Consequently we can surmise that as the system's purpose or function changes the architecture needs to evolve to support its new purpose or function.

In this context, the model illustrated in Figure 4.3 defines how a system's architecture supports its purpose and function and ensures its viability through maintenance and evolution (self-production/creation).

According to Hitchins' model, storing transient information and the knowledge of information location strongly contributes towards acquisition and sharing of knowledge regarding the performance of the system and the fitness of the architecture that supports it. This in turn enables the architecture to adapt, evolve and self-maintain, thus enabling the architecture to provide a framework for system cohesion. For example, different parts of a building and their functions are integrated into the whole building through the civil engineering architecture. This framework in turn enables the system to reconfigure its assets in anticipation of internal and external threats, ensuring the availability of the system (i.e. the system does not break down very often) and also survivability of the system. For example, rooms in a building can be converted to serve a different function when the main purpose of the building needs to change. Reconfiguring assets within the system enables groups within and outside the system to be linked so that synergy is achieved in coordinating and controlling these assets and groups in the system. These linkages serve to identify closed linked parts within the system so that they can be grouped or located together to ease communication and relationships, thus reducing system complexity. This in turn provides a resilient framework enabling the system to recover from any disruption. The framework in turn provides the foundation for progressive development whilst also supporting external entities (systems or parts of systems) that intermittently connect to or disconnect from the system. For example, parts of the building might be temporarily sealed in the event of fire. This ultimately supports the system's mission or purpose.

Figure 4.3 How a system's architecture evolves and supports the purpose, function and performance of the system

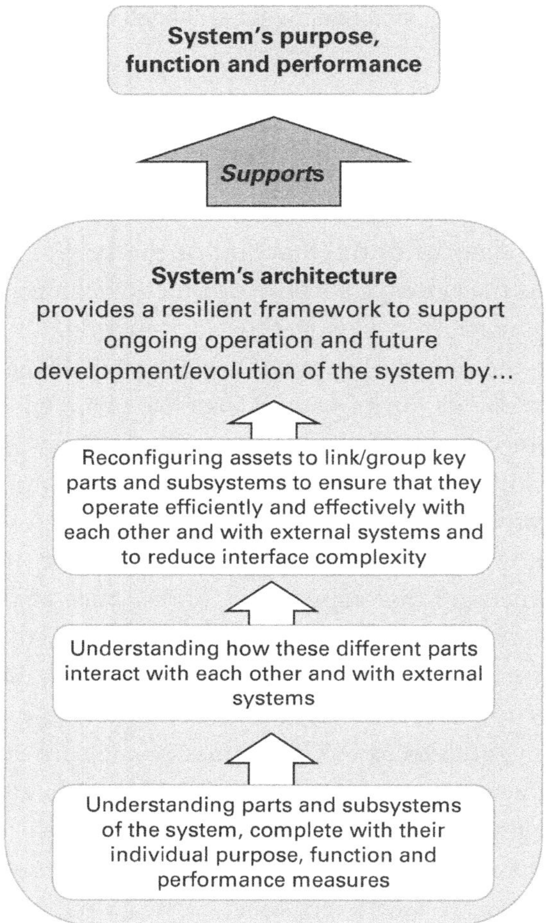

From this discussion one could see that Hitchins' approach to understanding the system's architecture is quite different from Miller's Living Systems Theory or Beer's Viable Systems Model discussed in the previous sections. Apart from having a strong engineering and technical systems bias, Hitchins' main focus is on understanding the characteristics that enable a system to maintain an effective architecture, i.e. a structure that organizes various parts of the system in relation to each other. Hitchins does not present us with a single unified model of an architecture, rather he presents a model that explains how a system's architecture is maintained and evolves over time. In the previous paragraphs when discussing the meaning of architecture we have already given examples of living systems such as an amoeba, worm, snake, cheetah and so on. From these examples, it is evident that as living systems evolve so does their architecture, albeit over very long periods of time. Have a look at the biological evolution in Figure 4.4 and think about the architecture of various creatures, i.e. different parts and how they are organized. You will see how their architecture has evolved over time.

The architecture of organizations also evolves over time, usually in response to adapting to changes in the operating environment. Some of these changes could be over long periods of time and some of them may be much faster as the organization responds to a disruptive event, such as the Covid-19 pandemic. For example, in response to the pandemic we have seen the shape of work changing in a very short period of time. Previously, for most organizations working from home was a luxury offered to a limited number of employees, and online meetings, although technically possible, were much less common. During the pandemic and the immediate aftermath (as during the writing of this book) we have seen a massive change in the attitude of the employees and the organizations. Many organizations and people found that they can be as effective, if not more so, working from home. As a result, a

Figure 4.4 Biological evolution

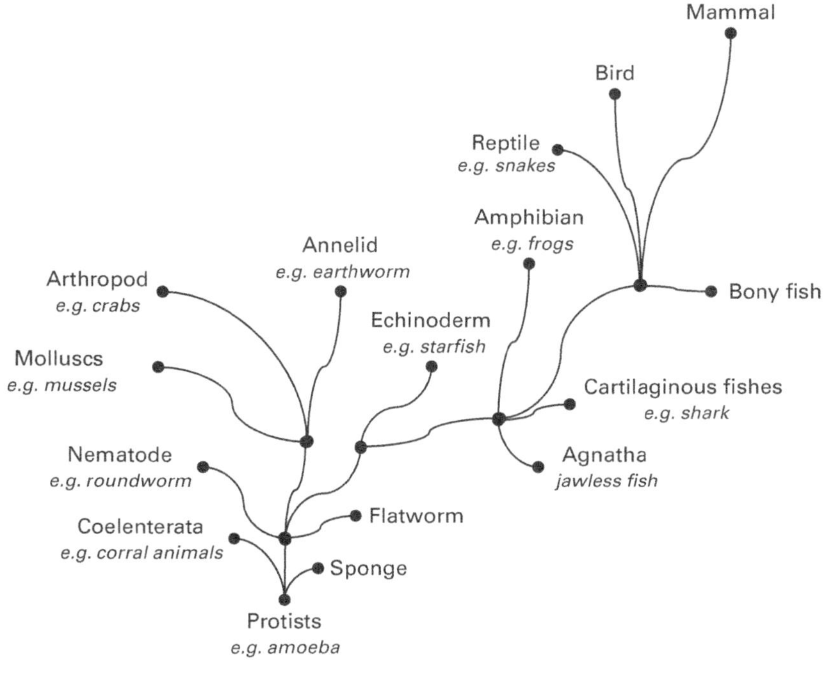

number of organizations downsized their office buildings and instead invested in systems and technologies that make their people more effective when working from home – for example Twitter, Square and Coinbase (Kelly, 2020). As one CEO of a technology company put it:

> ... since the pandemic we have vacated our building which we own and rented it out to another company. Today we are a virtual organization. All our people work from home, which saves them about two to three hours of travelling time every day, we do not have to heat and maintain a building including a canteen, which saves us money, employees get more work done, they spend more time with their families... We still have meetings but people can meet anywhere convenient, it does not have to be an office building. So far it is working better than we could have imagined.

In essence, they have changed their architecture. Previously, parts of the system (people) were connected together by being in the same office building. Today they are still connected together but the mechanisms that support this connection are no longer physical buildings and offices, they are technologies that underpin the internet and modern communications such as email, shared workspaces and video conferencing. In short, the purpose and performance expectations of the system are the same, but the function (i.e. how the system operates) has changed, and thus the architecture has adapted to support the new function.

4.4 Deming's System of Profound Knowledge

William Edwards Deming (1900–1993) was an American engineer, statistician, academic and consultant. He is recognized as the father of modern quality management and is often quoted as the influential force behind the Japanese industrial revolution and their reputation for high-quality products.

During his work on quality management and continuous improvement he widely used statistics where he observed variations in the systems, which became a core concept that underpins his System of Profound Knowledge (Deming, 2018). Deming suggests that in order to understand and predict the behaviour of any system, and particularly a human activity system such as the organizations we all work in, we need to focus on four elements as illustrated in Figure 4.5, namely The System, Theories, Human Behaviour and Variation.

Figure 4.5 Deming's System of Profound Knowledge

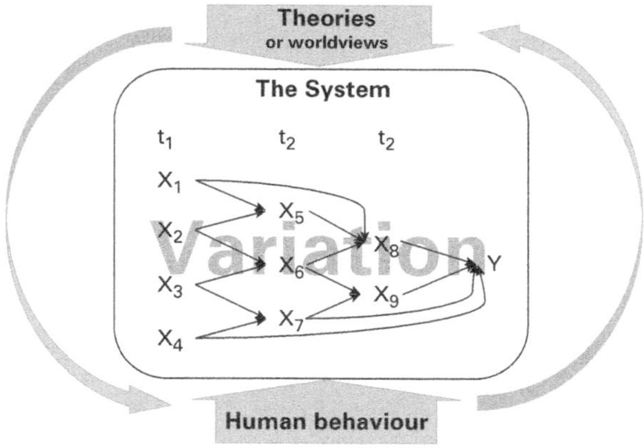

Consistent with the definition of a system, Deming's model also defines a system as a number of parts that are connected together, and as they interact over time that results in the emergent outcome or behaviour of the system. He conceptualizes each part of the system as a variable and suggests that the output or behaviour of each part is never consistent and is subject to at least some natural variations. He argues that these variations within each part of the system (represented by Xs in Figure 4.5) interact with each other either directly or indirectly over time (t in Figure 4.5), thus making the outcome or behaviour of the system (represented by Y in Figure 4.5) difficult to predict. In essence, with this approach Deming captures the complexity of everyday life. For example, think about your commute to work or school and how long it takes. Let us say your commute to the office is about 15 minutes on a good day, but sometimes it takes 45 minutes. If you leave home at 8.30 am the time it would take you to commute to work is a lot less predictable because of the rush hour and it can sometimes take you one hour to get to your office. But if you leave at 9.30 am you can usually get to the office within 15 to 20 minutes. So over time, interactions between the variables make the outcome more or less predictable. In this system the commuters and the traffic control system (e.g. traffic lights) represent different parts of the system that interact over time.

Deming suggests that this complexity in systems can be overcome by creating a lens that integrates our understanding of:

- **the system** and its parts
- **the variations** inherent within each part of the system and their interactions

- **the theories or worldviews** of different people about the system that ultimately shape **human behaviour**

So far in this book we have already devoted considerable time to discussing what a system is, how its parts are interconnected and so on. However, this is the first point where we have introduced the concept of variation. Although we discussed worldviews in Chapter 2, we have not delved into how different people's theories or worldviews serve to shape their behaviour within the system. Below we will devote some space to expand on these points.

Variation

Variation is a well-known phenomenon in statistics as well as in quality and process management. In short, variation is defined as a change or difference in form, condition, position or amount. Examples of variation include:

- If a machine produces 30 pieces per hour on average, then sometimes the machine will produce 25 pieces per hour, while other times it might produce 35 pieces per hour. These variations will average at 30 pieces per hour over time. For a given hour we can never be certain how many pieces the machine will produce, but we can be more confident that it will be somewhere between 25 and 35 pieces. Here the variation refers to the quantity produced over a given unit of time.
- A light bulb's lifespan is measured in hours. Typically, a modern LED lightbulb will have a lifespan of about 50,000 hours as specified by a manufacturer. This is an average estimated lifespan of a lightbulb – some will last a lot longer and others a lot less. Here the variation refers to the time over which a product performs its function.
- Statistically an average American male is 175.4 cm tall. This does not mean that the next American male to walk through the door will be this height. Most certainly he will be shorter or taller. Here variation refers to measure of height.
- In a workplace the people skills of the leaders are likely to be quite different. Even the leadership style and people skills of a single leader may vary depending on their familiarity with and experience of a particular situation. In short, variation is not just applicable to things we can measure objectively, as in the examples above. It can also be in softer elements of the organization, such as management style, knowledge, information,

policies and procedures, and so on. The reality is that variation in any of these factors will impact on the overall behaviour and performance of a system.

In general, variation has two causes: natural causes and assignable causes. In the first example of a machine producing parts, if everything is working normally the machine will produce 30 pieces per hour with a minimum of 25 pieces per hour and maximum of 35 pieces per hour. This is a natural variation; in other words there is no assignable cause that would explain the variation. However, if the machine breaks down and it takes 30 minutes to fix it, and then there are only 14 pieces produced during that hour, the reason behind this variation is due to assignable causes, i.e. due to the machine breakdown. Similarly, for other examples assignable causes for variation could be a manufacturing fault reducing the lifespan of an LED light bulb to 1,000 hours, or a medical condition that would affect the height of a person.

Variation has a profound impact on systems as it impacts both stocks and flows in complex ways. To demonstrate this, let us consider a simple system perfectly designed and balanced, comprising five activities with each activity taking an average of 10 pieces of work per hour (Figure 4.6). This could be a manufacturing process in a factory, a tax returns handling process or a student registration process in a school. What would the average output of the entire system be?

The first logical answer that jumps to mind is that the overall system output will be 10 pieces per hour. But in reality, it would be very unlikely that this output can be achieved. Because an average of 10 pieces per hour means that sometimes an activity will produce 7 and sometimes 13 pieces per hour. This will result in inventory building up between some activities and shortages in other activities. For example, when an activity is ready to work there might not be any work pieces available because of the variation in the preceding activity. This variation over time would result in an output profile averaging less than 10 work pieces per minute for the whole process, with significant variation in the output. The exercise outlined below effectively demonstrates this phenomenon.

Figure 4.6 A simple system with work flowing through it

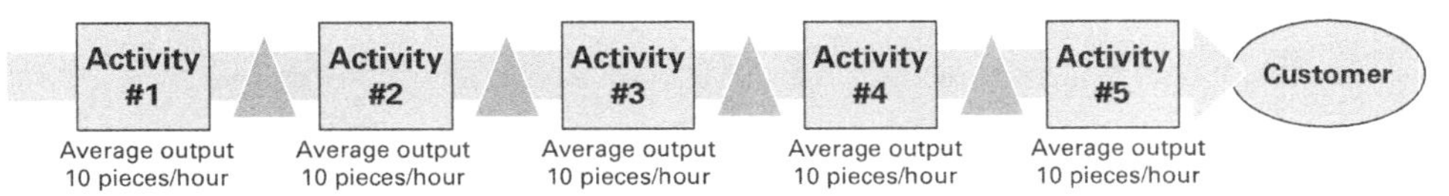

TEAM EXERCISE: IMPACT OF VARIATION ON PROCESS PERFORMANCE

This is a team exercise to help participants to better understand the concept of variation in a simulation of a simple process. To conduct the exercise, you will need seven people. Five people will work for five work centres, one person will represent a customer, and one person will be an analyst. If you have more people, you can have observers.

- Set up a production line with five work centres, as illustrated in Figure 4.6.
- Use coins as work pieces.
- Give each workstation a pair of dice.
- Start with six work pieces in each stock location with the first work centre having an unlimited supply of coins.
- The customer calls for product at regular intervals (say every 15 or 20 seconds).
- On the call of the customer, each work centre:
  - Throws the pair of dice.
  - Picks up the number of work pieces indicated by the dice (between 2 and 12) from the left-hand-side stock location and passes them on to the right-hand-side stock location
  - If there is no sufficient quantity of pieces on the left-hand-side stock, then the work centre will use the available pieces.
- Let the game run for about 20 calls.
- During the game the analyst records the number of work pieces received from work centre 5 for each call.
- Each work centre should record the dice value and the actual number of pieces processed at each call.
- At the end of the exercise discuss:
  - What does the overall output profile look like?... If you ensure that for each call the output coins are piled separately, you will see the output as a histogram.
  - What do you think the average output from the system is?... How did different parts of the system interact to deliver this behaviour?

Personal reflections

Having completed the exercise, reflect upon your own organization. Can you think of areas of the organization where variations (of time, practice, knowledge, skill, etc.) are causing problems? Can you identify sources of these variations? Can you eliminate or reduce some of these variations?

In statistics, standard deviation is used to measure the amount of variation or deviation from the average. The normal distribution curves in Figure 4.7 illustrate two systems with wider and tighter standard deviations whist having the same average values. A smaller variation suggests a tighter deviation with outputs closer to the average value. The widely popularized Six-Sigma process improvement approach focuses on understanding and reducing variations in a process.

Contrary to general belief that this line of thinking is only useful for repetitive manufacturing processes, this phenomenon becomes even more significant when the system increases in complexity.

Theories/worldviews and human behaviour

What Deming calls theories in his System of Profound Knowledge actually refers to the worldview of individuals, i.e. how they see and conceptualize the

Figure 4.7 Two normal distribution curves illustrating variations around the same average

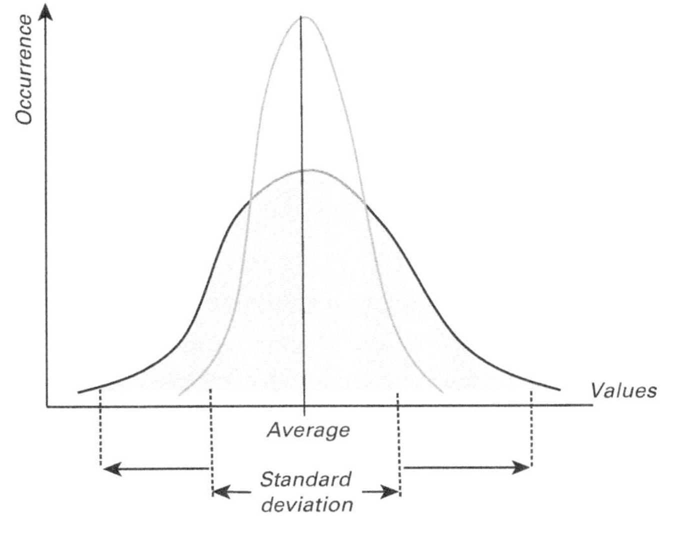

system, as their views inevitably impact on what they do and how they do things within the system – their behaviour. Consider this – have you ever come across someone in your organization who appears to be behaving irrationally? If you have worked in organizations of moderate complexity, we are certain that you will have encountered irrational behaviour, but have you ever wondered why?

In many cases, a behaviour that may appear irrational to you, from a different perspective would look perfectly rational. I have personally experienced this 'light bulb' moment many years ago (in 2005) when we were working on a multidisciplinary project to improve the performance of UK manufacturing companies. Some team members were talking about dysfunctional behaviours by people in organizations. A colleague, who was a psychologist and a behavioural scientist, interrupted and said, 'there is no such thing as dysfunctional behaviour, all behaviour is functional', which resulted in a heated discussion. The 'light bulb' moment came when another colleague commented that '… how would you describe what terrorists do, don't tell me they are functional'. And the response from the behavioural scientist was, 'of course it is functional behaviour, they would not do what they do if they thought it was dysfunctional'. At this point the coin dropped. Of course everyone has a different perspective on life, what is right and what is wrong, and we see this in organizations all the time.

In this context, in Chapter 2 when we asked 'What is a system?', we discussed how different students conceptualized their university differently. Also, at the end of Chapter 2, when we asked you to reflect upon your organization by asking a number of colleagues to draw a picture of the organization and narrate each picture to one another, you would have seen different worldviews of different colleagues emerging from their pictures and stories. These worldviews become critical to help us understand the rationale behind the behaviours of people in organizations. If you have not done this exercise, we strongly recommend that you do it with your classmates, friends or colleagues, members of your sports club or people from within the system you are trying to understand better.

In summary, Deming's System of Profound Knowledge provides further tools to help us think in systems. In particular, it helps us conceptualize and understand variation inherent within systems and their parts. It also brings individuals' worldviews, which he calls theories, into view to help us make sense of how variation in different parts of the systems may interact with different worldviews of individuals and can result in system-wide behaviour.

4.5 Goldratt's Theory of Constraints

Eliyahu Moshe Goldratt (1947–2011) was an Israeli business and management guru. He was the originator of the Optimized Production Technique, first published in the form of a business novel, *The Goal* (Goldratt and Cox, 1984), from which he developed the Theory of Constraints (Goldratt, 1990).

The exercise with coins described in the previous section should also be illustrative of the constraints within the system that determine the performance of the whole system. We have also talked about systems constraints earlier in this chapter when we introduced the Viable Systems Model and characterizations of different performance levels, i.e. **actuality**, **capability** and **potentiality**. In this context, a constraint is defined as anything that prevents the system from achieving its full potential. In the Theory of Constraints, a *constraint* is defined in a similar way as anything that prevents the system from achieving its goal.

The Theory of Constraints is a structured set of guidelines that helps us understand and manage the constraints in a system. The principle that underpins the Theory of Constraints is that organizational goals can be managed by controlling the variation in three measures: throughput, inventory and operating expenses:

- **Throughput** is the rate at which the system processes work, i.e. the rate at which the work flows through the system. For a commercial entity, throughput would also equate to the speed at which the system generates income through sales: the faster the throughput the greater the sales.
- **Inventory** is the accumulation of work through the system. In a commercial entity this would be the money that the organization has invested in purchasing things it intends to sell.
- **Operating expenses** are the resources (money in commercial terms) the system consumes to turn inventory into throughput.

According to the Theory of Constraints, a system's performance can be maximized by carefully managing and balancing these three performance measures by:

- maximizing throughput by getting as much work through the system as possible that meets the expectations of the system (i.e. effectiveness), whilst...

- minimizing inventory and operating expenses (efficiency) but not at the cost of throughput.

In Table 4.2 we have provided examples of throughput, inventory and operating expenses for different systems from different sectors to help you conceptualize these three performance measures in a broader context.

This way of thinking is in line with our earlier conceptualization (in Chapter 3) of a system comprising parts connected together through stocks and flows, illustrated in Figure 4.8.

The principle of the Theory of Constraints creates a focus on recognizing the stocks and flows. It enables the system to reach its goal whilst minimizing or eliminating the stocks and flows that slow down or even prevent the system from delivering its goal, i.e. the constraints. We can achieve this by focusing on resource relationships within a system, identifying the relationships that constrain the system, and then eliminating the constraint. This is best explained through an example.

Table 4.2 Examples of throughput, inventory and operating expenses for different systems

System	Throughput	Inventory	Operating Expense
Manufacturing system	The speed at which products are produced by the system	Quantity and value of raw materials and components present within the system	The cost of resources (human, materials, equipment, energy, etc.) that are consumed in the system
Mortgage application processing system	The speed at which mortgage applications are processed through the system	Number of mortgage applications awaiting in the queue to be processed	The cost of resources (human, materials, equipment, energy, etc) that are consumed in the system
National Innovation System	The rate at which new innovations/patents are generated and commercialized	Number and value of R&D projects in the system	The cost of resources (human, materials, equipment, energy, etc.) that are consumed in the system
Your email inbox	The rate at which you can deal with the emails in your inbox	Number of emails in your inbox waiting for you to process them	The time you spend processing your emails and the corresponding opportunity cost

Figure 4.8 A system, stocks and flows, and the three performance measures from the Theory of Constraints

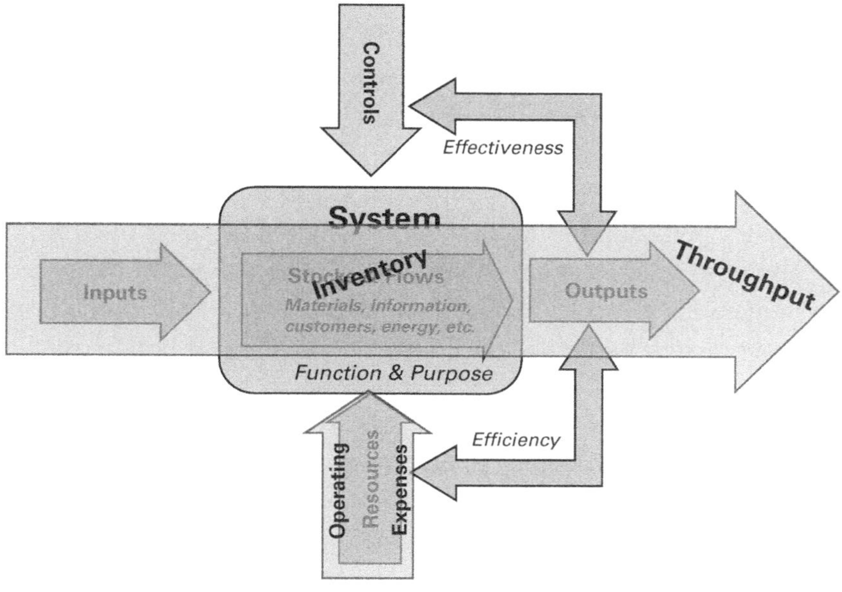

EXAMPLE: CHAIN AS A SYSTEM

Imagine a length of chain, how would you strengthen it? Essentially, a length of chain is a simple linear system with each link in the chain representing one part of the system. Each link is connected to the adjacent links. Through these links the force is transmitted through the entire length of the chain.

To strengthen the chain, we do not need to upgrade each link, because the strength of a length of chain is determined by its weakest link, i.e. the constraint. If we can identify the weakest link and strengthen just this one link, we would strengthen the entire chain.

Of course, with this intervention, although the entire length of the chain is a little stronger, the constraint will move to the next weakest link. To strengthen the chain further we would need to identify the next weakest link and strengthen that particular link and so on.

Just like in the chain example above, the Theory of Constraints provides a set of guidelines or rules to help us attain the goals of the system based around resource relationships to focus our attention on the constraints that slow down or prevent the system from attaining its goals.

These rules are based on simple resource relationships as illustrated in Figure 4.9. The figure contains three simple systems. All three systems comprise two parts, or resources, as referred to in the Theory of Constraints. In all three systems, Part A is capable of going through 100 pieces of work per hour and part B is capable of going through 50 pieces of work per hour.

In System 1, the two resources are not connected to one another. Thus, we can consider parts A and B as constraint resources because the capacity of each part constrains the overall output of the entire system, which is 150 pieces of work per hour. In this case, improving the capacity of either Part B or Part A will provide a net gain to the overall throughput of the system.

In System 2, the two resources are connected, with Part A, the non-constraint resource, serving Part B, the constraint resource. If both parts work at full capacity, the overall system output will be 50 pieces per hour, but because Part A is working at a rate of 100 pieces per hour and Part B can only use 50 of the pieces produced by Part A, inventory (shown by the dark triangle) will build up between the two parts at a rate of 50 parts per hour. In this system, to improve the system's throughput we would need to explore how we can improve the capacity of Part B. Any improvement in the capacity of part B would be a net gain to the whole system.

In System 3, the two resources are similarly connected, but this time Part B, the constraint resource, is serving Part A, the non-constraint resource. If both parts work at full capacity, the overall system output will still be 50 pieces per hour but because Part A is capable of working at a rate of 100 pieces per hour and Part B can only supply 50 of the pieces per hour, Part A will not be utilized for half of its time. In this system, like System 2, to improve the system's throughput we would need to explore how we can improve the capacity of Part B. As before, any improvement in the capacity of Part B would be a net gain to the whole system.

The Theory of Constraints provides us with the following rules to help us understand and manage constraints within systems:

- Rule 1: The level of utilization of a non-constraint resource is determined not by its own potential but by some other constraint in the system. As we have seen in Systems 2 and 3 (Figure 4.9), the system performance was constrained not by its own potential but by the capacity of Part B.
- Rule 2: Utilization and activation of a resource are not the same. In System 3 (Figure 4.9) it does not matter how hard we work Part A (activation), it can only be useful 50 per cent of its time (utilization).

Figure 4.9 An example of resource relationships in the Theory of Constraints

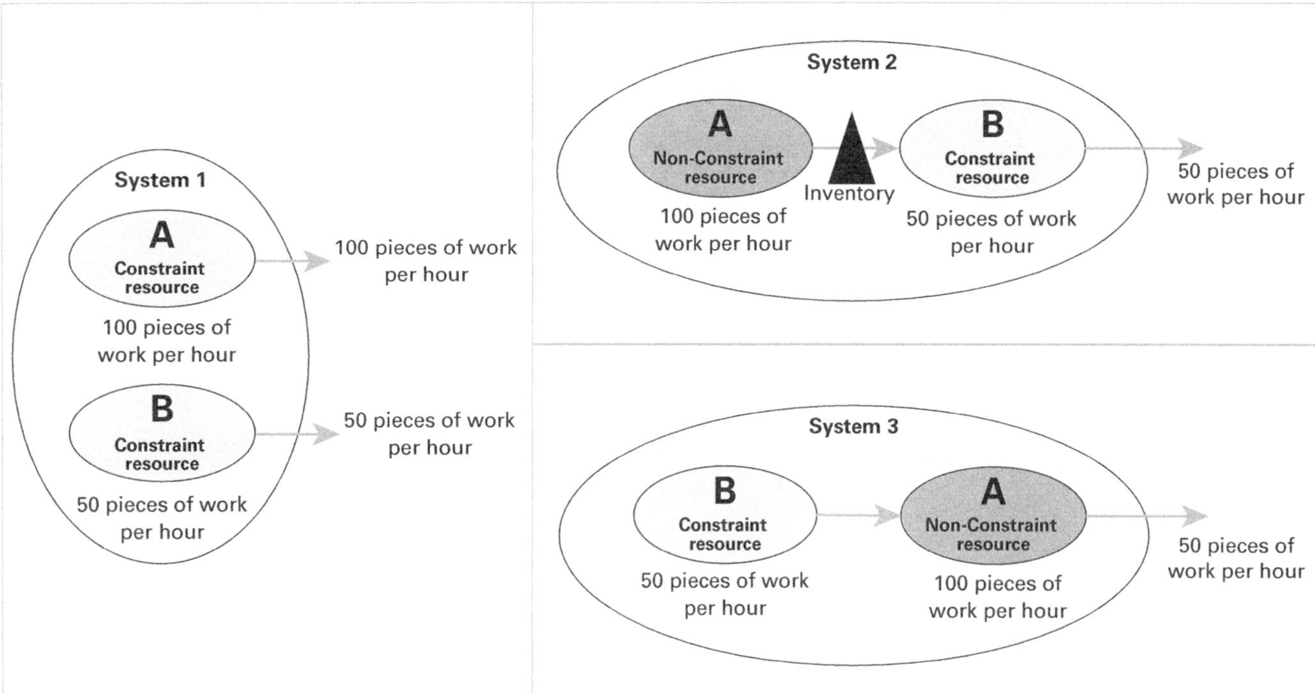

- Rule 3: An hour lost at a constraint is an hour lost for the whole system. In Systems 2 and 3 (Figure 4.9), if we lose one hour of productive time due to unavailability of Part B, which is the constraint, this hour of productive time will be lost to the entire system. Whereas an hour lost due to unavailability of Part A is not so critical because Part A can catch up as it has spare capacity.
- Rule 4: An hour saved at a non-constraint is a mirage. In Systems 2 and 3 (Figure 4.9), if we save an hour in Part A, a non-constraint resource, it will have no effect on the overall system's performance.
- Rule 5: Constraints govern both the throughput and inventory. In Systems 2 and 3 (Figure 4.9) we can observe that the nature of the relationship between Part B, the constraint resource, and part A, the non-constraint resource, governs the level of inventory in the system. In System 2, the non-constraint resource serves the constraining resource, and as a result the inventory builds up between Parts A and B. Whereas when the relationship is reversed as in System 3, there is no inventory build-up, and instead the utilization of Part A is affected.
- Rule 6: The sum of the local optima is not equal to the optimum of the whole. In Systems 2 and 3 (Figure 4.9), optimizing the performance of each part, i.e. Parts A and B, is not the same as optimizing the performance of the system as a whole. If we optimize the performance of each part, i.e. working Part A and B to their full potential, we create either excess inventory (System 2) or an unnecessary operating expense by activating Part A for longer than necessary (System 3). Within these constraints the system's performance would be better optimized if we activated Part A 50 per cent of its time, thus avoiding building up unnecessary inventory or operating expense.
- Rule 7: Balance the flow, not capacity. As throughput governs the rate at which the system attains its goal, balancing the resources to optimize the flow through the system is more important than trying to achieve a balanced capacity in the system. This is due to variations in different parts of the system. Over time it is virtually impossible to balance the capacity to enable the flow in the system. Thus, instead of trying to balance the capacity, you should focus on balancing the flow by building appropriate control mechanisms.

The **Drum-Buffer-Rope Principle**, illustrated in Figure 4.10, is a control mechanism that enables us to operationalize several of the above rules to balance the flow, rather than the capacity, in a system. In this production system we have a simple process that is flowing from left to right. The system comprises five operations (illustrated by circles), four of which are non-constraint resources (dark grey circles) with the constraint resource positioned in the middle (light grey circle). Based on the above rules, the constraint operation, the **Drum**, regulates the flow through the entire system (Rule 1), while the drumbeat represents the work rate of the constraint operation and ensures that all other operations are synchronized to the drumbeat. In other words, the non-constraint operations will be working at less than full capacity (Rules 2 and 4), but that is OK because working them any harder will not have any impact on the throughput of the whole system. The **Rope** represents the communication signal to synchronize the work rate of all the non-constraint operations with the work rate of the constraint operation.

The **Buffer** is a mitigation strategy against two risks. The *constraint buffer* mitigates against the risk of constraint operation running out of work due to a breakdown in upstream operations (Rule 3). The *shipping buffer* mitigates against the risk of downstream operations breaking down, thus negatively impacting on system's throughput (Rule 5). In principle, these buffers are a measure of time, as the amount of inventory will mitigate against these risks for a given amount of time, i.e. the longer these breakdowns can potentially last, the higher the inventory in these buffers would need to be. Thus, knowing the probability of breakdowns and the mean length of breakdowns would provide essential information to help us decide on the optimum size of these buffers.

Figure 4.10 The Drum-Buffer-Rope Principle

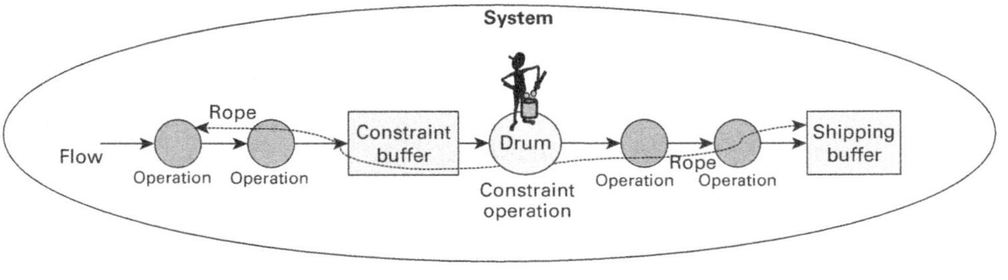

Finally, based on the above rules, the Theory of Constraints provides us with a simple approach to improving a system's performance. The process consists of five steps:

Step 1: Identify the system's constraint. There is no hard and fast science for doing this. Indeed we can model the flow of work through the system but often there are simpler and quicker indicators, such as looking for the machine with all the work piled up in front of it or looking for the person everyone needs to get a decision from. Remember sometimes the constraint can also be outside the system, in the market or even in the supply chain. Talking to as many people as possible within the system about what constrains their work, or what is it they are regularly waiting for, is an equally good way of identifying the system's constraint.

Step 2: Exploit the system's constraint. Spending a lot of money, buying a bigger machine or hiring more people is not always the answer. Usually, the constraint has capacity that we do not use. For example, a machine that is a constraint may be working only six hours a day from 9 am to 5 pm excluding lunch and coffee breaks. Staggering lunch and coffee breaks would enable the system to work for eight hours, increasing the capacity of the constraint by 30 per cent. Remember, an hour gained at the constraint is an hour gained for the whole system. As another example, there may be someone else who can take some of the workload off the constraint, even if it is lower-level, less-skilled work. This would alleviate the load on the constraint. In short, before spending money we should look to get everything out of the bottleneck by finding innovative ways of exploiting the constraint.

Step 3: Subordinate everything else to the above constraint. This is where we synchronize all other parts of the system to work at the same rate as the constraint resource by finding innovative ways of signalling the drumbeat to all other parts of the system. In this step we would also be looking at how we could create buffers in order to mitigate risks to the overall system performance.

Step 4: Elevate the system's constraint. This is where we would start considering additional investments to elevate the performance level of the constraint. However, it should be borne in mind that this step may not be totally necessary, as by exploiting the system's constraint we may have already moved the constraint to another part of the system.

Step 5: Go back to step 1. Just like the chain example at the start of this section, once we have elevated the performance of the system's constraint, it is likely that the constraint has moved elsewhere in the system.

In his book, *The Goal*, Eli Goldratt tells the story of Alex Rogo, a factory manager who has been given the ultimatum to turn the factory around or risk closure. The following is the precis of the story, which demonstrates the application of the Theory of Constraints in practice. The book is well worth a read and it is still available in print as well as in an audiobook format. A film telling the story is also available on various online outlets.

The Goal

The story starts with Alex Rogo, a fictitious factory manager, being given an ultimatum to turn the factory's performance around or risk closure. At first, Alex feels lost and does not know what to do. He then bumps into an old college professor at an airport, who asks him some questions about his challenges and questions whether he is using the right performance measure. The professor introduces Alex to the three measures of The Theory of Constraints, i.e. throughput, inventory and operating expenses, and advises him to look for his bottleneck (the constraint).

At first Alex is a bit confused about how the concept of a constraint could apply to his factory. But the coin drops when he is taking his son and his friend for a hike in the forest. One child, Herbie, is the slowest; he keeps falling behind and everybody ends up waiting for Herbie. Progress is slow. Clearly Herbie is the constraint. So, Alex puts Herbie to the front of the group – they no longer have to wait for Herbie to catch up, but they are making very slow progress and everyone is bored. Alex asks to see what is in Herbie's backpack. He has frying pans, cans of beans and many more things that are weighing him down. Alex asks everyone else to take one item from Herbie to lighten his load. The rest of the hike is completed in good time.

With this new insight, back in the factory, Alex shares his thoughts with his management team and after a bit of head scratching, they identify the constraint as one of the machines, the NCX10. They stagger the lunch and coffee breaks; they even recommission an ancient machine which was being scrapped to take some of the workload off the NCX10 and the factory performance improves within a few weeks. But Alex is informed that the improvement is not good enough to keep the factory open. Alex goes back to his management team and they go through the same process once again, but this time the constraint is in the market – they need more orders. Alex visits the marketing team at the company's headquarters and does a deal with one of the sales teams to alleviate this constraint. They get more orders, the factory performance improves further, and the factory becomes the best-performing plant in the group. Alex gets promoted and everyone lives happily ever after.

In short, the Theory of Constraints provides us with a set of thinking processes and guidelines to help us identify and manage constraints in systems.

CASE STUDY A systems thinking case study

In this case study we will look at how the models covered in this chapter could be used to help us understand an organization as a system. For consistency we will continue with the whisky company example we used at the end of the previous chapter as we are already somewhat familiar with the case.

As a reminder, the company manufactures and sells whisky in a global market; they have two business units, high-value products and low-value products, comprising about 45 and 170 specific products respectively. The manufacturing process consists of distilling the product, maturing it for a period of 5 to 25 years and then bottling it, including boxing and palletizing for transportation. The pallets are then shipped all over the world through various distributors to retail chains and specialist shops where customers can buy the product.

Using **Miller's Living Systems Theory**, we can start conceptualizing that the company system is a *concrete system* as well as a *conceptual system*. It is a *concrete system* because it exists in reality and consists of tangible objects (products, buildings, manufacturing equipment, etc.). It is a *conceptual system* because the two business units are based on knowledge and ideas. The company could have also easily been categorized into large products and small products according to their bottle sizes, or as US products, EU products and Rest of The World products depending on the markets the products are being sold in.

The company clearly processes materials (matter) and information. Based on Figure 4.1, at the *input stage*, the marketing and customer services functions can be conceptualized as the *input transducer* as they bring information into the system in the form of forecasts and customer orders. The purchasing function can be conceptualized as an *ingestor* as it brings materials into the system. At the *throughput stage*, the planning function can be conceptualized as both the *internal transducer* as it receives and converts the information received by the system, and *channel and net* as it also distributes this information… and so on.

Using **Beer's Viable Systems Model** and Figure 4.2 we can conceptualize the customers, suppliers, competitors, regulators, society and economy as the *external environment* the company operates within. The company then has two *System 1s* (business units), high-value and low-value products. The manufacturing planning function can be conceptualized as the System 2 as it interprets the overall business and production plans and coordinates the activities of two business units (System 1s). All parts of the company that are connected to the external environment, such as marketing, customer services, purchasing, accounts payable and receivable, can be conceptualized as *System 4*, as collectively these functions can bring in intelligence as to what is happening in the outside world. The strategic management and business planning function can be conceptualized as System 5, and the sales and operations planning together with sales, purchasing, marketing and operations management functions can be conceptualized as System 3 as they collectively manage the operation of the two System 1s.

Using **Hitchins' Systems Architecture** we have already conceptualized the systems architecture as the organizational structure and the infrastructure to support the purpose, function and performance of the system. It can include things such as the IT systems or proximity of buildings. For example, if raw materials need to travel long distances between operations, that would be counterproductive to the performance, particularly for low-value products.

Using **Goldratt's Theory of Constraints** we can analyse the end-to-end process from sales forecasts, customer orders and materials coming in from one end and products being shipped to customers at the other end. Through this analysis we may find that forecast accuracy together with the worldviews of the marketing people who prepare the sales forecasts are the key constraint to the performance of the high-value products business unit.

Using **Deming's System of Profound Knowledge** we can start identifying the differences in world views between marketing and operations and understand the key sources of variation. We can then analyse whether eliminating variation would significantly improve performance. We may also find that to reduce variation in the performance we need to formalize the planning process using hard system modelling tools (see next chapter), or maybe we need to co-locate marketing, planning and manufacturing functions to improve daily communications, thus improving the system's architecture.

Reflective questions

- In the above case study, we started describing how various functions of the company may map on to Miller's 20 subsystems (Figure 4.1) but we did not complete all 20 subsystems. Try completing the rest of the analysis and see if you can map the remaining subsystems and to company functions.

- Think about another organization you may know well, perhaps the organization you used in one of the previous exercises. Can you do a similar analysis of that organization using the models covered in this case study? And can you identify any improvements you could make?

4.6 Summary

In this chapter, our objective was to build upon various concepts and definitions we covered in the previous chapters and introduce you, the reader, to various systems thinking models and frameworks. The models and frameworks we have selected to include in this chapter, whilst not an exhaustive list of all the models in the field, are intended to provide different perspectives to systems and systems thinking.

On the one hand, Miller's Living Systems Theory and Beer's Viable Systems Model both look at complex systems, recognize the recursive nature of systems, i.e. systems exist within systems, and offer models of the mechanisms that enable living and viable systems to self-manage and self-create themselves. Even though the two models are quite different, there are a lot of complementarities between the two models. Hitchins on the other hand takes a different perspective by helping us understand the architectures that underpin systems and how these architectures evolve as systems change and adopt to their environments.

Deming and Goldratt provide different perspectives yet again. Deming identifies two fundamental factors that make complex systems difficult to predict. He identifies that when variation occurs in the performance of different parts of the system, their interactions are naturally going to produce at least partially unpredictable outcomes. He also identifies that this unpredictability is further exacerbated by the differences in the theories (worldviews) that different participants (people, animals, organizations, societies, etc.) may have about the system. He argues that we cannot begin to understand the behaviour of such complex systems without first understanding these variations in participants' theories or worldviews.

Goldratt takes a different perspective by focusing our minds upon the goal of the system and the constraints that are preventing the system from achieving its goal. He offers a process for analysing the system and improving its performance by identifying and eliminating a constraint.

These models and frameworks individually would not be sufficient to provide a comprehensive understanding of a complex system. However, in combination and together with the concepts we introduced in the previous chapters they equip us with the thinking tools and processes to help us understand and even predict the systems we are trying to manage or the systems within which we live, work and play.

REFLECTIVE EXERCISE

Think about a system you are interested in (e.g. the organization or department you work or worked in; your sports, art or drama club; your course or programme of study) and try to use all the frameworks and models we discussed in this chapter to gain a better understanding of the system by answering the following questions.

1. Is the system part of a larger system? What is the higher-level system that it is part of? What other systems exist within this higher-level system?
2. What are the parts of this system? Are they just simple parts or are these parts also systems (i.e. subsystem) in their own right?
3. Using Miller's model, think about what matter/energy or information is being processed through the system. Can you conceptualize the system in terms of input, throughput and output stages? Try to explain what happens at each stage.
4. Can you describe Beer's five systems within the system? Is this system a viable system?
5. What is the system's architecture? Was it always like this? Did it evolve over time?
6. How easy is it to predict the behaviour of the system? What are the primary sources of variation in each part of the system? And how do these variations interact to make the system's behaviour unpredictable?
7. Are there different participants in the system potentially with different worldviews? What are these worldviews? How may they be affecting the behaviour of the system?
8. Are there any constraints in the system? Where are they? What can be done to alleviate these constraints?

If you are unable to think about a system, think about your commuting system, i.e. the system you use to travel from home to work, school or club. We guess that the time it takes you to commute each time varies significantly. What are the reasons behind these differences? Try to use the questions above to think through the system and see if you get any new insights.

TEAM EXERCISE

Viable systems – asking participants to map the five systems of the Viable Systems Model and their interaction for their organization is a very good exercise. To get the ball rolling, you can ask them to think about how the company scans its external environment, competitors, technology, suppliers, etc. (System 4) and how this information is used to make strategic (System 5) and operational management decisions (System 3). Also, it is useful to ask the participants to think about the algedonic signal within their organizations, particularly if the organization is over- or under-sensitive to these signals. A healthy organization would have just the right reaction; an organization that is not so viable would either overreact to all signals or would be numb to signals and not react at all.

Variation – the variation exercise as part of Deming's Theory of Profound Knowledge (page 74) is useful and works in both small and large groups. It helps to demonstrate the point about variation as a simple linear system. Having completed this exercise, the instructor can motivate a discussion about other kinds of variation we may observe in organizations, such as variation in knowledge, management style, people skills, etc., to enable the group to develop a more fundamental understanding of the concept.

Constraints – although a little old, we still recommend showing the movie *The Goal*, which enables participants to hear and see what is going on, thus aiding their comprehension of the concepts discussed in the Theory of Constraints.

Notes

1 According to the Miller, Energy and Matter are same. He defines Matter as anything that has mass and occupies physical space, and he argues that Mass and Energy are equivalent as one can be converted into the other.

2 We discuss the concept of recurrence in greater detail in the next section when we discuss the Viable Systems Model.

References

Beer, S (1972) *Brain of the Firm*, Allen Lane, The Penguin Press, London, Herder and Herder, USA

Beer, S (1979) *The Heart of Enterprise*, John Wiley, London and New York
Beer, S (1985) *Diagnosing the System for Organizations*, John Wiley, London and New York
Deming, WE (2018) *The New Economics for Industry, Government, Education*, MIT Press
Goldratt, EM and Cox, J (1984) *The Goal: A process of ongoing improvement*, Routledge
Goldratt, EM (1990) *Theory of Constraints* (pp. 1–159). Croton-on-Hudson: North River
Hitchins, DK (2003) *Advanced Systems Thinking, Engineering, and Management*, Artech House
Hitchins, DK (2008) *Systems Engineering: A 21st century systems methodology*, John Wiley & Sons
Holliday, M and Jones, M (2015) Living systems theory and the practice of stewarding change, https://michelleholliday.com/wp-content/uploads/Living-Systems-Theory-and-the-Practice-of-Stewarding-Change-June-2015-min.pdf (archived at https://perma.cc/7WNX-YJPB)
Kelly, J (2020) Here are the companies leading the work-from-home revolution, *Forbes*, May
Miller, JG (1978) *Living Systems*, McGraw-Hill Book Company, New York

Hard systems thinking 5

In the previous chapters we introduced what a system is, developed various concepts and definitions that underpin systems thinking, and introduced a number of complementary systems thinking models and frameworks, which provide different perspectives on systems.

In Chapter 2, when we introduced systems, we differentiated between hard and soft systems and suggested the following definitions:

- **Hard system:** a system consisting of high-integrity parts that are connected through well-understood interaction patterns producing predictable behaviours.
- **Soft system:** a system consisting of autonomous parts that are characterized by high variability and unpredictable behaviours and connected through a loosely defined dynamic web of relationships, power structures, shared interests and values.

In this chapter, we introduce hard systems thinking and several approaches for modelling hard systems. We will start by outlining the characteristics of hard systems and then take you through some of the commonly used hard systems modelling techniques. The penultimate section will outline the key limitations of hard systems modelling techniques and provide examples of how organizations can overcome these limitations in innovative ways. These examples will serve as a transition to the next chapter on modelling of soft systems.

LEARNING OUTCOMES

- Understand hard systems and hard systems thinking
- Become familiar with different approaches to hard systems modelling including
  - flow charts and data flow diagrams

  - structured systems analysis and design method (SSADM) and the integrated definition (IDEF) method
  - process maps, including swim lane process maps
  - value stream maps
  - discrete event and agent-based simulation techniques
- Be able to use the hard systems modelling techniques to create models of simple systems
- Understand the limitations of hard systems modelling and hard systems thinking
- Develop strategies for overcoming these limitations

5.1 Characteristics of hard systems and hard systems thinking

Earlier we defined a system as consisting of different parts, which interact with each other, producing a certain kind of behaviour that could be more or less predictable. We also defined hard systems as consisting of high-integrity parts that are connected through well-understood interaction patterns producing predictable behaviours. From this definition we can deduce that the key characteristics of hard systems are their **predictable behaviours**, caused by **high-integrity parts** that are connected through **well-understood interactions**.

In this context, high-integrity parts mean that each part operates within tight tolerances and the amount of variation in each part is understood and predictable. Typically, the performance of each part of a hard system would not be affected by different worldviews, mood swings and other unpredictable behaviours associated with people and animals. Just think about why in show business they say *never work with animals*. In short, in hard systems there are no unpredictable variations in the behaviour of each part. We expect each part in a hard system to conform to a statistically and mathematically explainable, repeatable and reliable behavioural pattern. In a similar vein, in hard systems, we also expect to see well-understood (i.e. statistically and mathematically explainable) repeatable and reliable interactions to take place between different parts of the system.

Over time each part in a system will suffer wear and tear, particularly if not maintained. Consequently, the variation in the behaviour of each part as well as the interconnections will change (i.e. entropy). However, in hard systems even the rate of deterioration is predictable and well understood, and in many cases it is mathematically and statistically explainable. This is how manufacturers can define the service life of a light bulb or the maintenance schedule of your car.

> As an example, a car serviced by the manufacturer's approved specialist service centre with trained technicians using approved replacement parts is less likely to suffer from breakdowns compared to the same car serviced by a generalist mechanic. The specialist will have information on how different parts behave over time, and what parts wear faster and need to be inspected, lubricated or changed before they fail. The generalist mechanic is unlikely to have the same level of knowledge and will most probably apply the same maintenance routine to all cars; thus the car is likely to break down more quickly.

In hard systems, feedback from the system can be used to compensate for deviation from the expected outcomes by adjusting technical control parameters. In some systems this adjustment can happen automatically in the system based on some predefined rules. In other systems the feedback may be used to send a signal (possibly an algedonic signal in the Viable Systems Model) to an external party for a corrective action to take place. We can best see this feedback and automatic/manual intervention in the human body, wherein the body, if healthy, automatically controls the amount of sugar in the blood. When a person has diabetes, there are external sensors available that can send the person a message when the blood sugar level raises and the person can then manually administer insulin. In both cases, we are dealing with a hard system inside the human body that is measurable and predictable, enabling feedback to be used to compensate for deviation.

At this point we can summarize the characteristics of hard systems as follows:

- predictable behaviours
- high-integrity parts
- high-integrity connections

- feedback that can be used to compensate for deviation
- rate of deterioration/entropy that is predictable

Hard systems thinking is a way of thinking about systems whereby the analyst/thinker is assuming that systems behave as hard systems, i.e. they are predictable. In hard systems thinking it is assumed that the analysist can understand the system's current (or as-is) behaviour by modelling each part and the interactions between these parts. They can then go on and change parts and/or interactions of the system to define a new system with improved behaviour (make it more efficient or more effective, eliminate or reduce a problem, exploit an opportunity, etc.). The behaviour of this new (or to-be) system will be as intended, i.e. predictable.

In the following sections we will outline various techniques for modelling hard systems, or modelling systems from a hard systems perspective. This is not intended to be an exhaustive list of systems modelling techniques and indeed there are many commercial tools available that use these techniques, or variations of them, to help model hard systems. All of these techniques can be used to model the current (as-is) system as well as the desired new (to-be) systems.

5.2 Flowcharts

Flowcharts are one of the simplest systems modelling tools. A flowchart is a diagram that uses standard symbols to illustrate various activities of a process in sequential order. They are typically used to describe process flows in different processes including manufacturing, service, administrative and software. Although its main purpose is to model flows of activity within a process, it can be adapted for a variety of purposes, including modelling the flows within a system.

Figure 5.1 illustrates the most commonly used flowchart symbols together with an example of how these symbols are used to construct a flowchart that connects various activities (parts) of a customer order planning system. Essentially it describes the flow of work through the system by connecting various parts of the system in a logical sequence.

Figure 5.1 describes a simple customer order planning system which starts with the receipt of the customer order electronically as an entry into a database. It is then entered into the sales order processing system (SOPS). In the

Figure 5.1 Flowchart symbols and a simple example

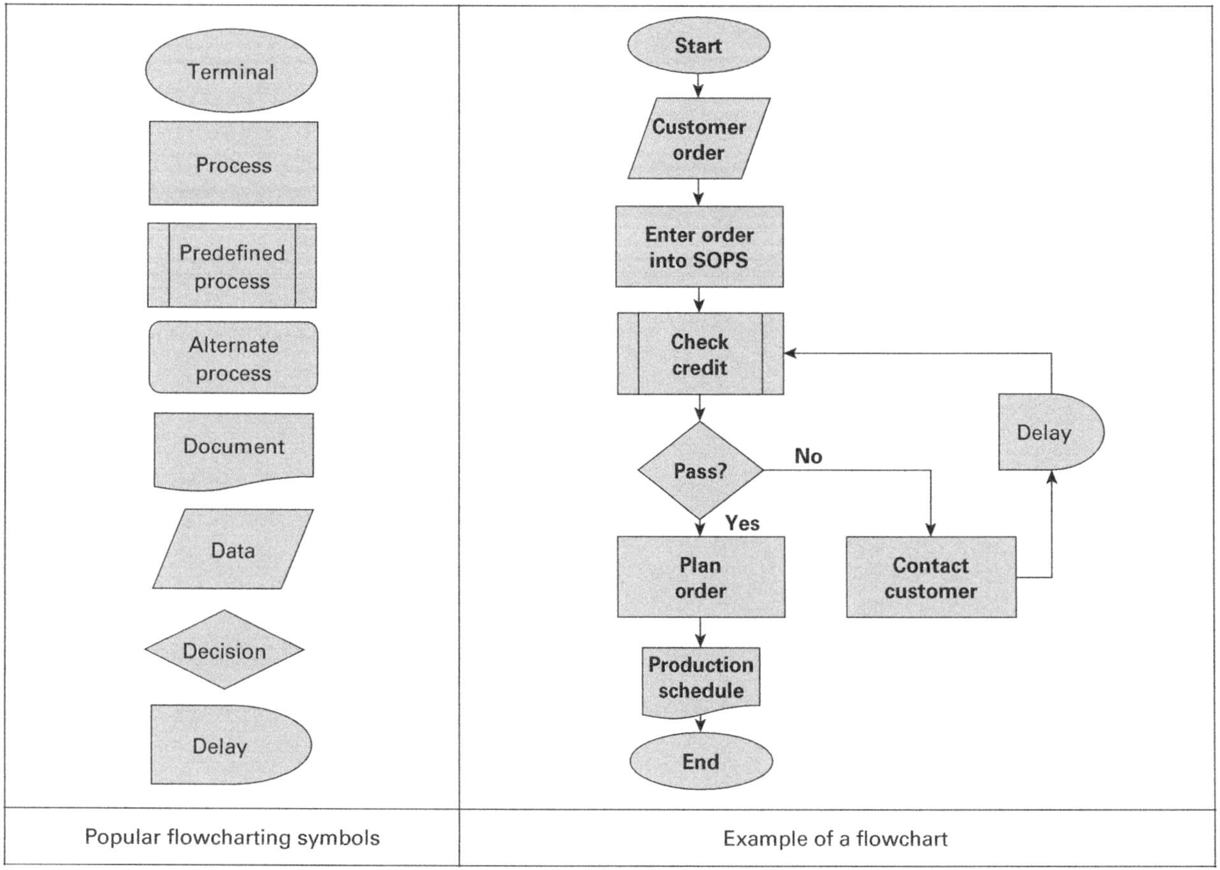

next stage, the customer's credit status is checked automatically using a predefined criterion. If the credit status is passed, i.e. the customer's credit status is within defined limits, then the order is planned into the production schedule and the output from the system is the production schedule in the form of a document. If the customer fails to pass the credit check, then they are contacted and the order is put on hold until the credit status is cleared.

Naturally, we can expand this flowchart to develop further detail around this simple system by flowcharting how the credit is checked, how the customer is contacted, etc. However, it might be more practical to describe these subsystems on different flowcharts to avoid overcomplicating the flowchart.

5.3 Data-flow diagrams

Data-flow diagrams (DFDs) are a form of flowchart that provide the means of representing flow of data through a system. Although DFDs use only four symbols to enable modelling of data flows through the system, the nature of the symbols can change depending on the notation used:

Entity, which is the process, function or subsystem that transforms inputs to outputs. Depending on the notation, the symbol used can be a circle, an oval, a rectangle or a rectangle with rounded corners.

Flow, shown in the form of an arrow, connects entities to one another. The arrow shows the direction of the data flow between the entities. Although originally conceived to illustrate data or information flows, it is now often used to also show other flows, such as materials, people, customers and decisions. Although we could argue that a decision is simply an information flow as illustrated in Figure 5.2. In some cases the flows can be bidirectional to illustrate that the entities are logically interdependent.

Store (warehouse, database or file) is used to illustrate storage of whatever is flowing between entities, represented by two horizontal lines. The store does not have to be a warehouse, database or a file – it can also be a filing cabinet where documents are stored or even a hotel or a hospital where people are staying.

External entity, sometimes referred to as terminal, stands outside the boundaries of the system but interacts with the system. It can be a computer system, an organization, a person, groups of people and so on. The key criterion here is that the entity sits outside the boundaries of the system and interacts with the system through flows.

Figure 5.2 Symbols commonly used for constructing data-flow diagrams

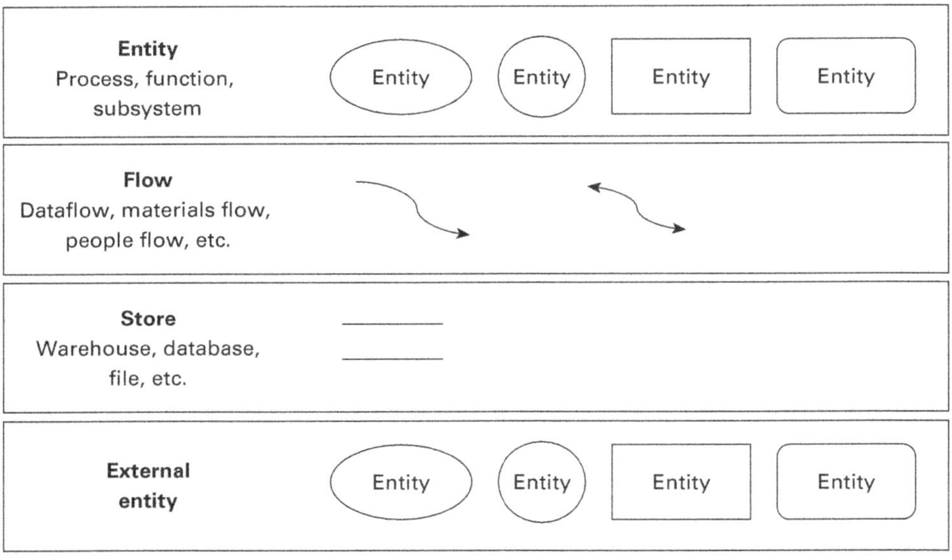

Figure 5.2 illustrates the symbols used in two common notations. Here you will notice that the symbols for entity and external entity are the same. However, usually the analyst would use symbols with different shapes to differentiate between internal and external entities.

Figure 5.3 illustrates the use of the DFDs to model the customer order planning system we described in the previous section. Here the customer and the production department are external entities shown as rectangles. The entities within the system are shown using oval symbols. The customer order is received from the customer and is stored in the sales orders database. The process outlined in Figure 5.3 is as follows:

1 The **customer order** is received from the **customer** and is stored in the **sales orders database**.

2 The **process sales order** function takes the customer's order from the sales database, processes it and passes it on to the **check credit** function for checking the customer's credit status against the **customer accounts file**.

3 If the order value exceeds the customer's credit limit the credit check fails, and this information is passed to the **contact customer** function (a decision flow); the function contacts the customer and a two-way dialogue takes place, illustrated by the bidirectional arrow.

Figure 5.3 A simple data-flow diagram

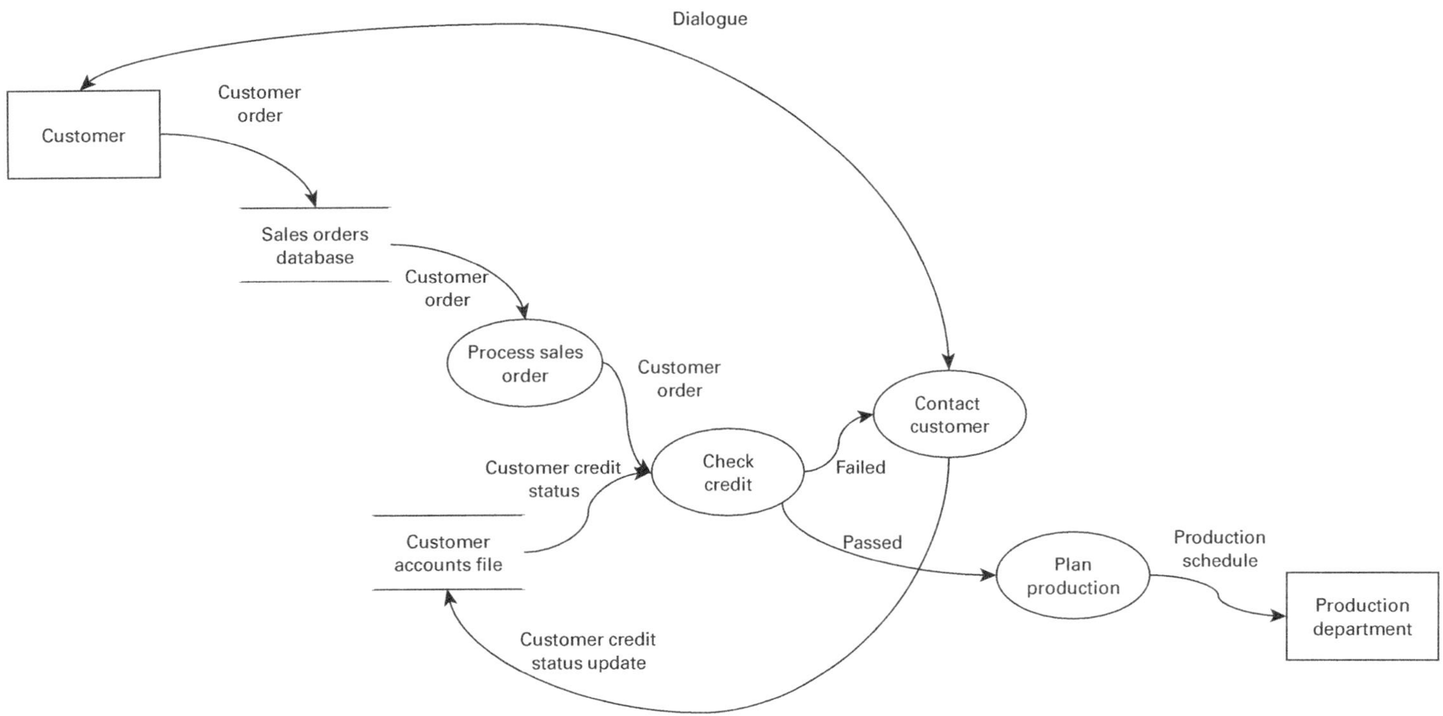

4 As a result of this dialogue, if the customer's credit issue is resolved, for example by increasing the customer's credit limit or the customer making a payment, then the **customer credit status** is updated.

5 As a result, the order passes the credit check and the order details are communicated to the **plan production** function which plans production and issues the **production schedule** to the **production department**.

The key differences between flowcharts and DFDs are that:

- DFDs use fewer symbols
- the flows between entities are annotated to describe the nature of the flows
- there is no time element represented, rather the sequence of activities is determined by the flow

5.4 Structured systems analysis and design method and integrated definition

The structured systems analysis and design method (SSADM) is a further development from DFDs. It was initially developed to deal with analysis and design of complex computer systems for the UK Government's Central Computer and Telecommunications Agency in the early 1980s. SSADM has evolved over the years and in 2000 it was repackaged as the business system development method. In summary, SSADM comprises three modelling techniques:

- **Data modelling** details the data requirements of a system. The data model contains *entities* about which business needs to record information, *attributes* that represent the facts about these entities, and *relationships* between these entities.
- **Data flow modelling** details how data moves through the system. Similar to DFDs this technique details *activities* that transform data from one form to another, *data stores* where data is stored, *external entities* that send or receive data from a system, and *data flows*.
- **Entity event modelling** details the *events* and their *sequence* that impact on an entity and consequently affect the behaviour of the system over time.

Integrated Definition (IDEF) is a set of modelling techniques that built upon SSADM and emerged from the field of systems and software engineering. These modelling approaches were developed for the United States Air Force and other public agencies to enable modelling complex information and engineering systems. The set of modelling techniques, identified as IDEF0 to IDEF14, covers a wide range of purposes including functional modelling, data modelling, simulation, object-oriented modelling, knowledge modelling, constraint modelling, organization modelling and network modelling.

In relation to systems thinking and modelling of hard systems, the most widely used technique is the IDEF0 functional modelling technique, which is similar to SSADM's functional modelling. In the following paragraphs we further explain the IDEF0 technique; however, we will refrain from going into additional detail on other SSADM or IDEF approaches as they are infrequently used in systems thinking and are more useful when analysing, modelling and designing complex software or engineering systems.

The IDEF0 or SSADM functional modelling approach uses the inputs, controls, outputs and mechanisms (ICOM) to model the relationship between entities, similar to our earlier conceptualization of a system in Chapter 3. In this context, the entity (system, subsystem or activity) transforms *inputs* to *outputs* under the rules, policies and/or constraints imposed by the *controls* and using the *mechanisms* (means or resources) available. These entities are linked together through these ICOMs, where an output from an entity can be an input, control (e.g. a policy decision) or even a mechanism (e.g. a tool) for another entity. A key feature of this approach is that the details of each entity can be modelled in greater detail in the next levels of analysis as illustrated in Figure 5.4, which is consistent with the recursive nature of systems discussed in the previous chapter.

In Figure 5.5 we have illustrated modelling of the customer order planning system using the IDEF0/SSADM approach through this simplified and rather abstract example. Here we can see the same customer order planning system described with additional details. At Level 0 we only see the process as a whole with the key input (Customer Order) and the output (Production Schedule), as well as controls and mechanisms summarized as Various Controls and Various Mechanisms.

At level 1 we see the next level of detail. The customer order is entered into the sales database (not shown) by the sales agent using the sales order processing system by the sales agent. We can also observe that this activity takes place during working hours (9 am–5 pm) five days per week due to the working hours policy of the company, indicating a potential constraint. Once the processed order is received by the financial controller (a mechanism), the check credit activity commences. Finance system (another mechanism) enables this activity and is controlled or constrained by the information

Figure 5.4 Nomenclate and structure of IDEF0/SSADM functional modelling

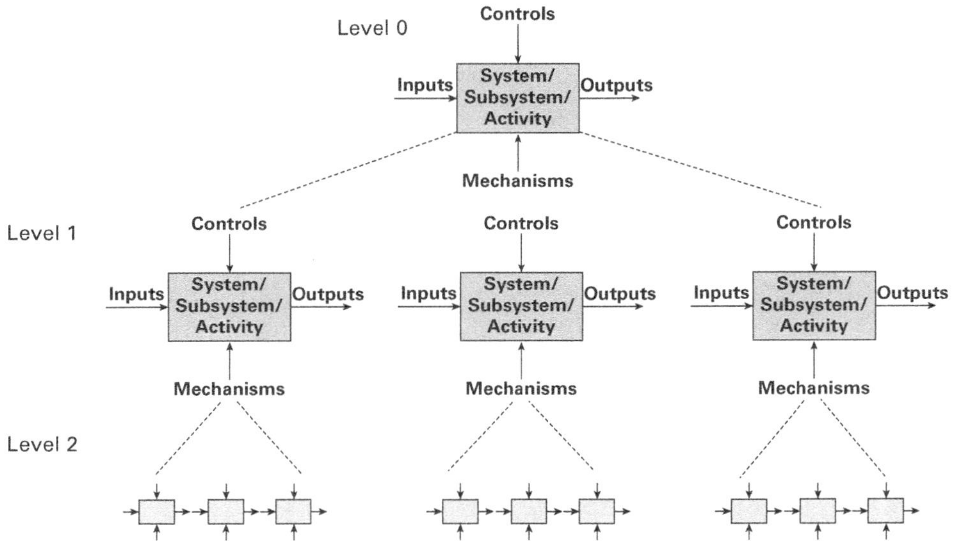

available from the external credit rating agency. If the credit check fails, the customer services department (mechanism) is contacted, and then in turn contacts the customer. As an outcome of this dialogue, if the credit issue is resolved (e.g. customer makes a payment) the credit status of the customer is updated. If the credit check is passed, then the order is forwarded to the plan production activity, where the production planner (mechanism) uses the planning system (another mechanism) to produce the production schedule. Here the control suggests that the production schedule is issued once a week on a Thursday, which may be another constraint.

At level 2, we see another level of detail that models the check credit activity. Here the credit controller (mechanism) compares the customer's credit balance to their credit limit. If the credit balance is within the limit the order is passed; if it exceeds the limit the credit check fails and the order is put on hold. If the credit check is failed then the first step is for the credit controller (mechanism) to contact the sales representative who is dealing with this customer to ascertain further information, as a result of which the credit issue may be resolved and the order passed. If the credit issue is not resolved, then the credit controller (mechanism) contacts the finance director together with information on the customer's credit rating from an external credit rating agency (control). The outcome of this can be that the customer's credit limit is extended and the credit is passed.

Figure 5.5 IDEF0/SSADM functional modelling example

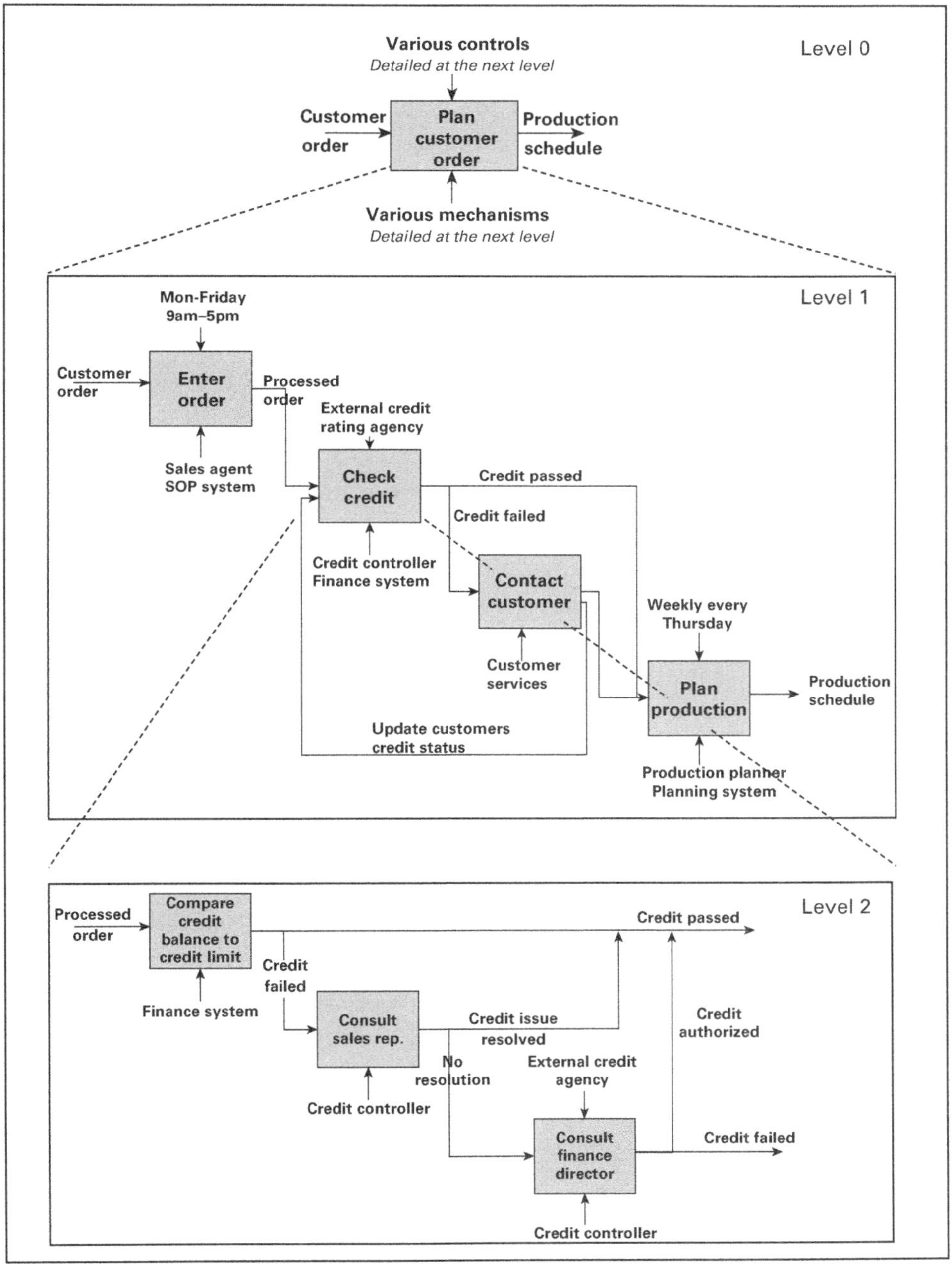

The IDEF0/SSADM technique comes with rigorous guidelines to help users to consistently apply and develop functional models of the systems. Although the rules and guidelines for constructing such models are outside the scope of this book, we will give some examples. One of the rules of this approach is that any system should have no less than two and no more than seven subsystems. Whilst the bottom limit of two is obvious, the top limit of seven is based on the psychology literature that states that any system with more than seven parts would be too complicated to comprehend. Another guideline is the numbering convention that should be used when creating these models so that it would be easy to relate various models to one another.

IDEF0/SSADM when used with rigour can help to uncover a lot of detail within a system. The only issue is that even with just two levels of analysis, as illustrated in our example, a lot of detailed documentation is produced representing a lot of person-hours of work. During the 1990s it was widely used to model the business processes of organizations before making investments into computer systems such as enterprise resource planning systems. In our experience, these resulted in models running into hundreds of pages of diagrams and associated narratives, which requires more time and effort to maintain and update as systems change.

5.5 Process mapping or business process modelling

Process mapping or business process modelling is widely used in business process management and systems engineering. It focuses on illustrating the processes, sub-processes and activities of an organization with a purpose to understand, analyse, improve and automate these processes. In fact, the techniques discussed thus far have all been used in one way or another to model business processes. However, some users have developed methods with fewer formalities and some of these approaches have been converted into software-based tools to help users model business processes. One of the simplest approaches for modelling business processes is the use of sticky notes on a wall or a similar surface, where the entire business process is modelled end-to-end on a single wall. Although this approach is less formal and less rigorous than DFDs or IDEF0/SSADM for modelling the system, it can generate results a lot more quickly whilst enabling the users to be creative with their modelling approach, capturing key details that may be missed through more formalized approaches. An example of such a process map is illustrated in Figure 5.6.

Figure 5.6 Example of an informal process map using sticky notes on a wall

Figure 5.7 Example of a simple swim lane flow chart

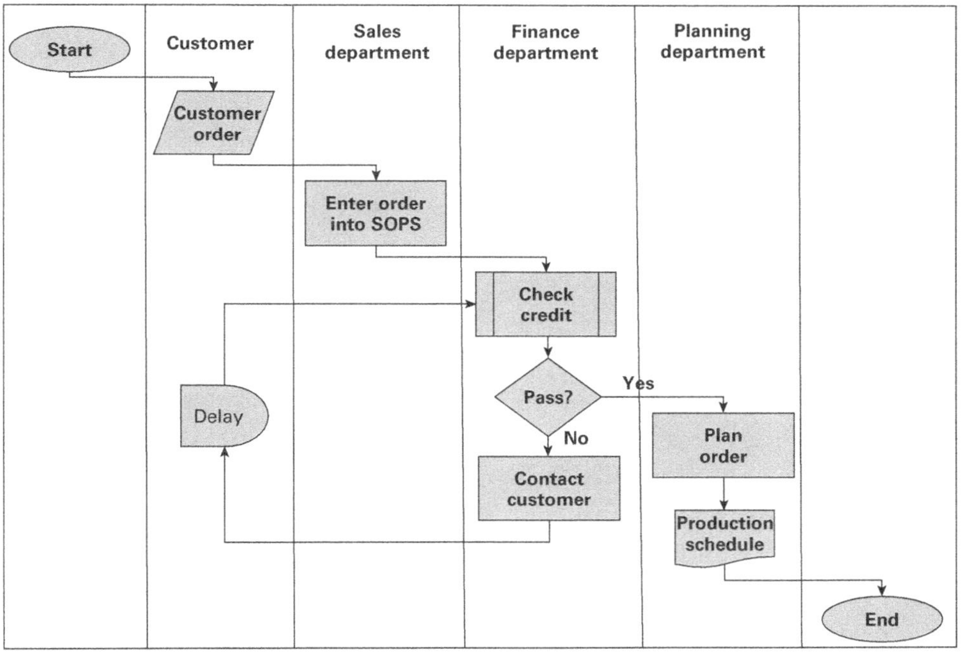

5.6 Swim lane process maps and flowcharts

This is a development of the simple process maps or flowcharts covered earlier in this section. It simply organizes the symbols into relevant lanes to show additional information on who or which function is responsible for the part of the process. An example of a swim lane flowchart for the customer order planning systems is provided in Figure 5.7.

5.7 Value stream mapping

Value stream mapping (VSM) is a technique that emerged from the lean thinking or lean management movement (Womack and Jones, 2003) which in turn is a development of lean manufacturing principles (Womack et al, 1990). Lean management is a methodology that focuses on minimizing *waste* within organizations while simultaneously maximizing quality, productivity and customer service performance. It is a customer-focused approach where *waste* is defined as anything that customers do not believe adds value and are not willing to pay for.

Value-stream mapping was developed specifically to address the needs of lean management by focusing on identifying waste in the system. This is achieved by focusing on activities that add value and eliminating, or minimizing, activities that do not add value. VSM visually analyses the series of events that take a product or service from the beginning (e.g. receiving raw materials) until it reaches the customer. As in previous approaches, it focuses on the flow of information, materials and/or people at each stage of the process, quantifies the time taken at each stage, and classifies this time as either value-adding time or non-value-adding time. The final output from the analysis is an in-depth understanding of waste across the system, which enables quantification of the value-added time as a ratio (value add ratio) or percentage of the overall time consumed across the system. An example of a value stream map is illustrated in Figure 5.8.

The value stream map starts with the customer at the top-right-hand corner. We can observe that the customer issues a long-term forecast against which they place weekly orders and they call off these weekly orders on a daily basis with variable quantities. Moving left, we can also observe that at any time the customer has about two days of stock available. The manufacturing company uses this information to produce and agree upon a customer delivery schedule, which takes around 20 hours per month to complete. This delivery schedule is used to develop a production plan (taking three hours per week) and a materials plan (taking 24 hours per week). The production plan is used for management of daily production priorities by the manufacturing supervisors. The materials plans are used to provide the suppliers with a long-term forecast, weekly demand schedule and daily expedites. The supplier delivers materials to the production site twice weekly and the time taken for these deliveries is unknown.

Figure 5.8 Example of a value stream map

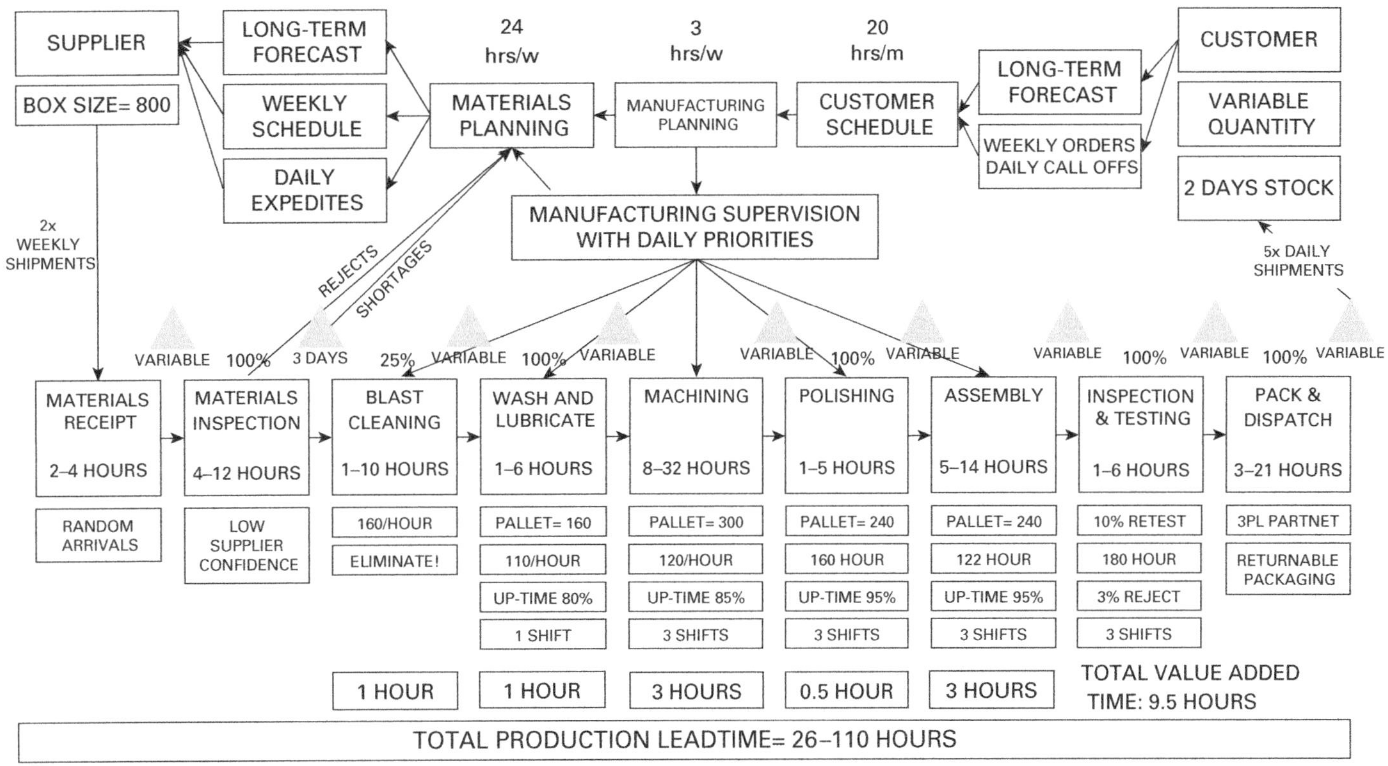

The lower part of the value stream map illustrates each stage of the production process starting from materials receipt through to packing and dispatch of the finished product to the customer. For each manufacturing stage the minimum and maximum time taken to complete each stage for a typical batch has been recorded along with other pertinent information relevant to each stage of the manufacturing process. This information includes inventory status between each stage of the manufacturing process, depicted by the triangle and the inventory level below the triangle, as well as the quality inspection policies used at each stage of the manufacturing process. At the very bottom of the figure, we can see that the total production lead time varies between 26 and 110 hours, whereas the value-added time at each stage is much smaller, totalling 9.5 hours across the entire production process. This makes the value-add ratio of 36 per cent at best and 8.6 per cent at worst. In this case the value-added time at each stage of the production process is computed based on the fastest time it takes to complete each stage for a typical batch with no interruptions, breakdowns and so on. We can also observe that stages such as materials receipt, materials inspection, final inspection and testing, and packing and dispatch, although they may be necessary, are not counted as value-adding activities.

VSM helps us to understand the waste within the system, as defined in lean management, thus helping us to optimize the system design to minimize waste. In this respect, different stakeholders may interpret the definition of waste differently. In the example above whilst packaging was considered a waste, in other instances it may be considered a value-adding aspect of the product, particularly if it makes the product more attractive and motivates the customer to choose your product over a competitor's product.

In this section we will refrain from providing further details on the construction of value stream maps and their variations. There are comprehensive guidance resources available online. We have also found Rother and Shook's (1999) book titled *Learning to See: Value-stream mapping to create value and eliminate muda* a valuable reference (*muda* meaning waste in Japanese).

Over the years we have also come across innovative ways of creating more visual value stream maps. This has been achieved by using videos or still photos of each stage of the process and organizing them in such a way that they tell a story of what is value-adding and what is not value-adding in the entire system. The video (see video link 5.1 in the online resources on the Koganpage.com product page) produced by Mercury Marine, although 13 years old, is a good example of applying this technique. These innovative approaches help us to more effectively tell a story about the system and its behaviour.

5.8 Discrete event simulation

Discrete Event Simulation (DES) is a simulation-based approach used for modelling systems (Allen, 2011). It models the flow of work through the system as a discrete set of events over time. Each event occurs either at a specific instant in time (e.g. 10:05 am every day) or following completion of a specific event (e.g. when the order entry event is complete, the credit control event will commence) and marks a change in the overall state of the system. DES assumes that the state of the system does not change between events, therefore the simulation time can fast-forward directly to the next event. DES is commonly used to model business and manufacturing processes. The customer order planning system we have used as an example throughout the system can easily be modelled using the DES approach. As DES is a time-based simulation, in addition to having the sequence of events, i.e. activities, we would also need to have variables such as *processing times* (e.g. the time it takes the sales department to enter the order into the system), *queue time* (e.g. the length of time the order has to wait in the sales department's inbox before they get around to processing the order), various statistical and computational algorithms such as probability distributions, confidence intervals, the Monte Carlo method as well as random number generators used to model variations in order/materials arrival rates and patterns, capacities, queue times and processing times of various events.

Although it is possible to develop DES models of very simple systems using spreadsheet software, due to the complexity of the systems and the volume of variables and associated algorithms and data involved it is more likely that DES models are built using proprietary or open-source DES software tools. Today, DES is commonly used to model in a variety of contexts. Some examples include:

- Understanding bottlenecks in a complex manufacturing or traffic flow system. By accurately simulating the system it is possible to gain a detailed understanding of the conditions (such as specific combination of variations at different events and times) that could create bottlenecks at critical resources.

- Optimizing queuing systems at road junctions, hospitals, call centres and other such systems by better understanding of the interplay between various factors and variations.
- Testing the potential impact of potential interventions to improve systems performance, including stress testing solutions to see whether a particular set of conditions would cause the system to fail.
- Evaluating investment decisions and potential alternatives by simulating their implications under different conditions.

In short, unlike other hard systems modelling approaches we discussed earlier in this chapter, DES provides an opportunity for observing a system under dynamic conditions, i.e. a working model of the system, rather than the static models offered by other approaches. This allows management to understand interaction between performance drivers and performance outcomes in a dynamic context. Although most DES software tools enable visualization of the system, such as various entities (customers, information, materials, people) flowing through the system, the real value from DES and other simulation models is the statistics, such as the arrival rates, resource utilization, queue times, etc. over time, which enables us to understand how different variables in the system interact to define the system's behaviour.

5.9 Agent-based modelling and simulation

Agent-based modelling (ABM) is also a simulation modelling method (Macal and North, 2009), but is different from DES as it focuses on modelling and simulating autonomous parts, i.e. agents, as well as their individual behaviours and interactions. In contrast, DES does not lend itself to the modelling of systems where each part of the system is an autonomous agent.

In ABM, different agents exhibit behaviours which can be described by a set of relatively simple rules. An agent interacts with other agents and their environment, which may influence their behaviour and, in turn, they may influence the behaviour of other agents. The modelling is constructed from the bottom up, describing each agent and the rules governing their behaviour and interactions from which a large-scale self-organizing system may emerge. This emergence of self-organization is the first of the two important features of this method. Each agent pursues its own interest in the system, and as the simulation progresses, the agents can have the ability to adapt to the changing environment. Diversity of agents is the second of the two important features of this method.

As a result, ABM allows us to construct the complex interrelationships of decisions of interacting agents while providing an environment for exploring the collective behaviour of agents. In other words, higher-level system properties that were not explicitly programmed in the system emerge from the lower-level subsystems. Hence ABM allows us to build and test models depicting particular behaviours that can then inform decisions about how to change the system. This approach allows us to simulate a complex system that is impossible to do using deterministic methods. The ability to incorporate the adaptability of the behaviour of the agents enables modelling of complex adaptive systems.

An agent-based model typically has the following three components:

1 Agents with their properties/attributes and behaviours.
2 Relationships or interactions between the agents (how each agent interacts and with whom) that create an underlying topology of interconnectedness.
3 Interactions of the agents with the surrounding environment.

The agents in the model have distinctive attributes that make them recognizable by other agents. They are autonomous and can execute their specific functions at least for a limited period of time. However, they also have dynamic interactions with other agents that might influence their behaviour over time. Agents also have access to only local information from other agents which is defined either by close proximity to them or from the local environment, or by their own network. Both are defined and controlled by the modeller. This makes ABM ideal for modelling decentralized systems with no central entity distributing information to agents or exercising control over the agents. However, this method can also be used to model systems with centralized control, with a main agent that can exercise some control. Information that agents obtain from the local environment can either be specific to their environment, such as their locations, behaviour or certain attributes, or relating to objects within their environment, thus enabling an agent's actions. For instance, in a transportation model an object within an environment might provide information about the available infrastructure and its capacity, thus allowing the agent to perform certain actions to make use of this infrastructure. If you would like to learn this method in more detail, the book *Agent-based Modeling and Simulation* by Simon JE Taylor (2014) is a good starting point.

Examples of using ABM include:

- Understanding water consumption behaviour of residents in response to different policies and demand management strategies. ABM allows us to examine water conservation tendencies among different groups of users each with their unique attributes, such as income level and access to information, and explore different scenarios determined by the application of different strategies.
- Analysing transport-sharing schemes (such as car- or bike-sharing schemes) and different incentives that might alter user behaviour. ABM allows us to test the effectiveness of different incentives aimed at encouraging users to choose alternative stations preferred by the system as their pick-up or drop-off points.
- Improving efficiency of logistics operations in retail by involving customers in making deliveries (customer crowd-shipping). ABM allows us to model the delivery of customer orders by a dedicated fleet (not autonomous agents) and customers as autonomous delivery agents making decisions about a delivery in response to different incentives.

In short, ABM allows us to observe the behaviour of a system under dynamic conditions and explore emergent behaviours under different scenarios. What makes it a distinctive approach is the focus on capturing the behaviour of autonomous agents and allowing for modelling adaptive behaviour in response to the behaviour of other agents. This makes it possible to model complex and adaptive system behaviours with emergent properties that are not programmed in advance, but are rather revealed over time within the simulation.

5.10 Hard systems modelling: limitations and innovations

In this chapter so far we have covered a number of different approaches that we can use for modelling hard systems. There are no strict formalities with these approaches unless one wants to or there are contractual obligations for using a formal methodology such as SSADM or IDEF. In many cases the system analyst will use one or a combination of these approaches to model the system to suit the needs of their project. In practice, we see many innovations around these approaches as exemplified by the use of still images and videos to bring the system to life as shown by the Mercury Marine example above. It is, however, important to emphasize that when we are modelling systems, the simpler it is and the more visual it is the more people will understand it and engage with it.

The key limitation of hard systems modelling techniques is that in business and management we tend to work with human-centred systems that have both technical/hard and social/soft dimensions. So, whilst using hard systems approaches helps to rigorously capture the procedural and tangible aspects of the system, it is likely that we will not be able to capture the softer social aspects (in memos and emails, behind closed office doors, informal conversations in corridors, around water coolers or coffee machines) that are most likely to shape the behaviour of the system. Recognition of these limitations has led some analysts to adopt further innovations as illustrated in the following case study.

CASE STUDY A systems thinking case study

Figure 5.9 shows a model of the end-to-end process for a large engineering manufacturing company, from receiving an enquiry, through proposal preparation, proposal issue, winning the order and so on, to delivering the order to the customer, gaining customer satisfaction, getting paid and closing the contract. In the photograph you can see some of the stages of the process identified by the labels hanging on the ceiling. On the floor you can see an SSADM approach to model the process in some detail. The company has chosen to use paper-based maps because having all these process maps on the computer or in folders was not user friendly and very few people other than the analysts (i.e. the team who compiled them) understood what they really meant. So, making the model visual and enabling people to walk through the system was the first development.

When the team started to walk people through the process, they discovered that those participating started sharing stories about what was really happening behind this process. It became apparent that the process maps, while describing the procedural and tangible aspects of the process, also helped to surface the social interactions that shaped the behaviour of the system. After walking many people through the process and listening to their stories they developed a range of stories and roleplayed these stories along the process (Figure 5.10) to raise awareness of both functional and dysfunctional aspects of the system.

Figure 5.9 Example of a hard system model displayed openly to enable different people to see and walk through the process

Figure 5.10 Bringing the process alive through roleplaying along the process

The following dialogue is a short extract from one of these roleplays where an order fulfilment process is being enacted. All the engineering and manufacturing has been done, the product is at the final testing stage and the customer is about the fly in to witness the final acceptance test...

Mark (production manager): Hi Jim (sales engineer), I just heard that we have problems with the final testing. We are trying to sort it out but we need more time. Any chance you can delay the customer a little bit?

Jim: Oh darn, how long do you need?

Mark: I need at least six hours, but to be on the safe side a day would be much better. Can you delay him until tomorrow afternoon?

Jim: He is flying in later this morning, I'll see what I can do – I think he likes playing golf!

Later at the airport Jimmy is meeting the customer's engineer (Tom)...

Jim: Welcome to the UK Tom. I thought that since this is your first visit to this part of the world, I have taken the liberty of booking us into the Golden Eagle hotel. I believe you play golf, so I am planning to take you out for a round of golf this afternoon. We'll stay at the hotel tonight and head down to the plant in the morning. Your test is scheduled for tomorrow afternoon, and we can still have you on the first flight the next morning.

Tom: I thought the test was scheduled for this afternoon.

Jim: To be honest I thought so too. I am not entirely sure what happened, but it was the planning department who changed the schedule. I do not think it affects our schedule; I hope you are OK with all this.

As can be observed through this interaction there is a hidden, arguably dysfunctional, dynamic within the system which was not captured by the SSADM-based hard systems thinking. In this example, the management team made the process visual by laying it out on the floor as a process map and then brought the real issues to the surface by storytelling and roleplaying along the process.

As we have demonstrated in this chapter, hard systems approaches can be used very effectively to capture the procedural and tangible aspect of a system, which is all that is needed for a computer program or an engineering system. However, in business and management where we have to deal with organizations, the key limitation of the hard systems approach is that it is largely impossible to capture the hidden social system using hard system techniques alone.

5.11 Summary

In this chapter our objective was to introduce you to hard systems thinking and help you to better understand the characteristics of hard systems. In doing this we also introduced you to commonly used hard systems modelling techniques. The techniques we selected to include in this chapter, whilst not being exhaustive, were intended to provide different perspectives and levels of sophistication to the modelling of hard systems.

Whilst most of the techniques used for modelling hard systems had their origins in the information systems field (such as flowcharts, DFDs and SSADM/IDEF), other approaches such as process mapping, swim lane process modelling and value stream mapping are innovations that emerged from business process management, quality management and lean management disciplines.

In the penultimate section we outlined the key limitations of hard systems modelling techniques with some examples of how organizations overcame these limitations in innovative ways. From these discussions it is clear that whilst being effective when dealing with engineered systems, from a business and management perspective, hard systems thinking and associated modelling approaches by themselves are not entirely sufficient to provide a complete understanding of a complex human activity system.

In the next chapter, introducing soft systems thinking, we will further reinforce the differences between hard and soft systems approaches by focusing on the characteristics of soft systems. We will also introduce techniques for modelling soft systems.

REFLECTIVE EXERCISE

Think about a small system you know fairly well. This could be a small part of the organization you work or study in. It could be a system related to a sports or arts club, your family or friends, or even a system you use regularly (e.g. a bicycle). Try to use three different techniques to model the system, like:

1 Flowcharts

2 Data Flow Diagrams

3 SSADM

4 Value Stream Mapping

Reflect on what you found easy while doing it. Then reflect on the aspects you found difficult. Was the problem in the modelling technique, i.e. it did not allow you to model what you wanted to explain? Or was it in your knowledge of the system? If it was the latter, a key function of any modelling technique is to make the analyst think about what they know and don't know about the system so that they know what questions they need to ask to develop a complete view. If it was the former, perhaps the technique is not suitable for the system you were trying to model, or you were trying to model some of the softer aspects of the system for which hard systems modelling techniques are not well suited.

TEAM EXERCISE

The objective of the exercise is to experience hard systems thinking and learn about relative merits and limitations of different hard systems modelling techniques.

Provide the participants with a bicycle or a detailed picture of a bicycle. Ask them to use SSADM in a rudimentary form to model how a bicycle works. The first thing they need to identify is all the subsystems of a bicycle. At this stage do not worry about the SSADM rule of a maximum seven subsystems. In general, the following are the subsystems of the bike:

- **Frame**, including the seat post where the rider sits.
- **Drive system**, including the pedals, sprockets, gears, rear wheel and tyre.
- **Steering system**, including the handlebar, front forks, front wheel and tyre.
- **Braking system**, including brake levers, brake calipers and break pads.
- **The rider**, including arms, legs, torso and head. We need the rider included in this system as the bicycle will not work without the rider.

Then ask the participants to try to model how a bicycle works using the relationship between the parts. For example, the rider sits on the seat post, which is part of the frame, and holds the handlebars and places their feet on the pedals. The rider exerts force in a circular motion on the pedals, which transmit this force through the chain and sprockets to the rear wheel, providing forward motion… and so on.

With the above objective in mind, it is worth doing this exercise with groups of two or three participants and then comparing what each group has done and sharing what aspects of the exercise they found easy and what they found difficult.

References

Allen, TT (2011) *Introduction to Discrete Event Simulation and Agent-based Modeling: Voting systems, health care, military, and manufacturing*, Springer Science & Business Media

Macal, CM and North, MJ (2009) Agent-based modeling and simulation. In *Proceedings of the 2009 Winter Simulation Conference* (WSC) (pp. 86–98), IEEE

Rother, M and Shook, J (1999) *Learning to See: Value-stream mapping to create value and eliminate muda*, Brookline, Massachusetts: Lean Enterprise Institute

Taylor, S (Ed) (2014) *Agent-based Modeling and Simulation*, Springer

Womack, JP and Jones, DT (2003) *Lean Thinking: Banish waste and create wealth in your corporation*, Simon and Schuster, p 10

Womack, JP, Jones, DT and Roos, D (1990) *The Machine that Changed the World*, Rawson Associates, New York

Further reading

Downs, E, Clare, P and Coe, I (1992) *Structured Systems Analysis and Design Method Application and Context*, Prentice-Hall, Inc

Goodland, M and Slater, C (1995) *SSADM A practical approach* (version 4), McGraw-Hill, Berkshire

Hanrahan, RP (1995) *The IDEF Process Modelling Methodology*, Software Technology Support Center, pp 1–8

Soft systems thinking

6

In the previous chapters we have introduced what a system is, developed various concepts and definitions that underpin systems thinking, and introduced a number of complementary, commonly cited systems thinking models and frameworks providing different perspectives to systems. In the previous chapter we elaborated further on the earlier discussion of hard and soft systems introduced in Chapter 2, and went on to develop hard systems thinking and introduce a number of techniques for modelling hard systems.

> As a reminder, our earlier definitions of hard and soft systems were as follows:
>
> - **Hard system:** a system consisting of high-integrity parts that are connected through well-understood interaction patterns producing predictable behaviours.
> - **Soft system:** a system consisting of autonomous parts that are characterized by high variability and unpredictable behaviours and connected through a loosely defined dynamic web of relationships, power structures, shared or conflicting interests and values.

At the end of the last chapter, we discussed limitations of the hard systems modelling approach, primarily its inability to incorporate social dynamics within the system model, i.e. the soft aspects of systems. We also alluded to some soft systems modelling techniques, such as storytelling and role playing when we introduced innovations for overcoming the limitations of the hard systems modelling approach.

In this chapter we will introduce Soft Systems Methodology and several approaches to modelling soft systems including storytelling, role playing, rich pictures and causal loop diagrams. However, before we introduce the methods, we will start by outlining the characteristics of soft systems, which will further reinforce your understanding of the differences between hard and soft systems and the thinking that underpins these two paradigms. The last section will introduce causal loop diagrams as a means of capturing the social dynamics of a system, which will provide a segway to the next chapter where we build upon causal diagrams to introduce causal mapping and its use in group decision making.

LEARNING OUTCOMES

- Understand soft systems and soft systems thinking
- Become familiar with Soft Systems Methodology including concepts such as root definition, CATWOE and trim-tab
- Understand the relative merits and limitations of different approaches to understanding and modelling soft systems, including
    - storytelling and roleplay
    - rich pictures
    - causal loop diagrams
- Be able to model, analyse and improve systems using soft systems thinking and approaches

6.1 Characteristics of soft systems and soft systems thinking

Earlier we defined a soft system as a system consisting of autonomous parts that are characterized by high variability and unpredictable behaviours, connected through a loosely defined dynamic web of relationships and power structures. From this we can deduce that the key characteristic that defines a soft system is the **unpredictable behaviour** of the system, which is caused by **autonomy of each part** together with **loosely defined dynamic relationships between these parts.**

Autonomy of each part means that each part may have its own worldview, which may be quite different from the worldviews of other parts of the system. It would also mean that as an autonomous agent each part would operate to maximize its own purpose, which may be related to financial outcomes such as profit, career outcomes such as promotion, or social outcomes such as recognition or acceptance. This autonomy creates a high degree of variation in the behaviour of each part.

To further complicate matters, in soft systems the relationship between each part of the system is loosely defined and highly dynamic. This is best explained in modern-day politics when we see nations who were considered allies not long ago become enemies. In soft systems, the nature of the relationship between two entities can change over time. Sometimes the change can occur over a long period of time; at other times it can happen almost instantaneously. Just think back over your relationships with family, friends and colleagues. Can you think of an instance where you had a close friend and suddenly, over something very minor, they appeared to have fallen out with you and you were left puzzled? Most of us have experienced this kind of change in relationships in our lifetimes, which can often be explained by different worldviews or values, i.e. something you would see as a minor issue maybe a very important issue for them.

In soft systems it is the combination of **the autonomy of each part** together with the **loosely defined and dynamic relationships** that makes the system behaviour unpredictable. For these reasons the behaviour of soft systems cannot be reliably explained through mathematical and/or statistical models. To add to the complexity of soft systems, just like any system, soft systems also suffer from entropy. If they are left to their own purposes, they will gradually or sometimes rapidly deteriorate into disorder. Whilst in hard systems the entropy is somewhat predictable, in soft systems entropy is a lot more difficult to predict. In most organizations it is therefore necessary to have constant change, renewal and improvement just to maintain the steady state.

With this level of unpredictability, in soft systems, feedback is used to compensate for deviation from expectations through social mechanisms such as trust, fear, influence, motivation, coercion, engagement and persuasion as well as through more technical mechanisms such as target setting, benchmarking, reward and discipline.

Based on this we can summarize the characteristics of soft systems as follows:

- unpredictable behaviour;
- autonomous parts with high levels of variation shaped by different worldviews;
- loosely defined dynamic relationships that can change significantly in the short and long term;

- parts connected through a defined dynamic web of relationships, power structures, shared interests and values;
- feedback is used to compensate for deviation through social as well as technical mechanisms.

Soft systems thinking is a way of thinking about systems whereby the analyst/thinker is assuming that systems behave as soft systems as defined above. From this definition one can surmise that we would use soft systems thinking to analyse, understand and improve soft systems, while hard systems thinking is used to analyse, understand and improve hard systems. However, this is only partially true, as in principle, we can use hard and soft systems thinking to analyse, model and improve both hard and soft systems. This is best explained through an example.

Let's consider a bicycle and its rider as a system. The bicycle itself is an engineered system. It clearly is a hard system and there is little benefit in trying to understand the bicycle from a soft systems perspective as each part of the bicycle is deterministic. A bicycle has no autonomy, feelings or sense of purpose. So, it would be safe to limit our analysis of a bicycle to a hard system modelling approach. In contrast, if we consider the bicycle and a rider as a system we have the human component, which makes the system much less predictable. In this case we can still take a view and model the bicycle with a rider from a hard systems perspective. Taking this approach, we would focus on the mechanistic aspects of the system as illustrated below.

BICYCLE AND RIDER AS A HARD SYSTEM

The rider sits on the seat, holds the handlebars with his hands and places his feet on the pedals. The rider then exerts downwards pressure on the pedals, alternating between the left and then right pedals. The pedals and the crank convert this force to rotational motion and transmit it to the back wheel through the chain and the gears on the back wheel. The wheel turns and moves the bicycle forwards. The rider moves the handlebars left and right to steer the bicycle. The rider can squeeze the brake levers that tighten the cables and engage the brake pads on to the wheel rim, slowing down or stopping the bicycle.

From previous trials and measurements of the rider's strength and stamina, we know that the rider is capable of exerting 200Nm of toque onto the pedals constantly for two hours, which will generate about 660 watts of energy, giving the bicycle an average speed of 38kmh over the two-hour period on flat ground. Specifically, we can predict this system's performance.

In the above example, the analysis considers the rider and the bicycle as deterministic parts with predictable capabilities that are likely to deliver predictable results. In this analysis we do not consider the rider's mental state, health or motivation. If we take a soft systems approach, we can develop a very different picture of this system.

BICYCLE AND RIDER AS A SOFT SYSTEM

Prior to a race the next day, the rider has a sleepless night worrying about rising interest rates and energy prices. He is worried whether he will be able to continue funding his daughter's private education.

The rider is also thinking about the race tomorrow where a good friend is competing against him, which may make things awkward. Furthermore, in the morning he finds that the batteries on the central heating controller have gone flat. When he gets up the house is cold and there is no hot water for a shower, so he leaves home feeling rather grumpy. He is tired, his mental state is not what it should be and he is not fully motivated to win his race today.

Given these conditions the rider is unlikely to be able to perform as previously predicted, but we cannot really say how these factors are going to combine to affect his performance. In fact, we may even be surprised. We may find that he is angry, and he takes his anger out by cycling a lot harder than he usually does, breaking his own record.

In this example, by analysing the bicycle and the rider as a soft system we have overlayed the social factors onto the more deterministic hard systems perspective to give us a more complete understanding of the factors that may contribute to the performance of the system. As in this example, even though we may still not be able to predict the behaviour of the system, we can at least use relationships between parts of the system to retrospectively explain the system's behaviour. In short, hard and soft systems approaches are not alternative or competing ways of looking at organizational systems, but rather, in many cases, they provide complementary views to help us to develop a more complete understanding of the systems we live and work in.

In analysing and modelling soft systems the analyst tries to capture the inherent complexity from multiple perspectives to present an explanation of the system's current (as-is) behaviour. In some ways, modelling soft systems is potentially a wicked problem, as it would be near impossible to incorporate everyone's worldview in exactly the way they see the system. Thus, when modelling soft systems, the analyst is trying to integrate the views of different people whilst developing a credible and shared explanation of the system's behaviour. Therefore, building consensus and developing a shared understanding of the system is an integral part of the modelling challenge before we can think about what needs to change to improve the behaviour of the system. Even then, due to the high degree of unpredictability, it would be prudent to think about any improvement or change proposition as a hypothesis and test this hypothesis before implementing the proposed change in a wider context as unexpected and unpredicted side effects are likely to emerge. Such experiments can give us further insights into the way the system is working and responding to intervention.

In the following sections we will introduce Soft Systems Methodology together with various techniques for modelling soft systems, or modelling systems from a soft systems perspective. Once again, this is not intended to be an exhaustive list of systems modelling techniques and indeed there are many commercial tools available that use these techniques, or variations of them, to help model soft systems.

6.2 Soft Systems Methodology

Soft Systems Methodology (SSM) was developed during the early 1960s by Peter Checkland and his colleagues at Lancaster University in the UK to help in dealing with complex organizational and societal problems and situations that have divergent views about the problem and potential solution (Checkland, 1981; Checkland and Scholes, 1990 and 1999). As previously defined, when we are dealing with soft systems it may be difficult to agree on the actual problem to be addressed. SSM was developed specifically for dealing with situations where we are not sure what to do, why the problem exists, how urgent the situation is, who is involved, who the stakeholders are and what their views about the problem are. Essentially, SSM provides an organized way of thinking through these kinds of soft systems problems.

SSM comprises seven iterative steps as illustrated in Figure 6.1. In this figure the part above the black line is associated with real-world thinking and the part below the black line is associated with systems thinking. The first two steps of SSM focus on exploring and finding out about the problem in the real world. Steps 3 and 4 are about applying systems thinking by developing the root definitions for the relevant systems and building conceptual models of the system. The final three steps are about exploring the models in the context of the real-world situation, experimenting with potential solutions, and taking actions to improve the situation. The methodology is not intended to be a linear process, rather it is an iterative process between steps as it is often necessary to revisit the previous steps before progressing to the next steps. The overall process might also have to be repeated in cycles as it is often necessary to review the outcome of an action or an intervention to understand the unexpected emergent behaviours (i.e. side effects) to refine the interventions and continuously seek improvement of the system.

There are numerous examples of the successful use of SSM to resolve diverse problems, including ecological, environmental, political, economic, business and military problems. In fact, in the 1990s it was the recommended complementary planning tool for the UK Government's SSADM. This advice demonstrates the synergy and added value that a soft systems approach can bring to help us understand complex systems.

In terms of its limitations, SSM has been previously criticized as being too linear, too functionalist, and supporting the status quo and existing power structures. However, these claims are often rebutted by users arguing that these limitations are attributable to the users of the methodology rather than the methodology itself.

The overall methodology is supported by several techniques to help the users through the process. Below we summarize each step of the methodology

Figure 6.1 Soft Systems Methodology

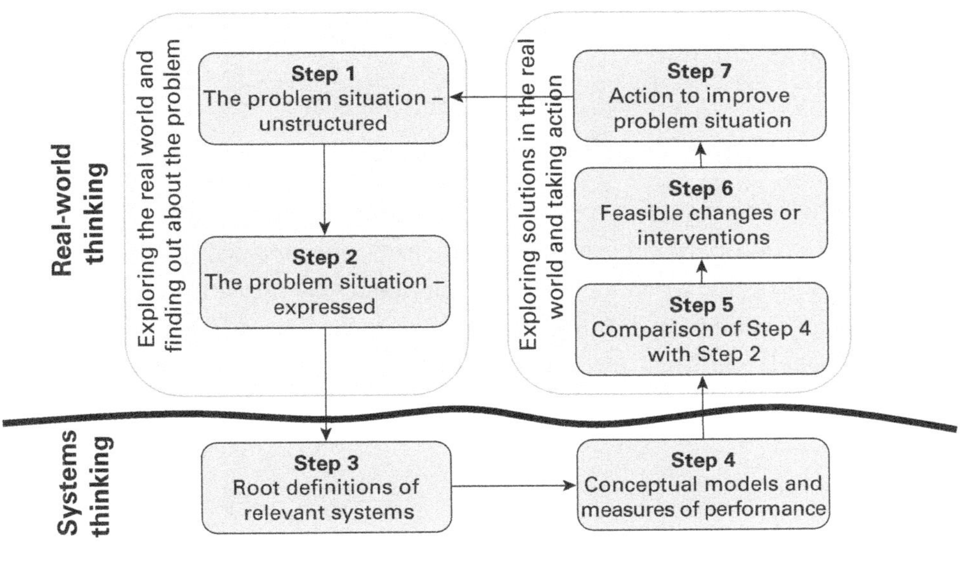

and include references to some of the commonly used techniques. In the following sections we will expand on some of these techniques to provide a complete understanding of the overall methodology.

Step 1: Problem situation – unstructured

This step is about engaging with various people concerned with the problem and gathering information about the situation that is considered to be problematic. Essentially, in this step the analyst is interviewing various people and getting them to explain what the problem may be, who the stakeholders may be, how the problems and potential solutions are being described by various people, and what the current performance measures and issues may be.

Although interviews are commonly used for data collection, we have observed that asking each person to compile short (five-minute) video diaries (daily or weekly) over a period of time describing what has happened and expressing their feelings and frustrations can be an alternative technique for collecting useful information about the current situation.

In this step it is important to interview people with different worldviews to ensure that we get as broad a picture of the situation as possible. For example interviewing people new to the system (e.g. new employees) is as important as interviewing people who have some experience of working in the system. Similarly, interviewing customers, suppliers and external advisors of a system will help to bring wider diversity in worldviews. This is important because, if people with similar views share slightly different but overlapping interpretations of the problem, it's less valuable than if such overlap emerges from conversations with people with divergent backgrounds and worldviews.

Step 2: Problem situation – expressed

The purpose of this step is to capture multiple perceptions or views of the situation. As each person consulted in the previous step will have their own unique background, worldviews and experiences of the situation, the challenge here is to identify common themes and develop different pictures of the situation. If we have interviewed 10 different people to understand a particular situation, it is unlikely that we will get 10 completely different views. It would be highly likely that a number of these perspectives would be similar to each other, and if we integrate these similar and complimentary views, we may end up with three or four quite different views of the situation.

An important outcome from this step is to note the differences in interpretation of the situation. As these differences are made explicit, further discussions and exploration of these differences enable the decision makers to arrive at accommodations/compromises or even a consensus over the situation.

To enable capturing and sharing the problem from different perspectives, Checkland and his colleagues developed the Rich Picture approach. The argument for the use of pictures is that words cannot adequately capture and describe a complex situation on their own. However, pictures used in conjunction with words (i.e. narratives) can help to develop a much richer picture of a complex situation, thus Rich Pictures. This approach has also proven to inspire people and help them talk more openly about problems and issues.

Step 3: Root definitions of relevant systems

In this step the objective is to capture the **root definition** or the purpose of the system that is relevant to the problem or situation at hand. A critical aspect of the root definition is the transformation that is performed by the system to deliver its purpose, which is captured by the verb in the root definition. For example, if we think of an education system we can formulate the purpose and therefore the root definition of the system in different ways as illustrated below. In this example, the transformation is highlighted in bold italics, and is significantly different in each root definition.

Higher education system...

... a system to ***drive economic growth*** through innovation and enterprise

... a system to ***make money*** through international student fees

... a system to ***develop new knowledge and global impact*** through leading-edge R&D

To help us ensure that the root definition is appropriate, Checkland and colleagues have developed a completeness test based on the mnemonic **CATWOE,** which stands for Customer, Actor, Transformation, Weltanschauung (Worldview), Owners and Environmental constraints. Below, each of the components is described in more detail:

- **Customers** are people or organizations that receive and are impacted (positively or negatively) by the output from the transformation. More recently this concept has been further developed by splitting the customers into two categories: beneficiaries and victims of the system.

  Beneficiaries of the system are those customers experiencing a positive impact from the outputs of the system, and **victims** of the system are those customers experiencing a negative impact from these outputs. With this distinction, sometimes you may encounter the mnemonic BATWOVE appearing instead of CATWOE.

  At this point, it is also important to point out the difference between customers and clients. Clients are not the same as customers, rather they are actors (see below). In SSM many systems that serve one group (clients) will often impact a different group (customers).
- **Actors** are those individuals, groups or organizations that make the system work. They carry out the transformation. According to this definition actors would include clients, suppliers and business partners.

  Sometimes actors could also be customers or even owners (see below) of the system but more often they are not. A good test to consider if an individual or a group of individuals are also customers is to think about whether they are positively or negatively impacted by the system. Similarly, considering if the actors also have the power to change the system or disband it would help us to decide whether an actor is also an owner.
- **Transformation** in its simplest form is the purposeful activity that transforms inputs to outputs. However, in complex systems the input-output view is often too complex to express simply in one sentence, thus it is often better expressed as *a system to deliver a purpose through some function*; for example an education system is a system to *drive economic growth* (purpose) through *innovation and enterprise* (function).
- **Weltanschauung** is the German word that means 'worldview' and it has somehow become part of the terminology often used in systems thinking. It captures the underlying and often uncommunicated beliefs that give meaning to the root definition. In this book we chose to use *worldview* but

we have included the often-quoted German equivalent here to highlight alternative terms and avoid any confusion in the future.

- **Owner(s)** is/are the key decision maker(s) who are concerned with the performance of the system and who can change the performance measures of the system. As previously explained, an owner can also be a customer or an actor.
- **Environmental constraints** recognize that all systems exist as parts of larger systems thus their operations and performance are constrained by factors outside the system's boundary. Thus, environmental constraints are those constraints that come from outside the boundaries of a system and are significant to the system's operation and performance. Therefore, the 'root definition' should include anything special in the environment of the system that is likely to affect the transformation.

Based on the CATWOE test as described above, a complete root definition of the system could be structured as follows:

> A system owned by 'O' in which actors 'A' perform transformation 'T' for customers 'C' within the worldviews 'W' and the environmental constraints 'E'.

Thus our earlier definition of the higher education system could be developed into a complete root definition as follows:

> A system owned by the **government** (O) in which **universities** (A) in collaboration with **schools, further education colleges** and **enterprises** (A) **drive economic growth** (T) by creating and growing enterprises for the benefit of the **wider society** (C) underpinned by **the values of responsible and sustainable business** (W) and within **technological capabilities** (E).

In general, there are no particular rules about how to develop root definitions as long as they conform to the CATWOE test. Some users prefer to identify all the CATWOE elements first and then start compiling a root definition; others may prefer compiling alternative root definitions first and then using the CATWOE test to refine them.

Whichever approach is taken, it is important at this stage to note that as part of this step (Step 3) it is likely that we end up with a number of competing root definitions due to different views about the purpose of a system. Such an outcome was illustrated with the example we provided earlier in this section about the purpose of the higher education system (i.e. drive economic growth vs make money vs develop new knowledge).

At this stage it might be appropriate to conduct the first cycle of the iterative process. If you are faced with multiple root definitions it would be appropriate to reduce these to a smaller number by scrutinizing each of the definitions and through further discussions with key stakeholders. In some cases it is also possible that the different root definitions could co-exist within the same system but as different subsystems within the larger system as discussed in Step 4.

Step 4: Building conceptual models

Once we have agreed on one or several root definitions, we can move on to building conceptual models of the system and its behaviour. If after the discussion with key stakeholders you have not reached a compromise on the common view, it may be that you have more than one root definition representing different distinct subsystems within the wider system. If this is the case, you would need to develop a separate conceptual model for each one of the subsystems.

At this stage it is worth noting that it is not uncommon to discover a number of distinct subsystems within an organization with different root definitions. Often some of the problems and issues we are trying to address can be attributable to the internal conflicts between these subsystems. Therefore, recognizing these as different subsystems with different root definitions can be a key step towards addressing these problems. To illustrate this, we have provided two examples below.

EXAMPLE 1: PUMP MANUFACTURING

A large engineering company is engaged in the design, manufacture and installation of pumps for their customers in the mining, oil and gas sectors. On the one hand, they design, manufacture and sell standard pumps. These standard pumps are made to stock based on a forecast. The customers buy them from a product catalogue, they expect short delivery lead times and make buying decisions primarily based on the price.

They also design, manufacture and install custom-engineered pumping solutions that have been engineered and manufactured as one-off products to meet specific customers' requirements. The main order-winning criterion is the organization's capability to design, develop, manufacture, deliver and install a pumping solution fit for purpose, to budget and to timescale. Thus, these products are significantly more complex and uncertain when compared to the standard products.

Clearly, here the company has two different systems, each with a different root definition:

A system where marketing, engineering, manufacturing and sales departments collaborate to create value by designing, manufacturing and selling market-leading standard pumping solutions.

A system where clients, engineering, manufacturing and projects departments collaborate to create value by designing, manufacturing and selling customized pumping solutions to address the needs of each client.

EXAMPLE 2: EDUCATION

A UK-based research-intensive university has undergraduate and postgraduate programmes as well as being active in local innovation and enterprise development activities. In this context, their undergraduates are mostly UK-based students who undertake five-year engineering degrees. The university actively coaches these students to develop innovations that could be transferred to the private sector or developed into start-up enterprises. In contrast, the postgraduate programmes are mainly popular among fee-paying overseas students undertaking standard one-year master's programmes. The university also has an active research and development culture and is one of the leading UK universities in terms of research intensiveness.

In this case it is conceivable that the university has three distinctive systems, each with a separate root definition:

A system to drive economic growth through innovation and enterprise.

A system to fund R&D and economic growth initiatives through international student fees.

A system to develop new knowledge and global impact through leading-edge R&D.

Once we have finalized our root definition(s) we can move on to building conceptual models of the system. To build the model we start by identifying the key activities that underpin the root definition. Often these activities can be ascertained from the verbs contained in the root definition, which helps to start building the models. However, in complex systems it is not always possible to ascertain all the key activities from the root definition. For instance, in the pump manufacturing example above, activities such as collaborating, designing, manufacturing and selling are part of the root definition and would provide a useful starting point for building a conceptual model. In contrast, however, the root definitions for the education system are less helpful in this regard. Whilst 'driving economic growth', 'innovating' and 'enterprise' are not useful to enable us to start building conceptual models, we can always go back to the data from stories, interviews and rich pictures in Step 2 to establish how these outcomes or functions are achieved.

Building a convincing conceptual model involves capturing the key activities and other elements that shape the behaviour of the system together with the logical links that connect the elements together. For example, if one of the outcomes of the system is leading to poor customer experience, there must be logical links from different parts of the system that lead to poor customer satisfaction; this could be product quality, late delivery or even unhelpful staff. Taking the latter as an example, when we look for the cause of this unhelpful staff behaviour, we may find that it is mostly attributable to staff morale and motivation, which in turn may be caused by other things.

Although using storytelling and rich pictures can help us to develop conceptual models, from experience we find causal loop diagrams more useful as a formalized way of developing these conceptual models. Indeed, they also enable us to explore solutions more easily in the real world before taking actions (i.e. Steps 5, 6 and 7).

In this section we will refrain from going into further detail on storytelling, rich pictures and causal loop diagrams, as we will discuss these in greater detail later in this chapter. However, at this point it would be appropriate to include a health warning. In the literature and wider internet there are some examples of soft systems models using rich pictures and causal loop diagrams that are rather simplistic and arguably focus on modelling the hard aspect of the system. The real value of soft systems modelling is to help us understand and model the social dimensions of the system, which helps us develop a profound understanding of why complex systems behave the way they do. Thus, when reading other sources on systems thinking in general and Soft Systems Methodology in particular this point should be borne in mind.

The final but important part of building a conceptual model is to identify and agree on the measures of performance for the system. According to SSM there are three measures of performance: effectiveness, efficiency and efficacy (which we discussed in Chapter 3). It is thus important that before proceeding to Step 5 we agree on the performance measures that enable us to evaluate and compare the current state of the system to any future improved state considering efficiency, effectiveness and efficacy.

Step 5: Comparing the conceptual model with the problem as expressed

In this step the main concern is to identify the *potential changes* that can be made to the system to resolve a particular problem/issue or improve the performance of the system. A simple way of doing this is to focus on the key elements of the system (from the root definition) and compare real-life issues with what could be done in the future. This is illustrated in the example in Table 6.1, which is based on the root definition of the higher education system introduced earlier. As a reminder, the root definition was:

> A system owned by the government (O) in which universities (A) in collaboration with schools, further education colleges and enterprises (A) drive economic growth (T) by creating and growing enterprises for the benefit of the wider society (C) underpinned by the values of responsible and sustainable business (W) and within technological capabilities (E).

Commonly our initial exploration of the real world (Steps 1 and 2) would have surfaced assumptions about the underlying causes of the problem and what needs to be or should be done to resolve the problem. This approach enables us to test these assumptions, which may be ill-founded. It is these differences between what happens in reality and the logical model that raise the questions that will ultimately lead to change.

Step 6: Feasible changes or interventions

This step is primarily concerned with identifying the *feasible changes or interventions* that would improve the behaviour of the system and consequently its performance. A table such as 6.1 is likely to contain several

Table 6.1 Starting to identify potential solutions

Root definition	Issues in the real world	What can be done?
… universities (A) in collaboration with schools, further education colleges and enterprises	Poor alignment between schools, colleges and universities, little or no collaboration with enterprises	• Review the purpose and objective of schools, colleges and universities • Create measures and incentives
… drive economic growth	In the fourth quartile for developed (OECD) economies	• Increase financial support for start-ups • Increasing support for collaborative growth initiatives
… creating and growing enterprises	Enterprise death rate is higher than birth rate	• Fund enterprise education • Start-up competitions • Advisory support for growth
… benefit wider society	Not visible. No clear benefits	• Measure the increase/decrease jobs versus higher value jobs
Owned by government	Primarily concerned with measuring and reporting outputs	• Focus on measuring and growing underlaying capabilities

possible interventions that would bring the real world closer to our conceptual model. However, there are a number of pertinent points here that need to be at the forefront of our minds when deciding which changes to implement.

In line with the fundamentals of systems thinking discussed earlier in this book, the *first point* is that once we make a change to the system, the system is changed, and it would need to be restudied and reanalysed in order for us to understand the new system and the new constraints. To give you a simple example, if we take a length of chain, how can we improve the strength of the chain? The simple answer is that we find the weakest link in the chain and strengthen it. If we need to improve the strength of the chain further, we would need to study the chain again, find the next weakest link and improve that link and so on. In summary, identifying and making several changes to the system may not deliver the expected results. In fact, it is likely to be counterproductive, with greater likelihood of delivering unexpected and undesirable side effects.

The added benefit of this approach is that by focusing on one change/intervention at a time we are more likely to get the change done, do it well and do it quickly. We must recognize that all change initiatives consume resources. One scarce resource is people's time. People have to work on their 'day job', i.e. designing products, serving customers, operating machines, loading trucks, etc., and in addition, they have to work on 'the project'. So, in terms of people's time, the change project is already in competition with the day job. If we introduce several projects simultaneously, there is a good chance that they will be competing for the same resources.

The *second point* is that the change and intervention should focus on identifying the most significant constraint that is preventing the system from getting one step closer to its purpose or delivering its performance measures. That is, the change or the intervention should be subordinate to the purpose and performance measures of the system.

The *third point* is that we should focus on finding the one simple change we can make that will have a profound effect on the behaviour of the overall system. 'Call me trim-tab' is the phrase engraved on the gravestone of Buckminster Fuller (1895–1983). Fuller, an American architect, systems theorist, author, designer and inventor, is frequently quoted for his use of trim-tabs as a metaphor. In 1972 Fuller said:

> Something hit me very hard once, thinking about what one little man could do. Think of the Queen Mary [the ocean liner] – the whole ship goes by and then comes the rudder. And there's a tiny thing at the edge of the rudder called a trim-tab. It's a miniature rudder. Just moving the little trim-tab builds a low pressure that pulls the rudder around which brings the whole ship around. [It] takes almost no effort at all...! (Kowalski, nd)

This trim-tab analogy, which goes by different names such as levers or pressure points in the system, captures an important feature of a systems approach. That is, one small change in an almost insignificant part of a complex system could end up changing the behaviour of the whole organization. The trick is knowing where or what the trim-tab is, or even how to find it. We will further discuss the techniques for finding the trim-tab when we look at causal loop mapping in detail later in this chapter. We will then discuss different types of trim-tabs or levers in the system in Chapter 9 after introducing system dynamics as a method for simulating the future behaviour of a system.

The *fourth point* is that people are not always motivated to implement change, particularly when people involved in the potential change have conflicting views or even see themselves as the victims of the change even if the logic of the conceptual model is undeniable. Therefore, when selecting which change to implement, it is important to understand the potential resistance to change. In this context, the good thing is that during the earlier stages of SSM we should have understood different worldviews of different people and this will give us a good idea as to how the change will impact the customers of the system, and whether they will become beneficiaries or victims. Needless to say, where a change is going to produce more victims than beneficiaries, it is going to be harder to implement. In this context, a simple change that might produce a lot of resistance is not as simple as it seems, and thus we must either find ways to mitigate resistance to change or seek alternative interventions that would be simpler to implement.

Step 7: Action to improve the problem

Once we have identified the change that we would consider feasible then we take action to implement this change. As stated above, this change will result in a new system that may even affect the wider system within which our system exists, leading to more problems and opportunities. Thus, the process starts again from Step 1.

REFLECTIVE EXERCISE

Think about a system you know well. This could be a business or a department you work in or a university, school or department within which you are studying. Use the CATWOE model and the examples from earlier in this chapter to develop a root definition for this system.

Then talk to some friends and colleagues who also work or study in the same system to see how they conceptualize the system, but at this stage don't share your root definition with them. Also, you do not need to educate them about systems thinking and all the concepts associated with it to do this. Just ask them a few questions around what they think the purpose of the system (business/department/club/school) is, who (people and organizations) they think are the key players in the system, and who organizes the system, measures its performance and is ultimately responsible for the system.

Compare their answers to the root definition you developed earlier. Do they agree with your root definition? Are they similar or wildly different? How can you further develop your root definition to incorporate their views?

Having introduced Soft Systems Methodology in some detail, in the following section we will introduce different but complementary techniques for modelling soft systems.

6.3 Storytelling and roleplay

Just like playing is the most elevated form of learning and investigation, storytelling is also an effective way of communicating and learning that has been developed and refined by different cultures over centuries. Storytelling is a social activity of sharing stories, sometimes including props, artefacts, pictures or roleplay/theatrics. Every culture has its own stories or narratives, used as a means of communication for the purposes of cultural preservation, education or entertainment. Therefore, it is considered a useful way of capturing and sharing information about the real world as well as sharing and communicating information about the conceptual model.

Essentially, a story is a narrative that is structured around a plot and characters, as we already observed at the end of Chapter 5 when we discussed how one organization overcame the limitations of hard systems modelling (SSADM) by roleplaying and storytelling along the process. In this particular case, when finding out about the real-world problems (Steps 1 and 2) the team captured various individual's stories about the company (the system) from different perspectives. These stories covered numerous themes explaining what worked, what did not, how and why, from different perspectives. Some were factual, some were sad and others very funny. These stories became infinitely valuable when identifying different root definitions for the system.

In a similar vein, vignettes are brief stories of events that may describe a particular situation. Typically, they are 800–1,000 words, but they can be just a few sentences long, as exemplified by the following episode demonstrating the (lack of) value placed on annual performance reviews in an organization:

> … in our organization we do annual performance reviews, but we just pay lip service to them, we do not really value them. Last year my manager told me that we will do my performance review next week on the flight when we are travelling to Milan, which I was not happy about…

Vignettes are commonly used in research to understand a particular phenomenon. Collecting numerous stories about the phenomenon from a diverse range of people with different perspectives enables the investigator to analyse the vignettes for patterns to identify themes and help them build theories to explain this phenomenon.

In similar ways, storytelling and roleplaying can be used to share, gain feedback and build consensus about the current state of a system, helping to pave the way towards identifying a common solution that is acceptable to all. There are no hard and fast rules to storytelling and roleplay as it is considered an art form, and requires a certain degree of creativity, vision, skill and practice. Having said that, the basic skills of storytelling are not beyond the capabilities of most people, they may just need some good examples or some advice and coaching to point them in the right direction. The internet is full of advice and guidance about how to tell effective stories, most of which would be useful for developing basic storytelling skills required to capture and tell stories about systems we are studying.

Roleplaying is an effective way of bringing a story to life. Similarly, roleplaying is also an artform that could be developed by most people over time. It comes more naturally to some people than to others. In most situations there are people who have some experience of roleplaying either from school or a local theatre group. Tapping into people who have some experience of roleplaying or who are eager to participate is a good way of getting people engaged in the story and communicating the current situation within the system.

6.4. Rich pictures

The rich picture technique was developed as an action learning mechanism to help learn about complex and ill-defined systems. There are no formal rules, nomenclature or syntax to follow; instead they rely purely on the user's creativity in using symbols, cartoons and sketches to help them to tell a story. The real value of the technique is that it forces the creator out of their comfort zone and makes them think more deeply about the system or the problem. Combined with the narrative that accompanies the illustration they provide a powerful way of telling a story about the behaviour of a system, as exemplified in Figure 6.2.

Figure 6.2 Rich picture example: how the head of a university department conceptualizes the department he is trying to manage

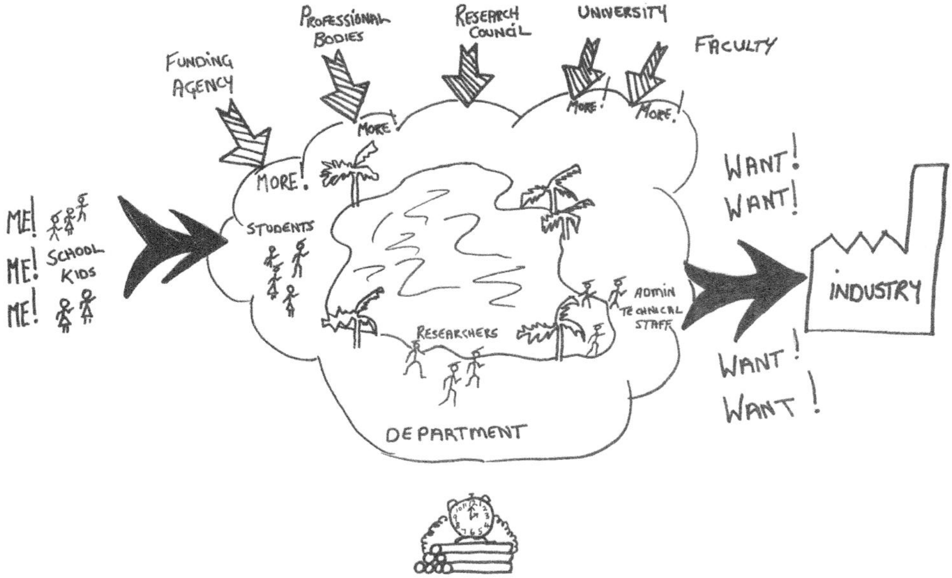

The following is his narration of the picture, with our comments inserted in brackets:

> As a management team, we are trying to create this tranquil environment [oasis with palm trees] where academics, students, administrative and technical staff have some stability and can perform. However, we have a number of forces that we have to battle with on a daily basis. On the one side we have kids [school pupils] wanting to come and study with us, on the other hand we have industry wanting more and more from us and our students. We also have the faculty, university, funding councils and professional bodies throwing more and more demands on us [illustrated as people firing arrows]. Quite frankly I cannot help but think that we are sitting on a time bomb [note a clock and dynamite at the bottom of the picture].

From the above example we can see that the picture alone is of limited use to communicate the message behind the picture. However, in this case the technique has enabled this person to express his frustrations with the current system and the situation as he sees it. It becomes much clearer when the picture is accompanied by his narrative.

Earlier in this book we introduced the concept of rich pictures, albeit without referring to them as rich pictures. The pictures in Figure 2.1 illustrate how different students conceptualize a university. Effectively these are rich pictures that could be useful, particularly if accompanied by a narrative, for communicating and sharing each student's conceptualization of a university from their own viewpoint. In fact, rich pictures are commonly used to help management teams in an organization to understand each other's viewpoints, which can help ease some of the underlying frictions with the organization. The example, Figure 6.3 illustrates rich pictures drawn by three different senior managers from the same organization. You will notice that the three stories have certain similarities and differences.

Although free-form pictures as illustrated in Figure 6.3 are useful to understand how to conceptualize a particular system or problem, the

Figure 6.3 Rich pictures and narratives by three managers from the same organization

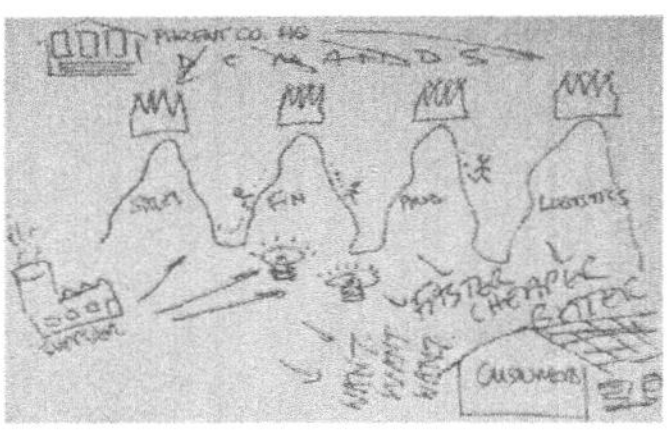	*'Our business is like four kingdoms who do not talk to each other. We have customers continuously demanding faster, cheaper and better products. Our suppliers keep on throwing new bright ideas our way. We also have our parent company coming up with demands about financial reporting, performance and so on. I am the little man running between these kingdoms, often uphill, sometimes downhill, to make sure that we do what we are supposed to do.'* [Operations manager]
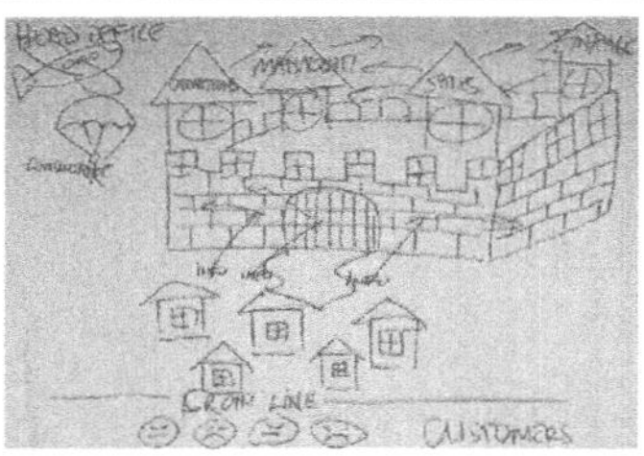	*'We are like a castle with the frontline staff outside the castle trying to deal with dissatisfied, angry, frustrated customers. We pass information about what needs to change, but the gate to the castle is closed and the information is not getting through. Inside the castle everyone is too busy fighting with each other. Head office is aware of the situation, and they are parachuting in a consultant.'* [Customer services manager]
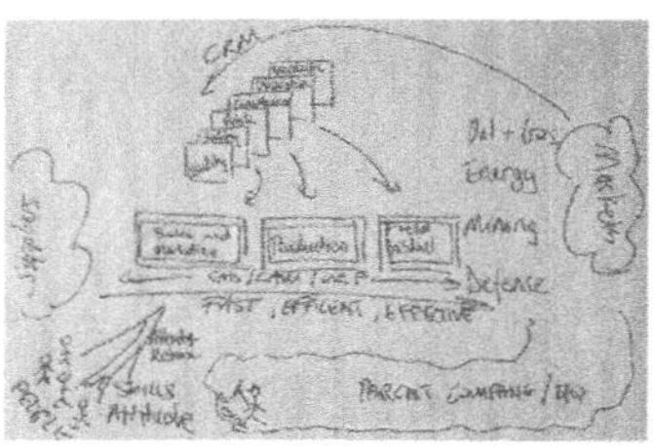	*Our business should be straightforward but we make it more complicated than it ought to be. We sell, make and sometimes install products for known markets with known requirements. Quality, safety risk, compliance are critical to what we do. We are also expected to be fast, efficient and effective, and our business systems are well positioned to help us achieve this. I see our key challenge as attracting and retaining good people with the right skills and attitude. The parent company is saying that they are trying to help us but I think they are undermining what we have achieved.* [Information systems manager]

more structure and process a rich picture contains the more useful it becomes to help us model the system later. As there are no hard and fast rules for developing rich pictures, we can often use the basic concept of a system, i.e. a system is a collection of interacting parts in which the interactions result in system-level properties and behaviours not attributable to the sum of individual parts. Based on this definition we can start building rich pictures that help us describe the parts and how they are connected to one another. In Figure 6.4 we have developed a rich picture, using standard PowerPoint icons, of the situation we described earlier in this chapter. As a reminder, the earlier story is as follows: *With the recent increase in interest rates and energy prices the rider is worried about his family's finances and whether they will be able to continue funding their daughter's education in the private school. The rider has a sleepless night worrying about finances. The rider is also thinking about the race where a good friend is competing, which is going to make things awkward. Furthermore, in the morning he finds that the batteries of the central heating controller have gone flat. When he gets up the house is cold and there is no hot water for a shower. So, he leaves home feeling rather grumpy. He is tired, his mental state is not what it should be, and he is not fully motivated to win this race today.*

In Figure 6.4, we can see that we can capture richer information which we did not identify from our earlier narration. This is because the act of drawing the picture makes us think more deeply about the situation and identify further linkages that had not thought about. Particularly, there are some self-reinforcing loops identified, such as the cyclist being angry at himself for not checking the battery in the central heating controller. Also, his awareness of little sleep, not having a clear head and lacking motivation are causing further anxiety. With these forces it would be safe to predict that this race will not be this cyclist's best performance.

In summary, rich pictures provide a flexible and unconstrained platform for communicating experiences and viewpoints of a given system or problem situation. Thus, it is a valuable technique for capturing and communicating how people see a situation individually and collectively. It is also worth noting that it is possible to produce rich pictures as a group by having everybody contribute to its creation. This approach can also help to develop and reinforce a shared understanding of the system or problem situation.

Figure 6.4 Rich picture showing the forces affecting a cyclist's potential performance in the race

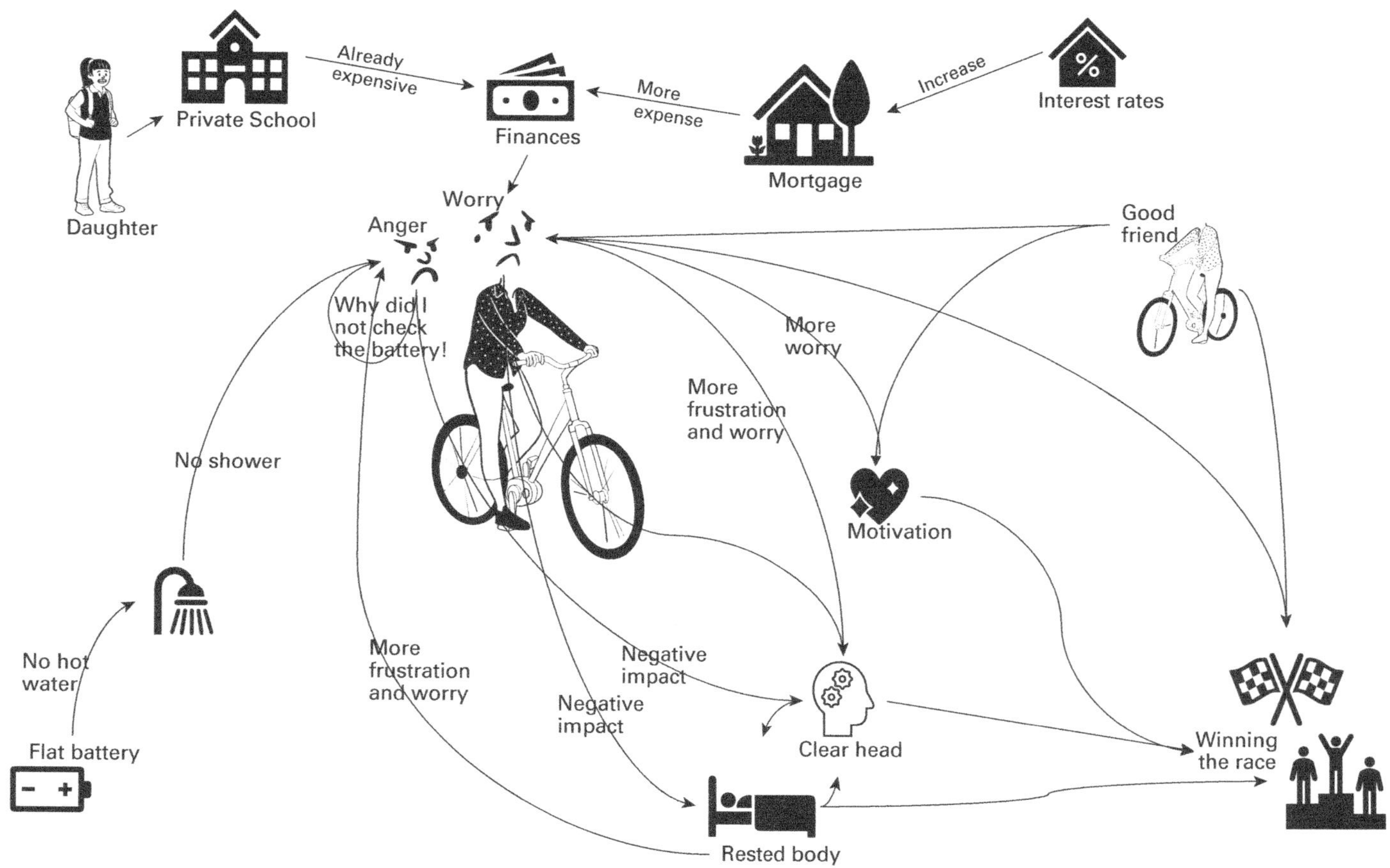

6.5 Causal loop diagrams

We have already introduced the concepts of causality and feedback loops earlier in this book (see section 3.7). In this section we will build upon the concept of causality and feedback loops as well as other things we have learned about systems and systems thinking so far, to develop an insight into how we can start modelling and understanding complex systems.

Essentially, a causal loop diagram illustrates the causal relationships between the entities within a system. As in rich pictures, they help visualize how different factors in a system are causally interacting to shape the behaviour of the system. In essence, one could argue that the rich picture we constructed in Figure 6.4 is an informal causal loop diagram. Whilst in rich pictures there are no hard and fast rules, in causal loop diagrams we have entities described in words and relationships between entities described by arrows. Furthermore, the relationships between entities can be characterized as positive (+) or negative (-) links. A positive causal link means that the two entities change in the same direction, e.g. both improving or both deteriorating. A negative causal link means that the two entities change in opposite directions, e.g. an improvement in one will cause deterioration in the other.

Let us develop these relationships through a simple example:

- If you are fed up, eating cake, after the initial sugar rush, will make you feel heavy and lethargic (Figure 6.5a). This is shown as two entities with a positive relationship.
- When you feel heavy and lethargic you feel more fed up, and you eat more cake, which makes you feel worst (Figure 6.5b). This is a feedback loop, which is self-reinforcing, i.e. a **positive feedback loop** which will continue getting worse if we do not intervene. This kind of feedback loop is known as a **reinforcing loop**.
- Instead, when you are fed up if you drink water, exercise and eat fruit, you will still get the energy from the sugar in the fruit but without feeling heavy and lethargic. When you feel less heavy and lethargic, you feel better and no longer feel the need to eat cake (Figure 6.5c). Now we have a **negative feedback loop**, which balances the effects of the reinforcing loop. These negative feedback loops are known as **balancing feedback loops**.

Understanding these feedback loops is important, as they are essential features of causal loop diagrams. It is important point to note that the arrows

Figure 6.5 Anatomy of causal loop diagrams

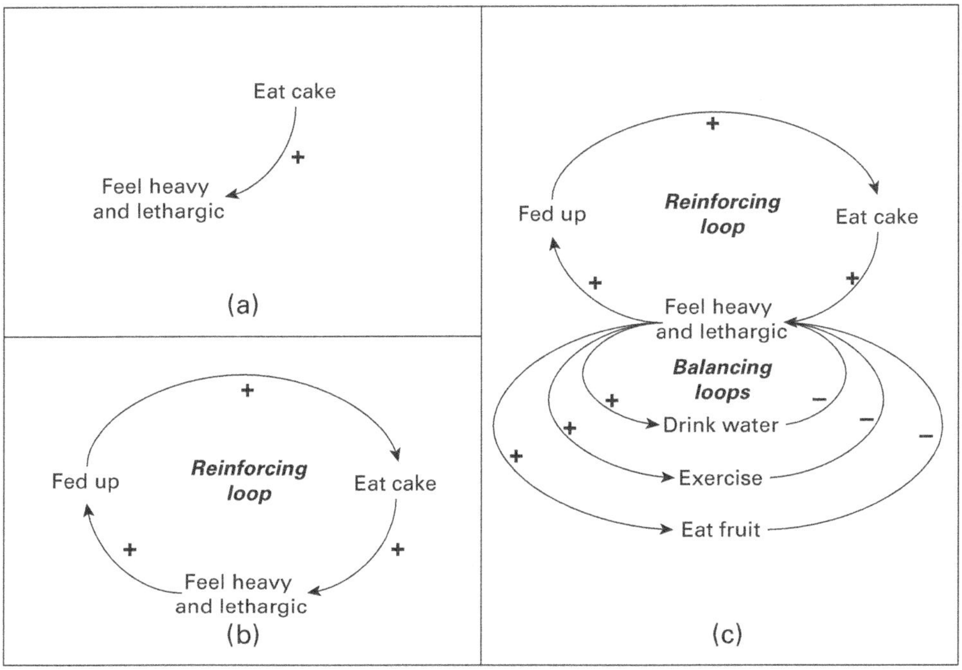

in causal loop diagrams represent causal relationships between entities, which are variables with values that can increase or decrease. Do not confuse this with data flow diagrams where the arrows represent material, information or even people flows.

Another important point to remember when constructing causal loop diagrams is the language we use when explaining the variables as this can impact on the nature (positive or negative) of the relationship between entities. When naming entities, you should refrain from qualifying them with phrases such as increasing, decreasing, improving, deteriorating or similar, as they can significantly change the nature of these relationships, from positive to negative or vice versa. This advice is the opposite of what is recommended in formulating statements in causal mapping discussed in the next chapter, whereby we are looking for the statements to be actionable. We can clearly observe the effects of such qualifiers in the example illustrated in Figure 6.6.

In Figure 6.6a we can observe each entity without any qualifiers and their relationships. In contrast, in Figure 6.6b we can observe the impact of using

Figure 6.6 Impact of qualifiers on the direction of the relationships between entities

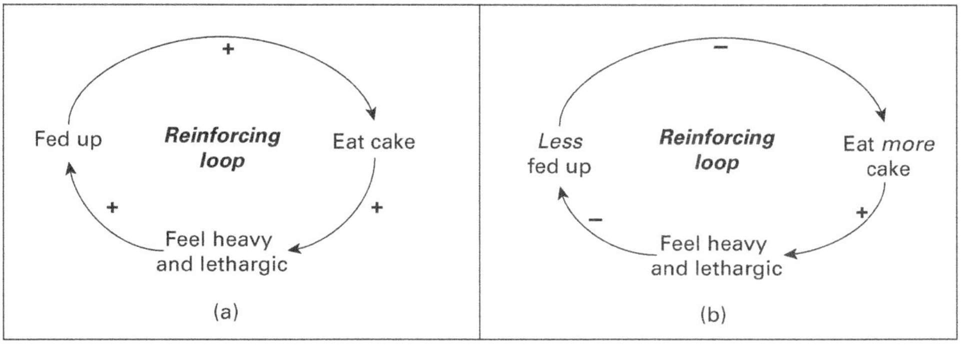

qualifiers on the same relationship. For example, when we qualify *Fed Up* with *Less Fed Up*, and *Eat Cake* with *Eat More Cake* the original positive relationship between *Fed Up* and *Eat Cake* reverses. Nevertheless, in practice we have found that some people find it useful to use qualifiers with entities when building causal loop diagrams as it enables them to keep all relationships either positive or negative to tell the story. This approach also enables the reader to follow the story more easily. For this reason, it is acceptable practice to build causal loop models using qualifiers. Naturally the model can always be edited to remove the qualifiers and correct the nature of the relationships. We will illustrate this in the example that follows.

Furthermore, to make casual loop diagrams comprehensible and easier to follow, diagrams are usually accompanied by a narrative that explains what is happening. To accurately relate the narrative to the diagram, sometimes the entities, relationships and feedback loops may be labelled, e.g. E1, E2 and E3 to represent entities and R1, R2 and R3 to represent relationships. This kind of labelling can also help you to tell the story of the model in a consistent manner.

In terms of Soft Systems Methodology, development of the causal loop diagram is understanding the system and developing a conceptual model that represents how the system behaves and the forces that make the system behave the way it does. Once we have completed building the causal loop diagram the next step is to analyse it to see what can be changed to improve the current situation and explore different solutions offered by different people (customers, owners, actors) in the system; we illustrate how this can be done in the case study which is included at the end of this section.

In searching for a feasible change to improve the system we go back to the causal loop diagram and look for a number of patterns:

- We explore the **balancing and reinforcing loops** to see what changes could be made to improve the system's behaviour.
- We look for **busy entities with a lot of inputs and outputs** as busy entities are influenced and are potential influencers of the entire system.
- We look for **entities with a lot of outputs** as they tend to influence a lot of other entities and can be the main influencer.

Finally, finding the changes to make to the system is not a straightforward task. Even after considerable modelling and analysis the changes we come up with may not deliver the expected outcomes. Even then, if we treat these as experiments, we can learn more about the system and eventually find the right intervention that will deliver the improvement we seek.

In the following case study, we illustrate this phenomenon together with various aspects of Soft Systems Methodology as well as the use of causal loop diagrams in understanding, modelling, analysing and then improving a complex system.

CASE STUDY Systems thinking case study

Understanding and modelling the system

We were invited by a national utility provider to help them resolve what they perceived as a wicked problem. To develop a causal loop model of the current situation we have progressed through steps 1 to 4 of Soft Systems Methodology. In summary:

Step 1 – we interviewed several people from the organization including senior management from corporate headquarters, middle managers managing the operations, customer service supervisors and agents, and even some customers. We summarized each interview into a short story reflecting their position in the system. In line with the CATWOE framework, we identified Customers – home residents and businesses who use the service and might call the call centre, Actors – customer service agents, supervisors and middle managers, and Owners – senior management from Headquarters, and described their worldviews and the environmental constraints (e.g. media and the wider society).

Step 2 – we consolidated different stories into a single story by discussing the problem situation and different views and making appropriate accommodations and compromises. By the end of this stage, we had most of the story developed, discussed and refined in the form of the causal loop model.

Step 3 – we explored various root definitions for the system and finally agreed it to be *a system owned by the senior management (owners), in which customer service agents, supervisors and managers (actors) work to serve the people at home and at work (reflecting household customers and business customers) to resolve service problems and address enquiries (transformation) efficiently and effectively (worldview) within the technical capabilities of our equipment (environmental constraints).*

Step 4 – we developed the causal loop diagram (Figure 6.7) and its accompanying narrative represented our conceptual model of the system as it existed at the time. The following is the abridged narrative for the causal loop diagram illustrated in Figure 6.7. We start our narrative at entity E1. The narrative follows the entity numbers in sequence.

Utility is a national company providing services to households in the UK. At the time of conducting this analysis it was criticized on a weekly basis on national television (E1) for poor customer service (E2) and poor customer satisfaction (E3). Combined, these three factors cause more customers to call the company, increasing call volumes (E4). To deal with increasing call volumes and to address poor customer satisfaction and national criticism the company hires more people, increasing headcount (E5) and costs (E6). Increase in call volumes and headcount leads to reduced productivity (E7). This together with increasing costs attracts attention from corporate management (E8), which leads to senior management micromanaging (E9) with daily monitoring of costs (E10) and increased emphasis on productivity management (E11), and this in turn leads to deterioration of management morale (E12). To improve productivity and costs, call targets (E13) are introduced, mandating that agents deal with each customer's call within eight minutes. To help manage this call target, egg timers (E14) are introduced on every customer services agent's computer screen. These egg timers change colour to amber at six minutes and to red at eight minutes to signal to the agent that they are near or at call target. Daily performance reviews (E15) are used to review the average performance of each agent to the eight-minute target and agents with lower performance are referred to the performance improvement programme (PIP), which essentially retrains the agents on how to serve customers and which they have already completed when first joining the company. Furthermore, the PIP is conducted out of hours so that it does not negatively impact productivity, and consequently PIP is seen as a punishment (E16). With the fear of missing the eight-minute target, daily performance reviews and the threat of PIP, agents defer complex enquiries from customers (E17) to remain within the time target. Examples

Figure 6.7 Example of a causal loop diagram using qualifiers where all relationships are considered positive

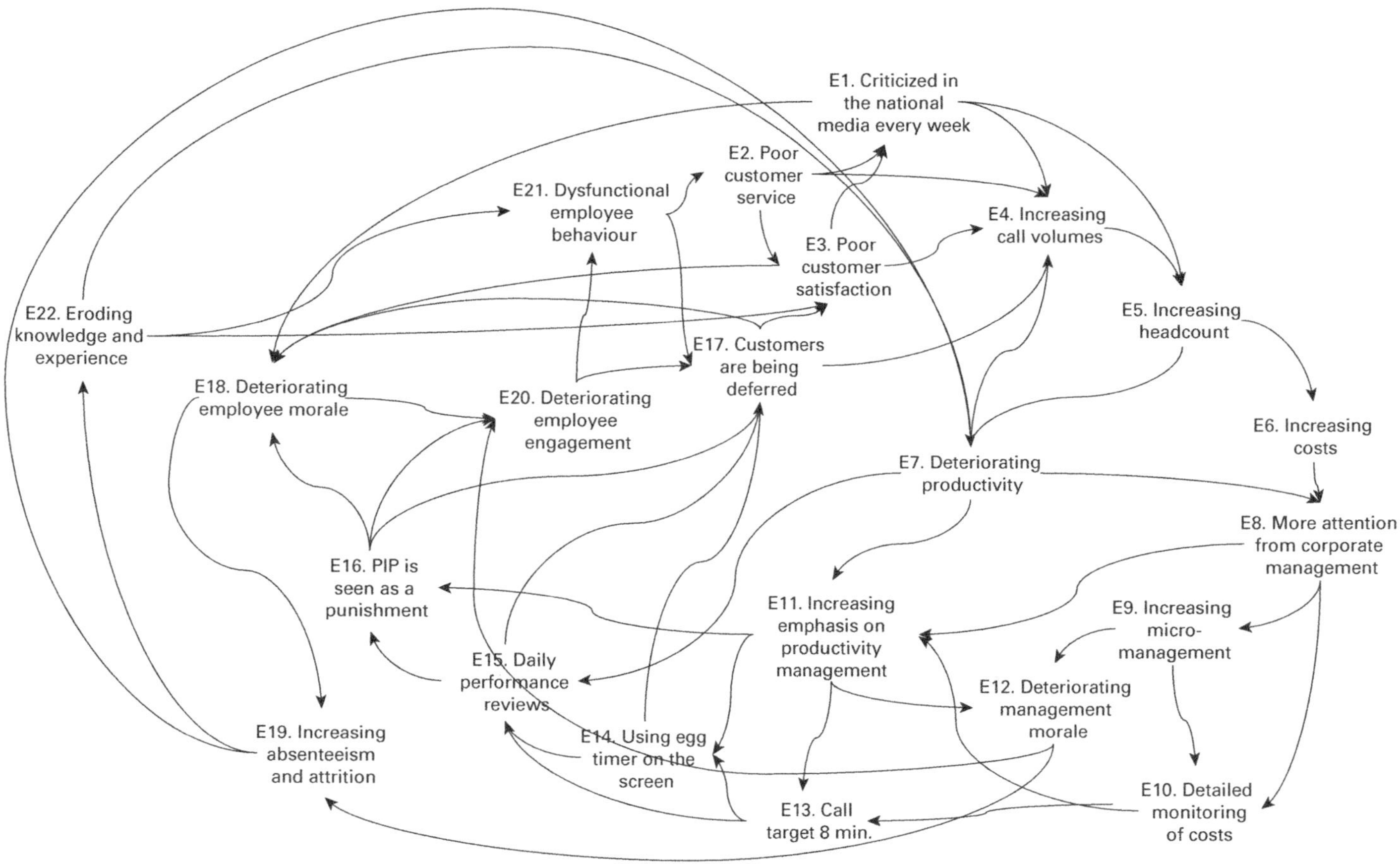

include, 'Sorry the computer systems are down, can you please call later?' and 'You have come to the wrong department, I will put you through to the correct department', and the customer is put back to the same telephone queue for someone else to deal with. This dynamic leads to deteriorating employee morale (E18), which together with deteriorating management morale (E12) leads to increasing levels of absenteeism and attrition (E19). This contributes to the deterioration of employee engagement (E20), which in turn reinforces dysfunctional behaviours (E21) such as deferral of customers (E17). This leads to poor customer service (E2) and satisfaction (E3). Moreover, whilst increasing absenteeism (E19) impacts directly on productivity (E7), increasing attrition (E19) leads to erosion of knowledge and experience, which further impacts on productivity (E7).

To be continued...

In contrast to the causal loop model illustrated in Figure 6.7, the model illustrated in Figure 6.8 is the same causal loop model with all the qualifiers removed and relationships expressed as either positive or negative relationships. Although this model better complies with the principles of causal loop mapping it is somewhat more difficult to follow compared to the causal loop model illustrated in Figure 6.7. In our experience in analysing complex systems, creating causal loop models using qualifiers and a narrative is sufficient to tell a story and start identifying opportunities for improving and innovating the system. While causal loop models with no qualifiers and positive and negative relationships become more useful if we are going to pursue a more quantitative modelling and analysis approach, such as systems dynamics modelling and simulation, which we cover in further detail in Chapter 8.

Figure 6.8 Causal loop model with all qualifiers removed and relationships expressed as positive or negative

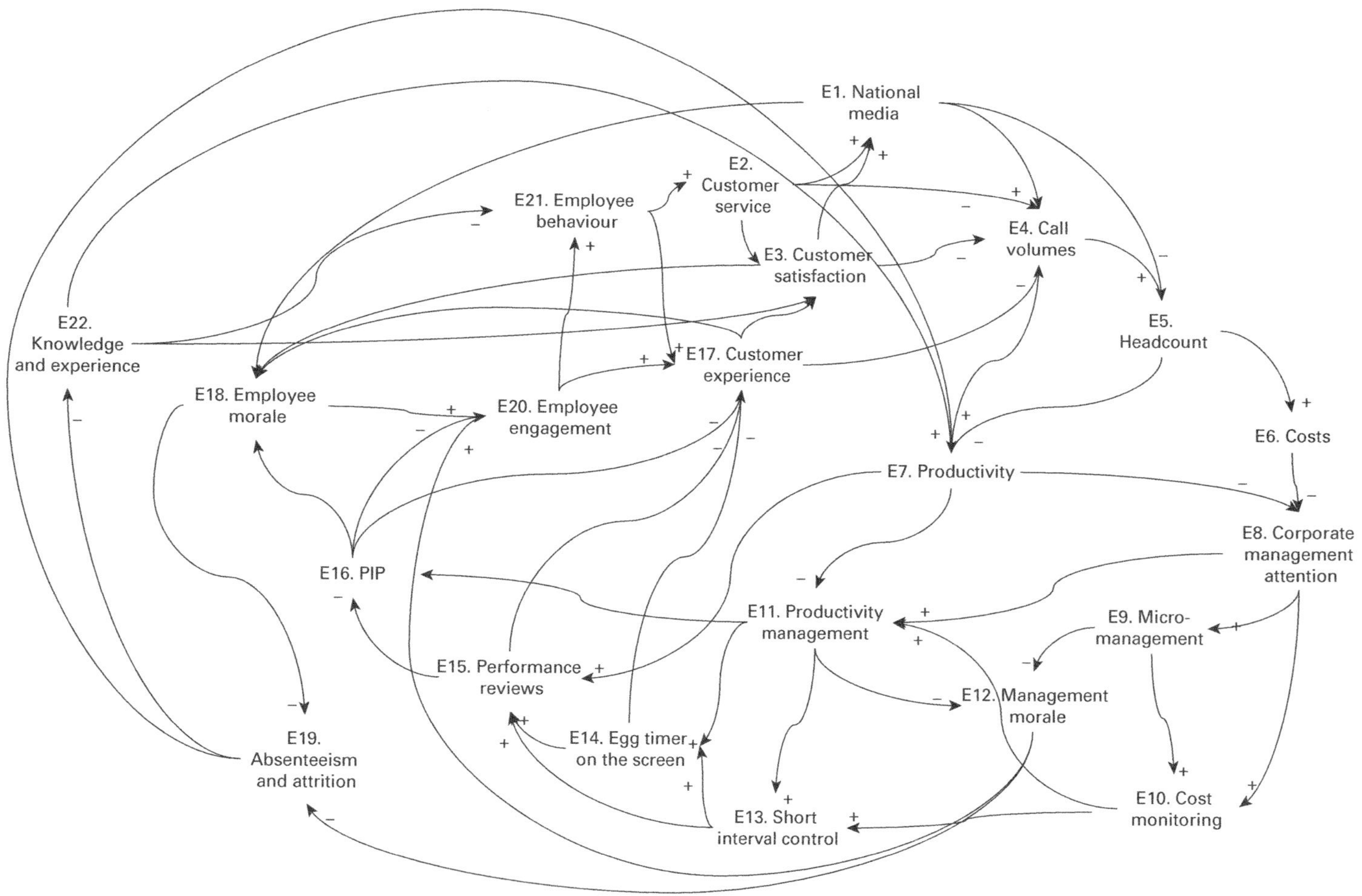

CASE STUDY ... Continuing the systems thinking case study

Analysing, improving and innovating the system

Earlier in this chapter we introduced the concept of the *trim-tab* when we introduced Step 6 of Soft Systems Methodology. In short, trim-tab can be defined as the single small change we can make to the system that would end up changing the behaviour of the whole system. In this section we explain how we can analyse our conceptual model (i.e. the causal loop model in Figure 6.7) to identify the changes we can make to change the behaviour of the system.

Step 5 – we analysed the conceptual model to see what can be changed to improve the current situation and explored different solutions offered by different people (customers, owners, actors) in the system. Table 5.2 illustrates an abridged version of the potential solutions proposed by various people. We have organized them against the root definition and the issues observed in the real world.

Table 6.2 Potential solutions

Root definition	Issues in the real world	What can be done?
To serve the people at home and at work	Unsatisfied, angry customers	• Employ more people • Customer service training for agents • Using process automation • More use of self-service technologies • Resolve customer problem/address enquiry at the first call
... in which customer service agents, supervisors and managers work	Deteriorating morale, poor engagement, dysfunctional behaviour	• Better technology support • Standard scripts • More team-building activities for staff • More social events for staff • Make everyone redundant and hire back the right people • Remove egg timers and 8-minute call target • Introduce self-managing work teams
... resolve service problems and address enquiries	Rarely solved at first call, average no. of calls unknown	• Improve pay to bring in more committed people with customer service experience • Focus on the customer

(*continued*)

Table 6.2 (Continued)

Root definition	Issues in the real world	What can be done?
… efficiently and effectively	Efficiency is managed on a daily basis, what about effectiveness?	• Increase focus on effectiveness • First call resolution
Owned by senior management	Increasing micromanagement	• Put systems in to remove the need for micromanagement • Trust you people and get out of the way • Introduce self-managing work teams

Step 6 – in searching for a feasible solution we went back to the causal loop diagram and looked for:

- **Balancing and reinforcing loops.** However, sometimes these loops are not as simple and obvious. In the causal loop model (Figure 6.7) we can see that the whole model is a reinforcing loop which starts and finishes with increasing call volumes (E4). Simply put:
  - increasing call volumes (E4) lead to increase headcount (E5), increasing costs (E6) and reduced productivity (E7);
  - this in turn leads to increased management attention (E8), micromanagement (E9) and emphasis on productivity management (E11, E13, E14, E15 and E16);
  - these elements all serve to create problems with employee morale (E12 and E18), engagement (E20) and behaviour (E17 and E21);
  - resulting in poorer customer service (E2) and customer satisfaction (E3), which drive call volumes (E4).
- **Busy entities with a lot of inputs and outputs.** If we follow the above logic, we can observe that entities such as call volumes (E4), deteriorating productivity (E7), increasing emphasis on productivity (E11), daily performance reviews (E15), deteriorating employee morale (E18) and customers being deferred (E17) are all busy nodes.
- **Entities with a lot of outputs**. In our example productivity management (E11) has comparatively more outputs and appears to be a key influencer for the entire system.

Based on this analysis together with the following evidence we can conclude that in this system there is an overemphasis on productivity management which creates the reinforcing loop we are seeing here without a balancing loop that reinforces the 'effectiveness' of the system. In this case, it was agreed that the first-call resolution would be introduced as a performance measure to balance the emphasis on productivity that is being driven by the eight-minute call target and the egg timers on the screens of the agents. Although this change resulted in some improvements, it did not solve the problem.

Clearly, having changed the system we have a new system. Theoretically, to analyse the new systems we would need to go through the SSM starting from Step 1. However, in this assignment we did not go through the second full iteration because we could clearly see that although first-call resolution was introduced as a measure, due to the learned behaviours at all levels productivity was being managed more actively. This was reflected in the following quotes by the customer service agents: 'I hate the egg-timer, it distracts me from getting the job done', 'Performance reviews are embarrassing, particularly if I spent ages trying to help a customer', 'The eight-minute target and PIPs force me to do things I do not like... I'd rather work elsewhere'.

From this it was clear that the balancing loop we created to resolve the problem was not strong enough to overcome the existing reinforcing loop. Furthermore, the data revealed that 68 per cent of the calls coming to this customer service centre were failure calls, i.e. because of not being able to deal with a customer's problem/enquiry at their first call. To continue refining the solution, we went back to the root definition and modified it as follows:

> A system owned by the senior management (owners), in which customer service agents, supervisors and managers (actors) work to serve the people at home and at work (reflecting household customers and business customers) to resolve service problems and address enquiries (transformation) on the customers' first call (worldview) within the technical capabilities of our equipment (environmental constraints).

The new root definition changed the worldview of the organization, which previously valued efficiency and productivity over effectiveness, i.e. first-call resolution. As a consequence, all productivity-related measures, such as the eight-minute target, the egg timer on the screen and individual productivity-related KPIs at operational level, were removed and the company operated using a single operational measure: first-call resolution. This resulted in a complete transformation in the way the system behaved. Customer service and satisfaction improved, call volumes dropped significantly, employee morale and satisfaction levels improved and the company no longer featured in the national media for their poor customer service. Furthermore, productivity improved significantly, despite management's concern that removing productivity measures would result in deterioration of productivity. This is because they were resolving more issues at the first call, which resulted in the number of failed calls plummeting.

At the start of this section, we started talking about the 'trim-tab', i.e. the one small change we could make to a system that would change the behaviour of the whole system. In the case study we demonstrated the use of causal loop diagrams for modelling, analysing, improving and innovating systems. We found the trim-tab to be a small change in the performance measures used. We have also observed that the introduction of first-call resolution measures was amongst the potential solutions (Table 6.2) that emerged from the analysis. However, modelling the system, understanding the reinforcing and balancing loops, and experimenting with the system enabled us to find the trim-tab. Even then, what worked was not just the introduction of the first-call resolution measures, it was a combination of this and the removal of the productivity measures.

6.6 Summary

In this chapter our objective was to reinforce the differences between hard and soft systems, introduce you to soft systems thinking and Soft Systems Methodology (SSM), as well as providing you with a working understanding of the approaches to modelling soft systems.

We started the chapter by looking at the differences between hard systems and soft systems in greater depth to reinforce your understanding of soft systems. We then introduced Soft Systems Methodology and the seven-step approach to understanding, modelling and changing soft systems that underpins SSM. We introduced storytelling, roleplaying, rich pictures and causal loop diagrams as techniques that enable us to navigate through the seven steps of the SSM. We illustrated the use of the seven steps and causal loop diagrams to model, analyse and improve a problematic system in a national utilities provider. Throughout the example we also highlighted the importance of finding the one small change we can make to the system that would change the behaviour of the whole system, i.e. the trim-tab.

In the next chapter we will build upon the causal loop diagrams introduced in this chapter. We will focus specifically on the use of causal loop diagrams to enable group decision making in complex systems where decision making is often a messy or wicked problem as there is always someone the decision does not suit.

REFLECTIVE EXERCISE

Think about a system you are interested in and try using all frameworks and models we discussed in this chapter to gain a better understanding of the system by answering the following questions:

1. What is it about the system that would characterize it as a soft system? Are there people involved with different agendas and worldviews? Are the parts of the system autonomous decision makers?
2. Reflect on the earlier exercises from the end of section 6.2, where you used the CATWOE model to develop a root definition for your system. Did other people in the system agree with your root definition? Were there similarities or significant differences? Could you explain these differences?
3. Reflecting on pump manufacturing and education examples provided in Step 4 of Soft Systems Methodology, does your system have clear subsystems, potentially with different root definitions? If so, what are they? Do other people see it the same way?
4. Try drawing a rich picture of your system. This does not need to be anything sophisticated; you can use just pen and paper if you like. Some people find it useful to sit in front of a screen using a drawing tool, as the act of drawing something makes them think about the system and the picture emerges after several iterations. You may wish to try this approach as it makes it easy to move things around, erase, redraw, cut and paste, etc. Once you have finished drawing the rich picture, try narrating your story, i.e. explain the story behind the picture. You will probably find that as you are narrating the story you will want to go back and make some changes to the picture. Once finished, sit back and reflect on the picture and the story. Is this what you intended when you started or is it different from what you imagined at the start?
5. Try converting your rich picture into a causal loop diagram. How easy or difficult did you find to do this? Are there any parts you were not sure about? Did it make you think that you need to go back and find out more information about the system?

TEAM EXERCISE

Rich pictures – Take a system that all participants may be familiar with and ask them to draw a rich picture of the system. If the participants are from the same organization, it is usually easier to ask them to draw a rich picture of their organization. Try not to qualify what the picture should do, such as explain how the organization works or highlight the issues and problems in the organization. Let them work that out for themselves. Usually, giving an example of the sort of thing you are looking for helps. We usually use the example from Figure 6.2. Also, this exercise works best if each of the participants draws their pictures on a flipchart using markers. They will need about 15 minutes to complete this exercise.

Next, ask each participant to show their picture to others and talk through the picture (i.e. the narrative). During this process, note the similarities and differences in the pictures and stories. Are the different perspectives and worldviews of different people coming through? Also watch for participants' reactions to each other's models – often there are surprises and a-ha moments that you can observe from their faces and body language.

Next facilitate a discussion about the differences and similarities and ask each participant what they have learned from the exercise. Often, your observations of participants' faces and body language (from the previous stage) are useful material to facilitate the discussion.

Causal loop diagrams – The above exercise can be continued by asking the group to consolidate their rich pictures into a single causal loop diagram. This exercise takes a bit longer and depending on the complexity and number of people involved you will need to give at least one hour to enable people to complete it. Also, doing this exercise on a large whiteboard with several coloured pens works best. This allows the model to emerge through several iterations (rubbing off bits and redrawing). Using different colours to represent different part of the system, e.g. different people's views from the rich pictures, will also aid further analysis.

To finish the exercise, ask the group what they think of the final model that emerged from this. Does it reflect reality from their perspective? Does it help to explain some of the behaviours? And what have they learned?

References

Checkland, PB (1981) *Systems Thinking, Systems Practice*, Wiley

Checkland, PB and Scholes, J (1990) *Soft Systems in Action*, Wiley

Checkland, PB and Scholes, J (1999) *Soft Systems Methodology in Action: A 30-year retrospective*, Wiley

Kowalski, K (nd) Call me Trim Tab – Buckminster Fuller and the impact of an individual on society, Sloww, www.sloww.co/trim-tab-buckminster-fuller/ (archived at https://perma.cc/W39V-Q9SM)

Further reading

Bell, S and Morse, S (2013) How people use rich pictures to help them think and act, *Systemic Practice and Action Research*, **26**, pp. 331–48

7 Systems thinking in group decision making

In previous chapters we gradually built understanding of complexity and complex systems, and what makes improving them so difficult. When making decisions about how to improve a system, involving multiple participants/stakeholders is essential, but at the same time can add additional levels of complexity. In Chapter 6 we introduced methods used for analysing soft systems, specifically causal loop diagrams. In this chapter we will focus on using causal mapping as a more specific technique that stems from causal loop diagrams.

In modern organizations there are a number of trends. First, we need to be inclusive and ensure that everyone is involved in significant decisions. Second, the world we live in is becoming increasingly dynamic and uncertain, thus we need to be able to make decisions fast in response to changes and ensure that everyone is involved in these decisions. Systems thinking provides us with a set of tools that enables group decision making. In this chapter we will demonstrate its use for strategy making/formulation as an example to show how systems thinking enables group decision making. We will start with discussing strategy making in the complex world and open strategizing as a bottom-up approach in comparison with more traditional top-down approaches to strategy making. We will then introduce causal mapping and its use in problem structuring before guiding you through the process of creating and analysing causal maps and compiling an open strategy based on a causal map. The penultimate section will provide practical advice on designing a causal mapping workshop to maximize the benefits of this approach.

LEARNING OUTCOMES

- Understand
  - the benefits of causal mapping for strategy making in the complex world
  - the benefits of causal mapping for making and negotiating decisions in groups
- Learn to use action-oriented causal mapping to aid strategic decision making
  - build the maps
  - validate the maps
  - focus on a specific type of problem
  - analyse the maps
  - develop a decision plan
- Learn how to organize a causal mapping group workshop

7.1 Strategy and complexity in the modern world

Up to this point we have looked at various tools and methods that can be used to understand systems, system complexity and model them from a particular point of view. However, we all might have different views on a particular problem or issue. Does it mean that one view is better or more correct than the other? And how do we choose which one? And if not, how do we capture different views and combine them in a systematic manner?

In this chapter we are going to look at a specific type of causal mapping – action-oriented causal mapping – which is widely used to aid strategic decision making (Ackermann and Eden, 2011a; Bryson et al, 2004) This method allows us to capture aspects of an individual's thinking about a problem or question. If used in a group, it provides an environment for capturing participants' diverse views on the problem, negotiating the meanings and reflecting their changing minds.

We can use problem structuring, in particular the causal mapping approach, for strategy making that entails a high degree of ownership and practicality. These two conditions are quite important and not always obvious in strategic management and other areas of business.

We are living in a complex and changing world. Amy Edmondson, a professor from Harvard Business School, talks about the VUCA world, a world that is volatile, uncertain, complex and ambiguous, and the need to have approaches for dealing with it (Edmondson, 2018) In the past decades we have lived through several major crises and are currently facing one of the major challenges humanity has ever had to deal with, i.e. climate change. In such complex and dynamic environments, organizations have to adapt to change that does not just happen from time to time, but rather continuously. In most cases organizations cannot influence the crisis or challenge, rather it exists within their external environment. Instead, organizations try to manage risks to mitigate the ramifications of the crisis or adapt to the new environment. To do that, organizations need to understand what they are good at, so that they can create bundles of activities or capabilities, which will enable them to adapt to the changing environment (Eden and Ackermann, 2010)

If we look at the seminal works of strategy thinkers such as Igor Ansoff, then Michael Porter and Henry Mintzberg, we can trace the evolution of the ideas about what strategy should be. Initially it resembled more a financial plan for the next 5 to 10 years that was designed by a small group of strategists, often with the help of external experts. It had then to be enacted by the company as a plan to follow. However, such a traditional top-down view of strategy is very much contested today, because these great plans often do not work in practice because of the VUCA world we live in.

Instead, a new view of strategy emerged that is quite often referred to as **open strategy** (Whittington et al, 2011). It advocates for building on the experience, capabilities, wisdom and hunches of managers at different levels in the organization. Through the process of capturing their thinking about what the strategy of the organization should be, what the values are, what capabilities the organization has and what the organization is bad at, they also develop a sense of ownership of the strategy. In a way these first steps resemble a classic SWOT (strengths, weaknesses, opportunities and threats) analysis, which is often used in the preliminary steps of decision making to evaluate the position of a system. It helps to focus attention equally on strengths and weaknesses, which will then allow the organization to find strategic fit. Following this approach, the strategy is no longer pre-defined, but rather it becomes emergent and adaptable to the changing environment.

To support this process, the organization needs to have good methods for making strategy and support their decision making. It is people who make decisions and this process is highly unpredictable. Causal maps, which you

Figure 7.1 Causal mapping workshop

will find look very similar to causal loop diagrams, can help manage this uncertainty. They become a transition object that is amended as the conversation between strategy makers and facilitators unfolds. They support negotiations about the priorities, building consensus between all the parties involved, addressing trade-offs and tensions, and ultimately building a sense of ownership of the strategy (Figure 7.1) All these social processes are as important as building the map itself (Ackermann and Eden, 2011b)

Why is the sense of ownership important? Traditional top-down planned strategies that are then shared across the organization might be difficult to implement. When the strategy is shared across the organization, some might interpret it and take it in different directions, creating disjoint and incoherent efforts to implement it, resulting in strategic drift. Others might read the strategy and even use it to build a case for a new project proposal, but ultimately, the strategy remains on the shelf gathering dust. This happens because those responsible for implementing the strategy have not been involved in the conversation. If instead strategy making becomes a social process involving discussion, negotiation and building consensus over what is feasible, what can be done, what should be the priority, what the constraints are, then managers at different levels, who can make the strategy happen, develop a collective sense of ownership for the strategy. It incorporates their world-views and unifies their efforts in the agreed direction, and therefore they will commit to it and enact it.

7.2 Causal mapping for problem structuring

Causal maps are a variation of causal loop diagrams covered in the previous chapter. Action-oriented causal mapping method is based on the strategic options development and analysis (SODA) approach for capturing individual views of an issue, using interviews and cognitive mapping. SODA provides a framework for problem solving that highlights the need to capture multiple views on a complex issue. It is informed by George Kelly's Personal Construct Theory (Kelly, 1955), which highlights that an individual's construct of the world influences the way they interpret their observations and the way they make sense of experiences.

Causal mapping can help to better understand aspects of an individual's thinking about a problem or question. In essence it captures the perceptual reality by gathering participants' judgments, wisdom, understanding and sensing of the situation. The map is built by paying attention to the expressed causality ('because', 'in order to', 'and so', etc.) of a situation. The links between the statements help the group to have that discussion about the consequences of particular issues or options as well as the resources and capabilities required to support each option.

The use of causal mapping emphasizes idiosyncrasy: each viewpoint represents an individual's own understanding of the world around them. It also helps to draw on various voices to avoid one person dominating the conversation, which can happen in a more traditional setting. It is important to recognize that the map represents important aspects of the conversation and helps us to have a more robust, more interesting discussion, as well as support contributions from multiple stakeholders incorporating different world views. However, it is not assumed to be a perfect representation of reality, rather it is a model in its own right.

An advantage of causal mapping is that it allows you to capture the complexity and richness of empirical material without reducing it. The map will

Figure 7.2 Example of a causal map of a project focused on improving livelihood of smallholder farmers in Brazil

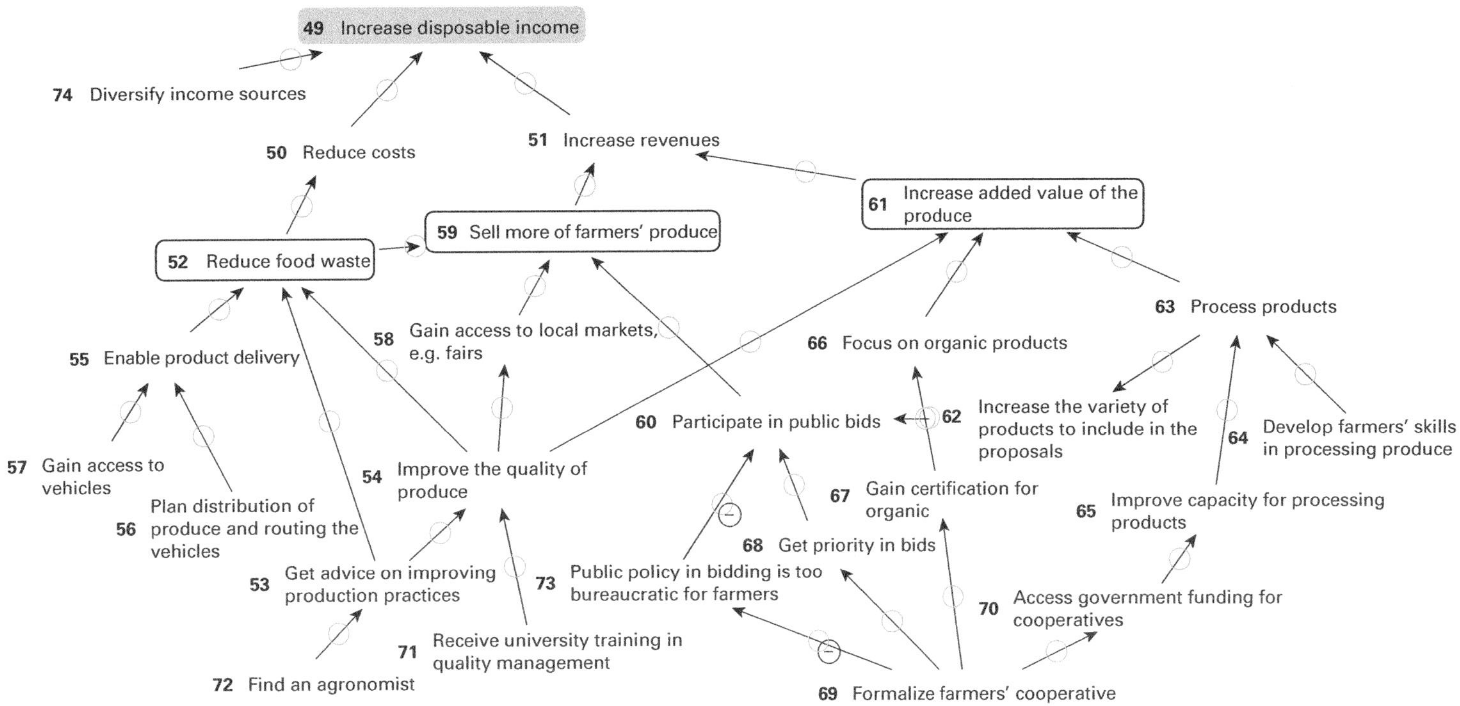

enable you to zoom in on one of the identified problems or opportunities, a knock-on effect the problem might cause, as well as a potential cascade of subsequent triggered knock-on effects, which become visible through the causal links. You may then ask what kind of mitigating actions and strategies, or what kind of decisions, the organization has to make to address and mitigate the knock-on effect. Within this space, you start exploring and prioritizing alternative options. Subsequently, you can zoom out to see a bigger picture and then choose another problem as the focal point on the map. That is why it is useful to think about the complex world using methods like this for problem structuring, because they can help you make a better sense of the reality.

This is particularly important when looking at organizational systems and addressing organizational issues. They never exist in isolation and are impacted by as well as impact other systems, such as other organizations, stakeholders, etc. They can often be improved or addressed in multiple ways. Causal mapping can help explore the interconnections and possibilities in a structured way.

Below is an example of a causal map that was developed during a workshop that discussed how to improve the livelihoods (i.e. disposable income) of smallholder farmers in Brazil.

Usually, the statements that emerge in the middle will indicate strategic issues and dilemmas such as 52 'Reduce food waste', 59 'Sell more of farmers' produce' and 61 'Increase added value of the produce', which are critical to solve. Part of the process of analysing the map described in the subsequent sections is to understand the critical issues (illustrated with a solid border on this map). It is by solving the critical issues that we can achieve the goal (with solid background), which will usually be located at the top of the map, whilst the bottom the map will usually contain more detailed actions, i.e. ways the issues can be resolved. This layout of the map is usually achieved by directing the links upwards towards the top of the map.

7.3 Constructing causal maps

Causal maps are constructed through group meetings or by merging cognitive maps obtained individually. In both approaches the facilitator follows the same steps outlined below. If individual cognitive maps are built, then the facilitator must join them together into one causal map before analysing the final map. In this case the facilitator would have to scrutinize the language and meaning of different statements, e.g. to ensure that there is no redundancy in the map (the same idea expressed in different words), or conflicting ideas with similar wording and the same meaning. In the following we have detailed a three-step process for constructing cognitive maps.

Step 1: Gathering data

The mapping process usually starts with one open-ended question, such as: What are the main distinctive competences, core capabilities or dynamic capabilities of our organization that we should be protecting rather than outsourcing? What should be the corporate strategy in the next five years? How should we divest the corporate portfolio? What should be our mergers and acquisition options in the next few years? What are the most critical strategic issues our organization is facing today? The question should be fairly simple at this stage.

Then the participants are invited to write statements in response to this question. The statements can be written on sticky notes or gathered using specialized software. If you are looking for a software designed specifically for this method, Strategy Finder (https://www.strategyfinder.com/) is a cloud-based option that can support group work. Decision Explorer (https://banxia.com/dexplore/) is a desktop-based alternative, which can be used by a facilitator during the workshop, but does not support group work. Kumu (https://kumu.io/) is a generic alternative that can support causal mapping through systems or causal loop diagram templates. It also has a free account option. It is useful to number all the statements to make it easier to navigate the map; specialized software can do this automatically. The list below provides guidelines for what a good statement should look like.

DO:

- use short statements (6–8 words)
- look for actions (imperative verbs), e.g. 'find more funding' instead of 'need to find more funding'
- retain ownership (use the participant's original language)
- break down long statements
- look for contrasts in meaning (opposite poles)
- watch out for possible key issues and general outcomes that are good in their own right

DO NOT:

- aggregate the statements
- use generic statements, e.g. 'management communication'
- make judgements about, or omit, things that you believe to be less relevant – they may turn out to be important once the map has been produced

Both positive and negative statements are welcomed during the data-gathering step. For instance, hiring new staff leads to having to spend more money, but it may also mean having better staff, which may result in having better capabilities.

The role of the facilitator at this stage is to check the statements for clarity and ask for clarifications or rephrasing. The most important condition here is to try and make as many statements actionable as possible, because then the causality can be captured much more easily. For example, you might want to formulate the statement as 'improve food quality' instead of 'high food quality'. During this step the facilitator also starts clustering the statements to look for emergent themes, without linking them just yet.

Step 2: Linking the statements

When the initial data gathering has been completed, the group usually starts with one cluster or theme that unites a group of statements, which is considered the most important, linking statements together in causal relationships. Deciding on the most important cluster can be done through voting or group discussion. Alternatively, if none of the clusters stand out, the facilitator can pick any to get the process started. Then the group moves to the next cluster, linking the statements within this cluster as well as looking for links with the first cluster. Sometimes halfway through it becomes evident that a new cluster needs to be added to the scope because the two are strongly interconnected.

Adding an arrow between two statements indicates at least a partial influence of the statement initiating the arrow on the statement receiving the arrow.

STATEMENT → influence → STATEMENT

Figure 7.3 Flow of the causal map

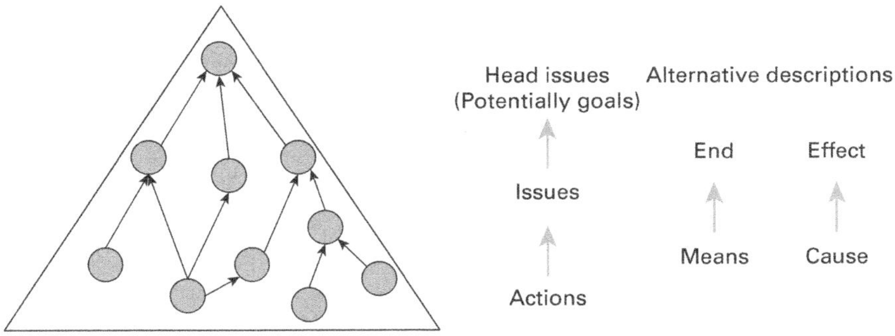

In combination, the links and statements create an issue system, which can be arranged hierarchically from potential causes through to ultimate effects.

The image shows a hierarchical schematic of connected statements, flowing into the top statements. Actions are connected to issues, which are connected to head issues (possibly goals) These may also be described as means to end or cause to effect relationships (Figure 7.3)

When looking for connections, it is useful to use two questions:

1 The statements coming out of the issues (in the middle) answer the question 'why?'.
2 The statements coming into the issues answer the question 'how?'.

Figure 7.4 shows an example of five statements reflecting on the issues that a university wants to address. The statements have been added and numbered in order of capture and then labelled with connecting arrows to indicate influence. For instance, the university wants to 1) 'attract more students from overseas'. Why do they want to do that? Because this will 2) 'increase university income'. How can this be achieved? One option would be to 3) 'improve university ranking position'; another option would be to 4) 'improve branding of the university'. Improved ranking will also have another positive consequence – 5) 'receive higher proportion of the government research funding', which will in turn contribute to the increased university income. Apart from linking the statements, this example also demonstrates how different options emerge and can potentially be prioritized.

Figure 7.4 An example of a simple causal map

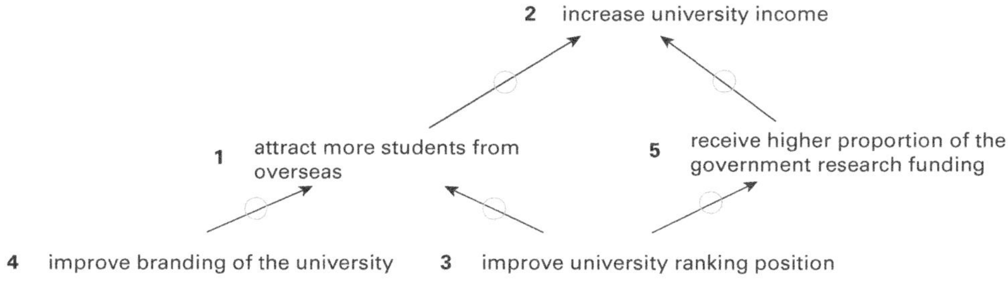

During the process the group is not limited only to the statements that have been brainstormed during Step 1. The mapping process might reveal gaps in thinking, unintended consequences or new opportunities (as in the example above), and the need to add new statements to fill in these gaps.

Step 3: Tidying up the map

Before and during the analysis you might need to tidy up and merge maps. Specifically, when tidying the map, you need to check that the correct wording is used, e.g. using overly generic wording may require clarification. You might want to check that there are no redundant summary links on the map. For example, on the map below the link between 8 'Transition to Net Zero by 2050' and 15 'Influence companies' behaviour to implement sustainability strategies with Net Zero targets' is redundant because the two statements are already connected through statements 13 and 14.

You would need to check the heads (those statements that do not have outgoing links) and ensure that they are indeed the high-level goals. You do not want to have goals that are not good in their own right. For example, on the map in Figure 7.6, statement '16 Address challenges of last-mile delivery: transparency, cost, unpredictability' does not look like an ultimate goal of a logistics consultancy, unless it is a very specific research project. Even then, this statement looks more like an issue that needs to be addressed in order to achieve a more strategic goal. And therefore it needs to be linked to one of the existing statements or prompt a new statement in response to a question 'Why this issue needs addressing'. Similarly, statement 21 'Younger consumers have an intrinsic motivation to become part of the sustainability solution and are willing to change their behaviour' looks more like an external factor

Figure 7.5 Example of redundant links

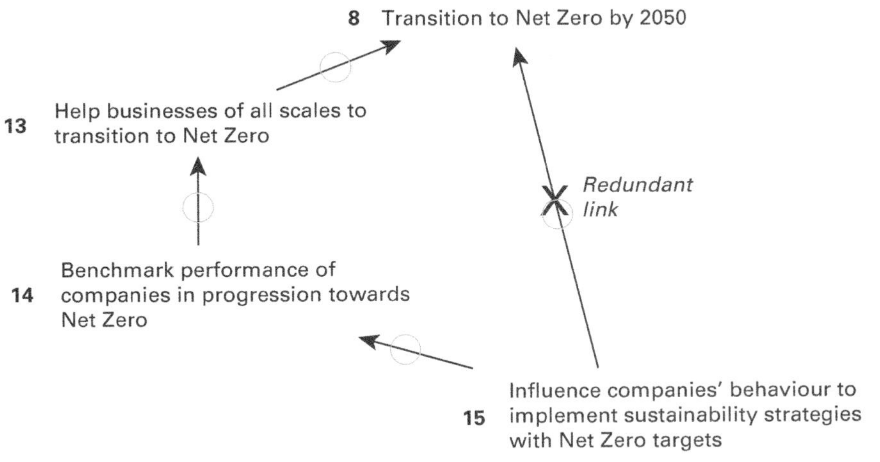

that impacts the studied system rather than a system goal. In this case, the statement might require a discussion about the validity of the direction of the link connecting statements 21 and 19. Both cases can be brought to the group as points of discussion during the tidying-up step before the analysis.

When looking at a recollection of events illustrating an underlying problem, it might be tempting to describe them through causal links in chronological order. However, it is important to try to capture causality rather than chronology or a timeline. This means looking for underlying problems and causes that are a generalization of the illustrative example.

If you identified feedback loops, you might want to scrutinize them to ensure that they are valid because, due to the action-oriented nature of causal maps, feedback loops are much less frequent than in causal loop diagrams. For example, you might discover that the direction of some arrows in this loop needs to be changed, as in Figure 7.6.

Then you need to examine if any statements duplicate each other and therefore need to be merged. However, it's important to pay attention to the context and perhaps, instead, the wording of the statement needs to be revised. For example, on the map in Figure 7.7 statements 6 and 10 are formulated using the same wording – 'passenger transport sharing'. However, statement 6 is used in the context of combining passenger and freight transport, while statement 10 refers to reducing the number of private vehicles on the road through sharing. The two statements have a very different meaning, and would need to be clarified to avoid confusion.

Figure 7.6 An example of questionable heads in a map

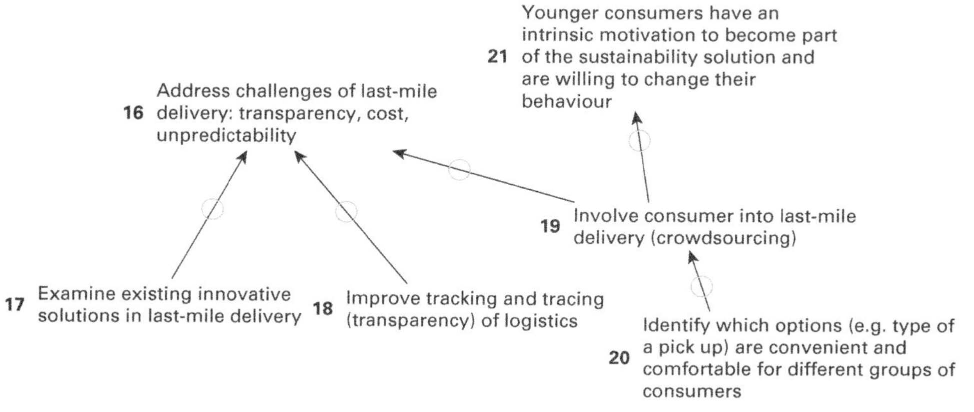

Figure 7.7 An example of similar wording with different meaning

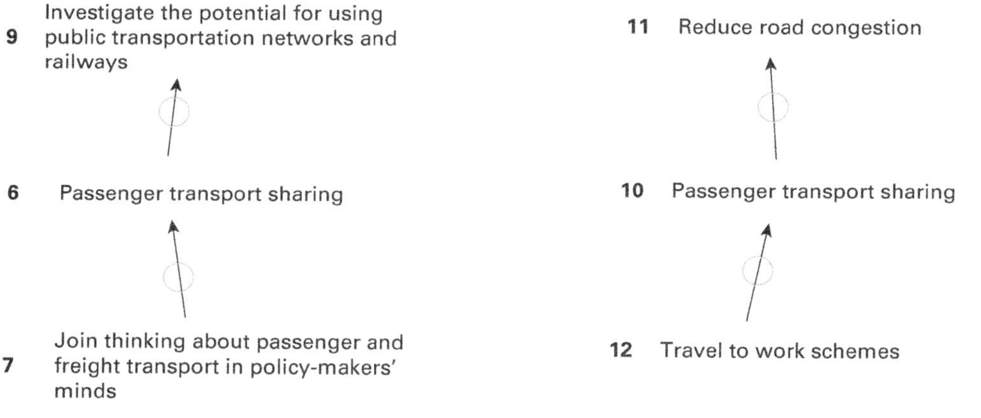

The resulting map normally resembles a tear-drop structure in shape. Once the map has been created, it needs to be validated with the group participants to ensure it is an accurate representation of the situation. For instance, you might want to check the direction of arrows and interpretation of causality between the statements with the participants. Below is a quick checklist of what to look for when tidying up the map:

- correct wording
- check the direction of arrows
- remove unnecessary summary links

- tying up heads
- check the validity of feedback loops
- emphasize causality, not chronology
- merging statements: similar wording can be an indicator for merging; however, it is important to pay attention to the context (ins and outs)

Now try constructing a causal map using the following case study.

CASE STUDY A systems thinking case study

The following is a story detailing the Landless Workers' Movement (*Movimento dos Trabalhadores Rurais Sem Terra* – MST) in Brazil and the formation of a Canudos settlement, one of the several settlements that resulted from this movement. Using this story as a basis for analysis, develop a strategic problem structuring map to identify the problems of this complex situation. Capture the viewpoints of the different participants involved.

A Canudos settlement of small farmers in Brazil was established when 12,757 hectares of land that belonged to the former president, Colemas Rezende, and his family was occupied. This first occupation occurred on 6 October 1997. 127 families stayed in this location for nine days under pressure from other farmers, the police and local politicians.

The solidarity Movement of Landless Rural Workers started a conflict with the local landlords to expropriate a part of their land. This provoked marches for peace, social justice and agrarian reform.

After four consecutive occupations and conflicts with armed forces, 48 per cent of the Legal Reservation and Permanent Preservation Area was given to the families.

In the following years, the government struggled to attract younger people from the already pressured cities. How could they make rural life more appealing? Perhaps they could improve living conditions by giving small farmers special credits, family scholarships and retirement income.

Maize was easy to grow but wasn't profitable for the farmers. In 2006, the Brazilian government signed a new law to support local farmers. This law included the stipulation that 30 per cent of school food must be sourced from local suppliers. This meant farmers could sell fruit and vegetables at higher prices and improve their living conditions.

However, the farmers had to meet certain requirements to be able to bid for contracts. For example, how would these farmers control the quality of their products? Or how would they organize their supply chain? The University of São Paulo offered help by educating the farmers on how to monitor produce and meet HACCP (Hazard analysis and critical control points) standards. This helped slightly, but more work and infrastructure was needed.

To begin with, try to draft your initial ideas on a piece of paper. It will not be perfect on your first attempt but you will refine it through iterations. Draft the statements, group them in themes and then begin to arrange the statements hierarchically to establish an issue system (potential causes through to ultimate effects)

To be continued...

7.4 Analysing causal maps

Once your basic map has been established, the next stage of the process is to analyse the map and explore the issues further. When you start analysing the map, as a first step to aid the analysis, you might want to consider visual support to help focus and reduce the map to manageable size, as well as conduct visual analysis of the map. Depending on the software you are using, you might be able to copy parts of the map to separate views to focus on a certain issue or category of issues. Then usually any changes you make in the separate view will be transferred back to the common map. You might also want to use styles to distinguish visually between different categories of statements, particularly when the resulting map has more than 100 statements. For example, if we are looking at the issue of integrating smallholder farmers into higher-value supply chains, then we might want to categorize different barriers into themes like cultural barriers, structural barriers, technology barriers, etc. At the early stages of a project, it might be also useful to separate styles into high-level objectives, identified problems and opportunities linking to these objectives and potential solutions addressing these problems and opportunities. The categories you created for styles will form your sets. If you bring them to a separate view, you will be able to zoom into the map and see what this part of the map tells you.

Then, you need to explore busy statements on the map, those statements that have a lot of incoming and outgoing links. In all that complexity, the busy areas are probably your strategic issues. However, you might find out that they are too generic and need breaking down into more nuanced statements. You can use centrality analysis. This analysis can also be referred to as central analysis, but we believe that the term *centrality* captures better the essence of the analysis. This analysis is used to aid you with identifying important statements to focus on using weighted sums of the first-, second- and third-degree connections. Those are likely to be the statements that have the most significant impact on the system. Most of them will be visible visually as busy statements, but you might also find a few surprising ones that do not look connected to many statements directly, but generate high impact through a lot of second- and third-degree connections.

However, the degree of proximity might also need to be taken into account. When central scores are calculated to identify the most central concepts, usually the highest weight is given to the first-degree links, then the weight is reduced for the second- and third-degree links. For example, in Figure 7.8, if you just count the links, concept B has 11 links while concept A has only 10. However, if you take a weighted sum, the central score of concept A will be high – 8 vs 6.6 for concept B. This is because concept A has more first-degree connections than concept B. What it means for decision makers is that issue A might be of a higher priority to focus on.

Some software packages allow for conducting centrality analysis that calculates a weighted sum of first-, second- and third-degree connections.

The next step in the analysis is to check the map for feedback loops. Feedback loops have already been discussed several times in the previous sections. In causal mapping feedback loops work the same way as in causal loop diagrams. Below is a summary of the two types of loops used in systems thinking:

- *Balancing feedback loops*, which can also be referred to as **self-correcting cycles** in causal mapping literature. They stabilize or balance the system. They lean towards an 'equilibrium' of a single value; however, sometimes such loops can create a state of alternating between two values.

Figure 7.8 Central scores and the use of weightings

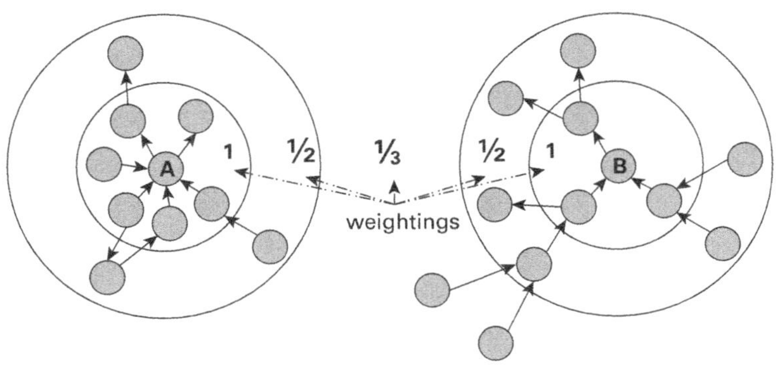

- *Reinforcing feedback loops*, which can also be referred to as **escalating cycles** in causal mapping literature. They can drive the value to infinity by reinforcing the feedback in the system. They are self-sustaining. If they contain issues, these loops can be vicious cycles. If they benefit the system and have a positive impact captured in them, they can be virtuous cycles.

As mentioned in the previous section, in action-oriented causal mapping feedback loops are less frequent because of how statements are formulated – focused on action and direction of action from cause to effect. Therefore, there is no reason to panic if there are no loops on the map. If the map contains loops, these are very important for the system to focus on. When a priority issue or goal is part of the feedback loop, the loop could represent a complex matter of high significance to the organization.

The next aspect to focus on is to look at the heads and tails of the map. The **heads** should have already been highlighted during the tidying-up step. During this phase, the remaining heads that do not look like the main objectives of the system, need '**laddering up**' on the map, i.e. responding to the question 'why' until the group reaches the higher-level objectives. **Tails**, or those statements that do not have incoming links, should be the actions that will form the action plan. If they look too generic or high level and lack detail to be included into the action plan, then you need to continue exploring and detailing the solutions to the problem by 'laddering down' on the map, or answering the question of 'how' the statement can be achieved/resolved.

As you continue exploring the map, you will focus on the relationship between different statements. During the exploration you might discover that some connections are too generic to the level of being pointless. The example in Figure 7.9 shows a very generic relationship between transitioning to Net Zero by 2050 and developing policies for limiting unsustainable consumer behaviour. This scenario calls for an unpacking of this relationship.

In what context should policies limit unsustainable consumer behaviour? If we look at it in the context of logistics, it would limit consumer-responsive modes of delivering things, whereby a company delivers orders whenever consumers want them, rather than engaging consumers in a more optimal (e.g. carbon neutral) solution. This in turn can be viewed as part of developing

Figure 7.9 An example of a too-generic relationship

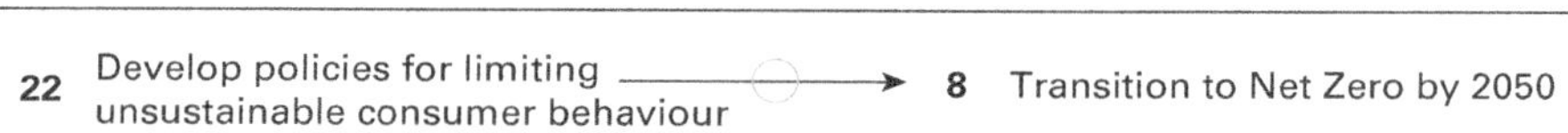

Figure 7.10 Unpacking the generic relationship

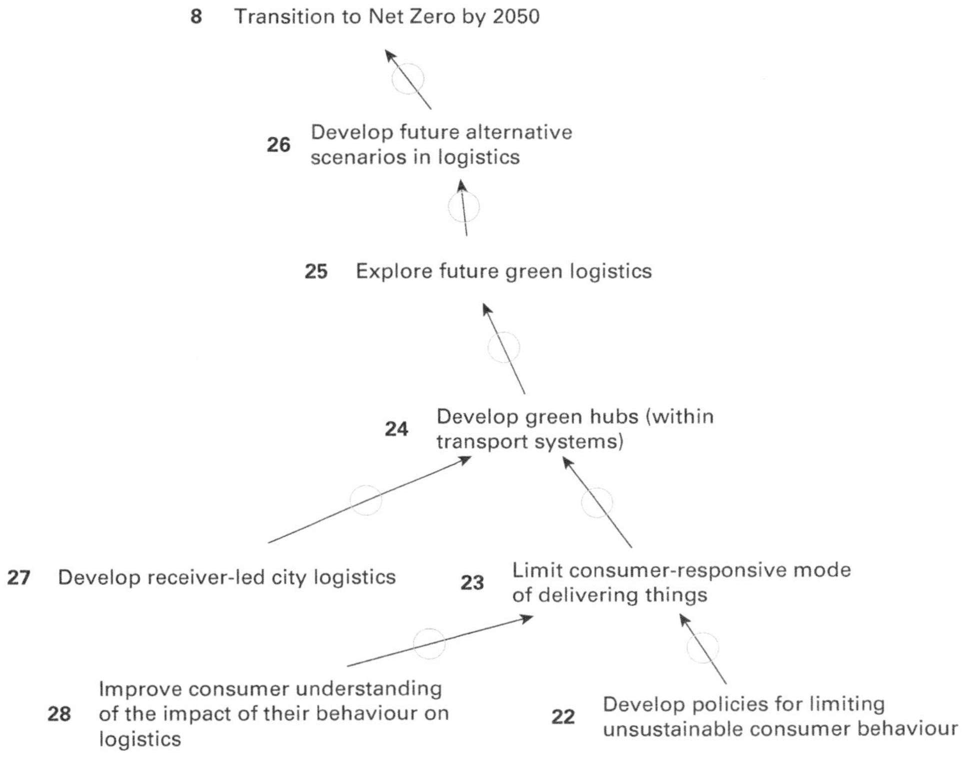

green hubs within transport systems, which might be one of the future approaches to green logistics. Green logistics is in turn viewed as one of the alternative scenarios in logistics of the future that is meant to transition to Net Zero. We can continue exploring this cluster further. For instance, something else that might limit a consumer-responsive mode of delivering things is improving consumer understanding of the impact of their behaviour on logistics. Developing green hubs might also require more than one approach, such as developing receiver-led city logistics (Figure 7.10)

Below is a quick checklist of what to look for when analysing the map.

- Focusing on the selected aspects of the map
  - Views – you can display parts of the map on different views to make it easier to focus on specific areas
  - Using styles – you can use different styles for different clusters or themes to aid visual analysis

  - Sets – you can split the map into different sets by theme or cluster to make it easier to manipulate the map during the analysis
  - Lists – you can look at different lists, e.g. heads, tails or most central concepts to aid the analysis and validation of the map.
- Elaborating relationships
- Exploring interesting options and issues
  - Reinforcing loops
  - Domain/central (watch out for catch-all phrases)
  - Heads (end goals) and tails (actions to achieve the goals)
  - Cluster and busy statements

7.5 Agreeing priorities

Using your (facilitator) judgement and group discussion, supported by analysis, you can identify a set of priority initiatives. You can then review these priority initiatives and grade them according to their relative priority (i.e. which of these priorities matters most)

You can consider factors such as:

- the relative urgency
- feasibility
- potential impact (or indeed any other criteria of importance to the organization as we decide on the relative priority of ideas within the priority set)

Setting up a vote to help decide relative priority can be a useful mechanism. For example, when working with a management team. Each participant can be given three to five votes/points which they can allocate to the statements that they think the organization should concentrate on. They can distribute the votes whichever way they want, e.g. allocate all of them to one concept or distribute them between several different ones. Normally participants are not constrained by the type of statements they can vote for, meaning that they can vote for any statement. However, if you want to steer them towards a more specific type by guiding them on what to focus on, you can suggest what the participants should be looking for when distributing the votes. For example, if they are asked to vote for the most important problems, they will naturally select statements that are positioned closer to the top on the map.

Once the relative priority has been decided, an indicator can be added in the text of the priority ideas, on the map, to capture the decision. You can use *** for top priorities, and then ** and * for other priorities, according to the sense of their relative importance, or you can use different styles to indicate the degree of importance. The identified priorities can be used to zoom in on the chosen areas and continue a more in-depth analysis of the parts of the map.

Do you agree with those actions? Do you think it's an important strategic issue? And once we have all the records, we can ask the group to vote. Do you think these are our long-term strategic issues? What might help to decide on the priorities is linking them to the budget/financial and non-financial resources. For example, you can give the group 100 credits and ask them to distribute them across five main priorities. At this point the group usually shifts the focus to the making of the resulting strategy. While doing this, it is important to keep in mind that consensus is more important than compromise.

CASE STUDY ... Continuing the systems thinking case study

Let us go back to the Canudos example. The map in Figure 7.11 is our interpretation of the story. When you build your map, it will most likely look different, which is fine – it does not make it better or worse. You need to remember that we are capturing a soft system and we are prone to our own biases that shape our viewpoints, so each map is likely to be different.

We can look at the busy statements (with solid border lines), statement 29 'Improve farmers' living conditions', which is the main focus of the story, and statement 40 'Sell higher-value products to local schools', as the key solutions to this objective.

We can also notice a feedback loop (with dotted border lines), a balancing loop for the government that they would want to reduce. In this story, people marched in support of the landless rural workers' movement for peace, justice and agrarian reform. In response, the government agreed to give 48 per cent of the claimed land to the families. They did it to keep their voters happy, so they would then be less likely to continue marching. And this decision in turn reduced the amount of people marching on the streets, as they saw the desired outcome of their protests.

Then we can look at the heads in the map. One might think that improving farmers' living conditions would be the ultimate goal in this system; however, for the government it is only a means to achieving another goal – stopping outmigration and reducing pressure on urban areas. The decision to give land to farmers also supports

Figure 7.11 A causal map of the Canudos story

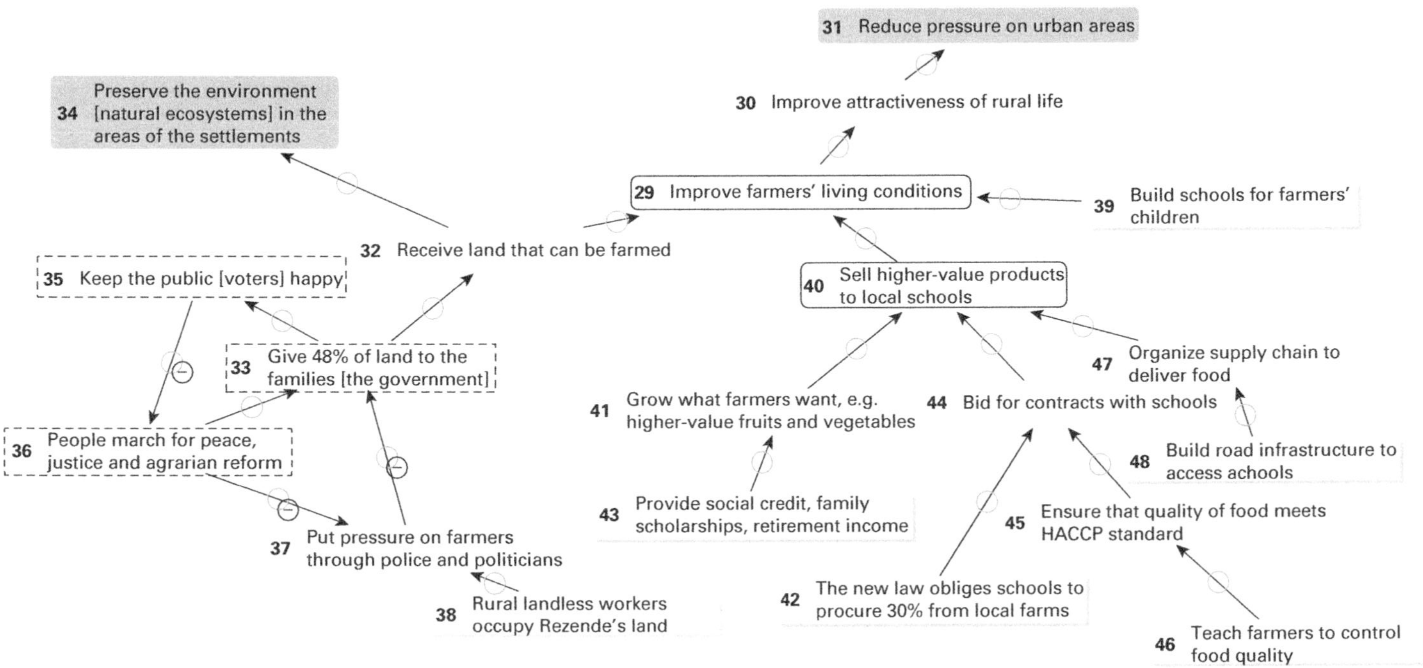

another higher-level goal (the statements with solid background) – 34 Preserve the environment in the areas of the settlements.

Finally, we can look at the tails (with shaded borders) all of which are the actions that need to be performed or have been performed to achieve different objectives in the systems.

Making an open strategy

Making strategy involves balancing the need to be thoughtful and intelligent about the future direction while at the same time accounting for the social and political pressures in the successful implementation of agreements. If the group discussion does not reach the space where consensus needs to be reached, it might mean that the discussion has not touched on the trade-offs. When trade-offs are brought up, participants become more involved and start talking about the alternatives, limited resources, prioritization. Mapping the complexity is only the start of the strategy-making journey. Deciding which option to take is where the real struggle with the strategy conversation is happening.

Initially the group focuses on using instinct, experience and wisdom to work with all the strategic issues and opportunities identified in the previous steps. This approach to strategy resembles negotiations (Ackermann and Eden, 2011b), because in the discussions of the priorities usually the politics come in, and they are unavoidable. The question of how we spend limited resources inevitably leads to the decisions about which team will receive more funding, for example, because that team is needed for supporting our core strategies.

As was mentioned previously, it is important to reach consensus rather than compromise. In the process of reaching consensus it is useful to think about the following questions: What if we choose option A for our strategic priority rather than option B? What will be the consequences? And what capabilities do we need to have in place to support option A and option B? And if we want to go for both option A and option B at the same time, do we have enough capabilities and resources to support both of them? And if not, which option do we choose? And this way compromise would mean choosing option A over B, and consensus building might require creating a new option C from options A and B. In other words, we might need to try to find an option where available different options have some representation in the strategy.

Negotiations that lead to consensus rather than compromise require a number of important features:

- Start from 'where each participant is at' – their immediate and personal/role concerns: issues.
- Seek to develop new options rather than fight over 'old' options: conciliation.
- Attend to 'procedural justice' (fair procedures, being listened to) – it is not about democracy but about good management.
- Use a 'transitional object' – a picture/model that is equivocal (fuzzy but meaningful) and changing, and that encourages shifting of positions. In our case the causal map can be such an object.

Following these principles throughout the process will help to ensure that the developed strategy is accepted by all the participants and can then be successfully implemented. The outcome of the identified consensus will be captured in the Statement of Strategic Intent (SSI), a report that is usually written after a strategy-making workshop. Developing the SSI usually involves creating focus, which can then be followed by strategic issues within that focus, which are then followed by actions that help to address these issues captured in the SSI. Below we will describe different types of focus that you might want to choose when deciding on the type of problem you want to address with causal mapping. We will then go into more detail of one type of focus – competitive advantage – which can be explored through assets, competences and competence outcomes. We will guide you through the analysis, which can then be used as a basis for formulating SSI.

Creating focus

The prospective strategy can differ in its focus, and it is recommended that the group tries to focus its attention on one of the following types. In particular, the focus might be on issue, purpose or competitive advantage.

- **Issue focus:** The group might be interested in the issues an organization is currently facing. In this case the strategy-making process will focus on various issues and their prioritization in order to explore potential solutions to the issues that are recognized by the group as the most important.

Figure 7.12 SSI focus types

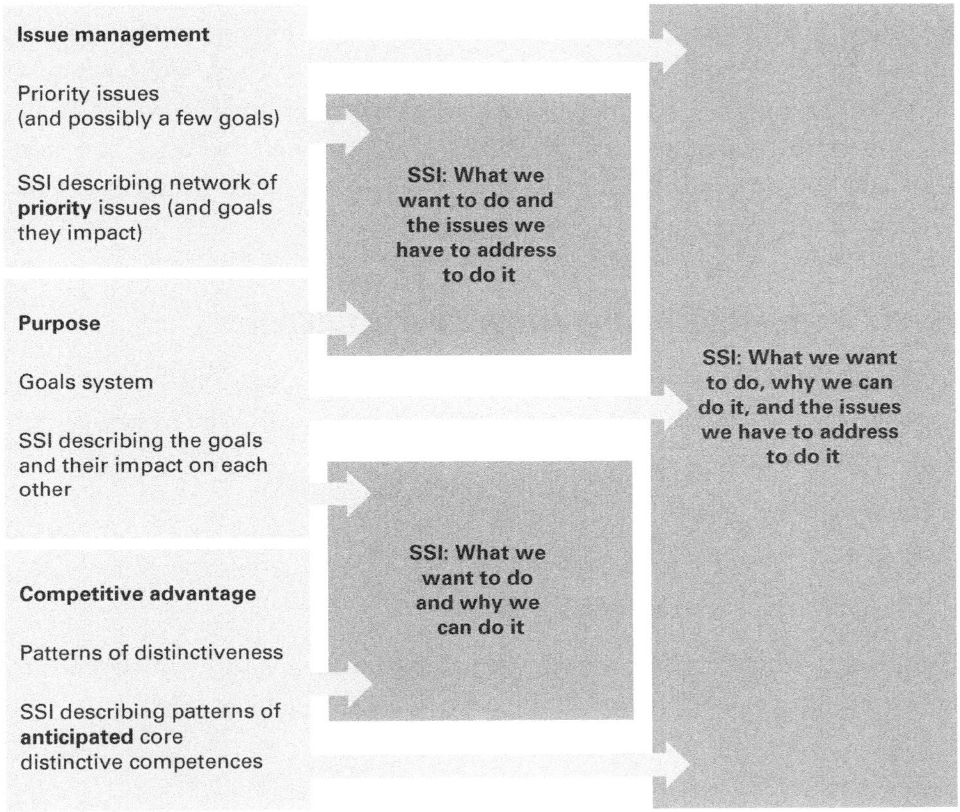

- **Purpose focus:** The group might be interested in organizational purpose. In this case the focus will be on the system of organizational goals and their interrelations.
- **Competitive advantage/differentiation focus:** The group might want to explore what makes their organization competitive. In this case the group will explore and identify patterns of distinctiveness that emerge from identified organizational competences.

The reason for choosing the focus is that organizations cannot be good at everything. But as far as we have that strategic focus, we have a better chance of success in today's complex, ambiguous and rapidly changing environment. Figure 7.12 summarizes the differences and combinations.

While issue management and purpose might be somewhat self-explanatory, productive use of resources or identifying competitive advantage usually requires further exploration. In open strategy, it is focused on identifying assets, competences and competence outcomes in the company, some of which are distinctive (Eden and Ackermann, 2010) Those are essential not only for strategy making, but also for developing core capabilities for fulfilling a purpose and function of an organization, which are in essence a combination of competences and capacity to perform determined by available resources (both financial and non-financial). In the following section we are going to focus on the competences and how causal mapping can help identify them.

Assets, competences and competence outcomes

Traditionally, we look at assets, competences and outcomes in a linear manner, as shown in Figure 7.13. Assets enable competences, which then lead to competence outcomes. In other words:

- What we have: **assets**
- What we do with the assets: **competences**
- What we achieve: **competence outcomes**

Competence outcomes then enable delivering business goals, which leads to delivering customer value and, ultimately, delivering generic goals.

Figure 7.13 Linear view of assets, competences and outcomes

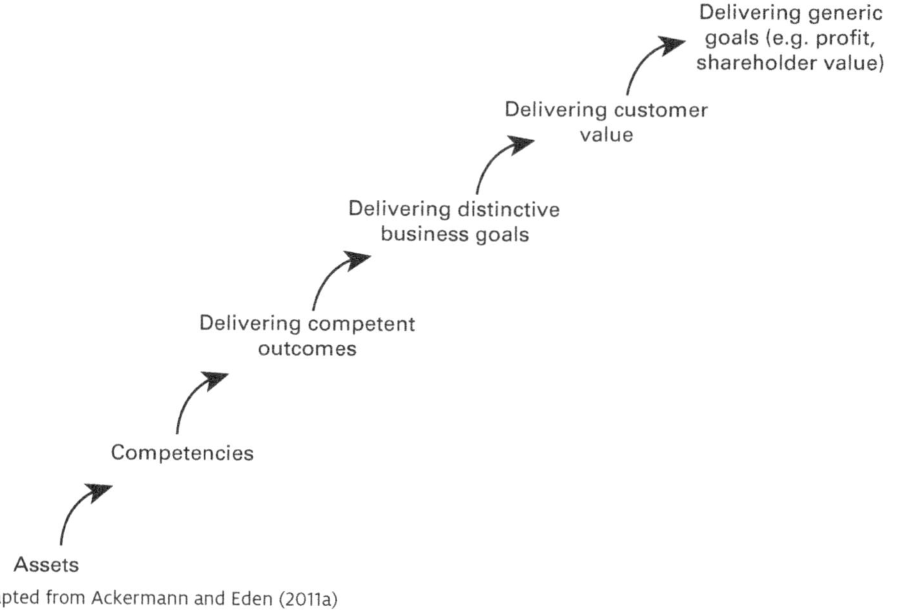

Adapted from Ackermann and Eden (2011a)

Individual competences are rarely distinctive – distinctiveness arises through patterns or bundles of competences. Distinctive competences develop through networks of relationships between competences and organizational purpose. Unlike **distinctive competences** (**DC**), **distinctive competence outcomes** (**DCO**) cannot be managed directly – they are more externally focused and support business goals directly. Historical and **distinctive assets** (**DA**) can be exploited by distinctive competences in order to achieve distinctive competence outcomes.

Identifying core competences allows the decision-making group to unpack more complex relationships between the different components described above, as shown in Figure 7.14. Core distinctive competences are the ones that lead to distinctive competence outcomes. We can also think of threshold competences, which are essential for achieving business goals but might not have much impact once the threshold is passed.

When trying to mark competence outcomes, competencies and assets on the causal map, you will usually end up with a sandwich-like structure. In the bottom, you will have assets or what the company has that allows it to stay competitive, for example, having a global training base or possessing a unique technology.

Right above the assets you will have competences that are to an extent enabled by the assets. For example, perhaps with the unique technology the company is able to create new products every year. Or perhaps the global training base partially enables finding and recruiting the best talent. At this point you will notice that all the competences start with 'ABLE'. This formulation makes the cluster of statements more distinctive on the map as competences and emphasizes that it is the company's ability to do something.

And finally on the top you will have competence outcome – those things that the company can achieve with the competences it has. For instance, recruiting the best talents and creating new products every year results in the perception of a company as a leader in innovation.

To build this map, you will usually start this exercise by generating statements about what the company is good at. At this point, you do not need to concern yourself too much with which of these concepts are assets, which are competences and which are competence outcomes. We are going to demonstrate this approach using an example of focusing on the competitive advantage of a university as part of its strategy. However, you can apply this approach in many different contexts that are not necessarily focused on strategy development. In Figure 7.15 you can see an example of 21 concepts generated for a university.

Figure 7.14 Non-linear view of assets, competences and outcomes

Adapted from Ackermann and Eden (2011a)

In the next step you start sorting out the statements into three groups and rephrasing them, competences in particular, to clarify the meaning. For example, competence 86 'Deliver courses and programmes across campuses in a consistent manner' turned into 86 'ABLE TO Deliver courses and programmes across campuses in a consistent manner'. It is recommended to use different styles for each category to make the map visually clearer.

In Figure 7.16 you can see that statements like 91 'Have local campuses in different countries', 94 'Strong industry connections', or 95 '200 years of history' have been classified as assets – what the university has. The statements like 86 'Able to provide equal opportunities for teaching and research-focused staff', 81 'Able to support flexible modes of teaching (synchronous and asynchronous on a rolling basis)', or 87 'Able to deliver applied and impact-driven research' have been classified as competences – the company's ability to do or accomplish something. Finally, statements like 77 'Reputation of a global university' or 75 'Legacy of a practice-oriented university' have been classified as competence outcomes – what the company can achieve.

In the next step you might want to regroup the statements within each category to put more distinctive items to the right. For instance, 91 'Have local campuses in different countries', 94 'Strong industry connections' and 92 'Have local teaching staff' have been recognized by the company as the

Figure 7.15 An example of statements generated for a competitive advantage-focused strategy

84 Send students and staff for an exchange to a different country

80 Can ensure reliable and transparent examination process

91 Have local campuses in different countries

95 200 years of history

92 Have local teaching staff

86 Deliver courses and programmes across campuses in a consistent manner

79 Degree is not location specific

94 Strong industry connections

77 Reputation of a global university

89 50 years of experience in distance learning provision and support

85 Equal opportunities for teaching and research-focused staff

87 Applied and impact-driven research

83 Supports bottom-up initiatives

78 Famous for online education

93 Have integrated IT support across the university

88 Partnership with the British Council

81 Flexible model of teaching (synchronous and asynchronous on a rolling basis)

76 Attracts students from all walks of life from across the world

82 Programmes have integration with industry

90 Strong partnerships with affiliated teaching institutions across the world

75 Legacy of a practice-oriented university

Figure 7.16 Statements classified into assets, competences and competence outcomes

- **75** Legacy of a practice-oriented university
- **76** Attracts students from all walks of life from across the world
- **77** Reputation of a global university
- **78** Famous for online education
- **79** Degree is not location specific

- **80** Can ensure reliable and transparent examination process
- **81** Able to support flexible modes of teaching (synchronous and asynchronous on a rolling basis)
- **82** Able to provide integration of programmes with industry
- **83** Support bottom-up initiatives
- **84** Able to send students and staff for an exchange to a different country
- **87** Able to deliver applied and impact-driven research
- **86** Able to deliver courses and programmes across campuses in a consistent manner
- **86** Able to provide equal opportunities for teaching and research-focused staff

- **88** Partnership with the British Council
- **89** 50 years of experience in distance learning provision and support
- **90** Strong partnerships with affiliated teaching institutions across the world
- **91** Have local campuses in different countries
- **95** 200 years of history
- **94** Strong industry connections
- **93** Have integrated IT support across the university
- **92** Have local teaching staff

most distinctive assets, 84 'Able to send students and staff for an exchange to a different country' and 86 'Able to deliver courses and programmes across campuses in a consistent manner' have been recognized as the most distinctive competences, and 77 'Reputation of a global university' has been recognized as the most distinctive competence outcome. As you can see, there is an international theme emerging on the map.

In the next step, you start connecting concepts with each other. Typically, assets will lead competences and competences will lead to competence outcomes, but this is not always the case. Assets can support competence outcomes directly. For instance, 90 'Strong partnerships with affiliated teaching institutions across the world' leads to 76 'Attracts students from all walks of life from across the world'. Competences might also support assets. For instance, 81 'Able to support flexible modes of teaching (synchronous & asynchronous on a rolling basis)' supports 94 'Strong industry connections'. However, it is unlikely that competence outcomes support anything other than other outcomes. Competence outcomes should be the heads in the map, otherwise you might need to re-examine them and scrutinize whether the identified competence outcomes are indeed outcomes.

To delve into the analysis, you might want to focus on part of the map. For example, in Figure 7.17 statement 86 'Able to deliver courses and programmes across campuses in a consistent manner' seems to be the core distinctive competence, supporting two competence outcomes, 77 'Reputation of a global university' and 79 'Degree is not location specific', and supported by distinctive assets, 91 'Have local campuses in different countries' and 92 'Have local teaching staff', and distinctive competence 84 'Able to send students and staff for an exchange to a different country'.

As we continue analysing the map, we can certainly see an international theme emerging – reputation of a global university, consistency in the delivery of courses and programmes, partnerships across the world. International-local ways of working appear to be a major pattern of distinctiveness for this university. You can continue analysing the map in this manner.

Below is a quick checklist of how to approach mapping competence outcomes, competencies and assets:

- start with the standard concepts
- assign DCO/DC/DA = 'jam sandwich'
- move more distinctive items to the right
- explore linkages
- explore the patterns of distinctiveness

Figure 7.17 An example of a major pattern of distinctiveness

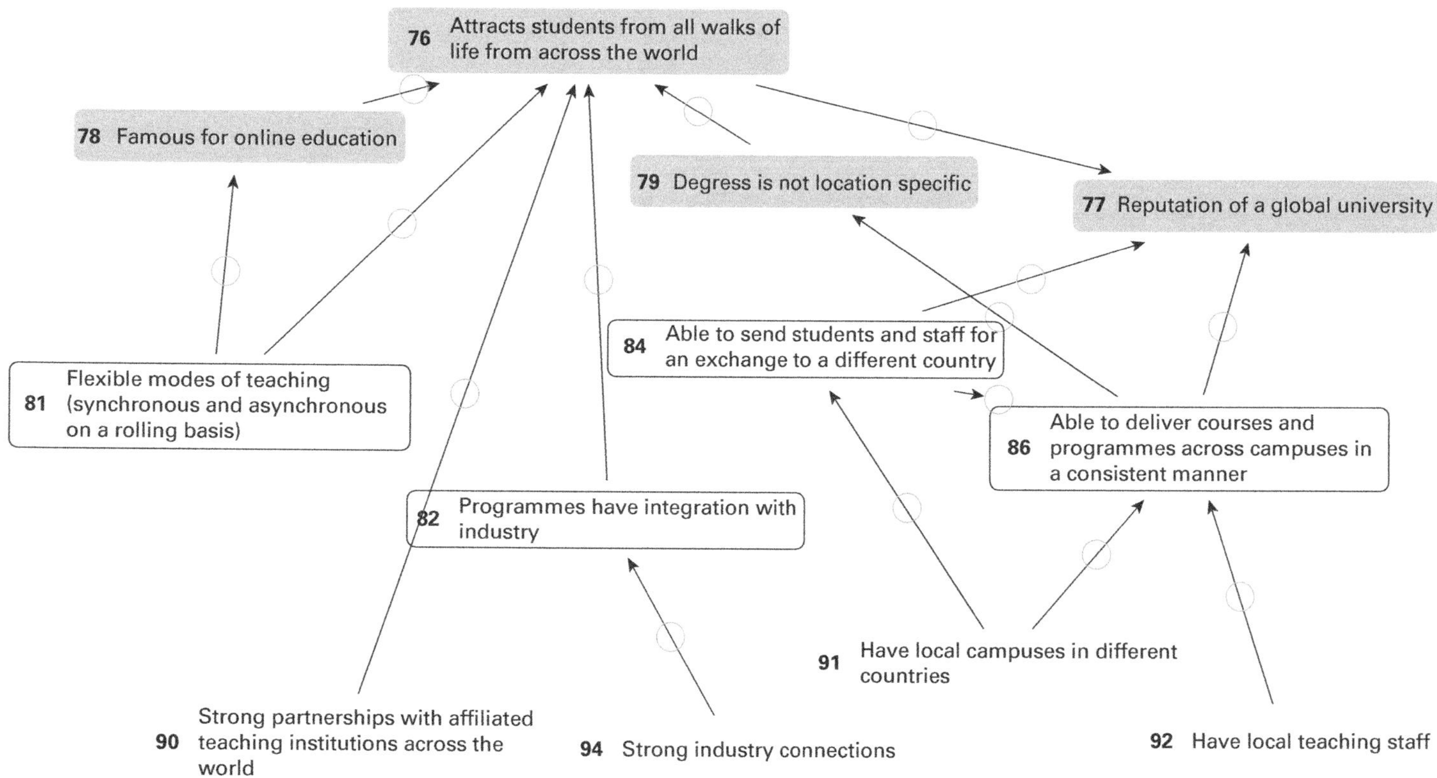

7.6 Designing a workshop for group decision making and open strategizing

Preparing for the workshop

There are four areas to consider when designing a session: client outcomes, process, participants and platform. As an important first step, you need to work with the client to be sure you are clear on the target outcomes, and the benefits or limitations, of the methods to be used. Understanding the outcomes will help you ask the right questions at the start of the workshop and guide the process in the right direction.

The process, participants and platform can be identified once the client outcomes are understood and agreed (Figure 7.18)

When preparing for the workshop, you need to detail the **process** of the entire session, including the following aspects:

- Decide on what questions to ask to guide participant responses.
- Decide on which frameworks, if any, to use to organize responses.
- Clarify the ordering, timing and instructions for key activities.

The other important aspect to consider is the **participants** who are going to provide the input to the process. The considerations might include the following:

- Work with the sponsor to identify the 'right' people to be involved.
- Think about the diversity of inputs required in order to achieve the best outcomes.
- Provide a formal invite from the session sponsor to legitimize proceedings.

Figure 7.18 Preparing for the workshop

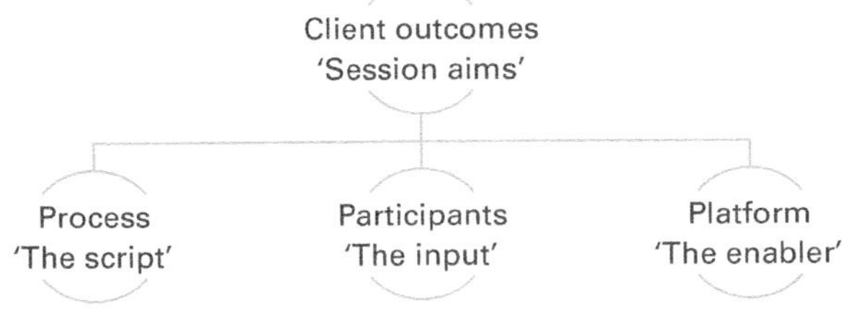

It is important to have power brokers on board, i.e. middle managers and senior managers need to be convinced in the method and agree to have a conversation together, otherwise the enactment strategy will not happen.

Finally, it is essential to decide how the workshop is going to be facilitated (**enabled**) in terms of tools (e.g. whether a digital platform is going to be used, and, if yes, what training might be required) The considerations might include the following:

- Decide on the role that technology and supporting materials will play in running the workshop.
- Think about the needs of the session: the time available, the abilities of participants, the practicalities of logistics.
- Own the organizing task.

Running the workshop

The mapping process involves four key areas: preparation, ideation, analysis and synthesis, as illustrated in the image below. The following is a recommended process to follow during the workshop:

1. Preparation
   - Understand the mapping rules. The participants might need an explanation of the purpose of the workshop and the mapping process.
   - Familiarize yourself with the mapping rules. The participants might need training in how to construct statements and link them together.
   - Develop the potential outcomes of the mapping process.
2. Ideation
   - Bring ideas forward: issues, goals, solutions. At this point the participants brainstorm ideas and put them forward.
   - Identify and mark issues. This involves the facilitator clustering ideas and identifying issues to work with as a starting point.
   - Start linking the statements. At this point the mapping process starts, with drawing links between statements.
3. Analysis
   - Discuss busy points.
   - Vote for the most pressing issue and the most interesting idea.
   - Have a break.

4 Synthesis

- Ladder up and down the chain of arguments by linking further statements.
- Connect between issues and goals, building a goal system.
- Run through each selected idea. The facilitator will focus on the ideas that were voted for the most and identify the gaps in arguments.

7.7 Summary

In this chapter we have introduced the action-oriented causal mapping method that is widely used to aid strategic decision making. You have learnt how to use this method to capture aspects of an individual's thinking or a group's diverse views on the problem, how to support strategy development or understand organizational core competences, and how to analyse the resulting maps. You have also learnt how to organize a workshop that would provide an environment for facilitating a group causal mapping exercise.

REFLECTIVE EXERCISE

To reflect on what you have learnt in this chapter, choose an issue in your organization that you would like to explore and devise an action-oriented strategy for an organization. Choose your 'client organization'. This could be a team, unit, division or the whole organization for which you can make meaningful strategy. Avoid selecting an organization that is too large – instead of selecting the whole of corporation XYZ, you could select an organizational unit defined by a regional territory, function or product category. You can select a current or previous employer.

Once you have decided on the issue and the organization, follow the steps outlined in the 'Constructing causal maps' section, starting with formulating a question to build the map, and then continue analysing the map to develop a plan of how the issue can be addressed and why it should be addressed. Show the map to your colleagues to help you validate your thinking about the issue and bring in different perspectives.

TEAM EXERCISE

In your team, select an organization and try to analyse its competitive advantage. Start with generating ideas about what this company is good at in terms of assets and competences and competence outcomes. The three questions mentioned in the previous section will help you formulate the right statements:

- What we have: **assets**
- What we do with the assets: **competences**
- What we achieve: **competence outcomes**

Continue through the process outlined in section 7.6 to build a map of competitive advantage for the chosen organization. Discuss how competence outcomes are supported by competences and assets, and which of them are the most important ones. Focus on those and formulate what this company is best at.

References

Ackermann, F and Eden, C (2011a) *Making strategy: Mapping out strategic success* (2nd ed.), Sage

Ackermann, F and Eden, C (2011b) Negotiation in strategy making teams: Group Support systems and the process of cognitive change, *Group Decision and Negotiation*, 20 (3), pp. 293–314, https://doi.org/10.1007/s10726-008-9133-y (archived at https://perma.cc/SRL8-JY8V)

Bryson, JM, Ackermann, F, Eden, C and Finn, CB (2004) *Visible Thinking: Unlocking causal mapping for practical business results*, John Wiley & Sons

Eden, C and Ackermann, F (2010) Competences, distinctive competences, and core competences. In R Sanchez, A Heene and T Ede Zimmermann (Eds.) *A Focussed Issue on Identifying, Building, and Linking Competences*, 5, (pp. 3–33) Emerald Group Publishing Limited, https://doi.org/10.1108/S1744-2117(2010)5 (archived at https://perma.cc/CS8M-3482)

Edmondson, AC (2018) *The Fearless Organization: Creating psychological safety in the workplace for learning, innovation, and growth*, John Wiley & Sons

Kelly, G (1955) Personal construct theory. In RN Sollod and CF Monte (Eds.) *Beneath the Mask: An introduction to theories of personality* (pp. 449–71) John Wiley & Sons

Whittington, R, Cailluet, L and Yakis-Douglas, B (2011) Opening Strategy: Evolution of a precarious profession, *British Journal of Management*, 22, pp. 531–44, https://doi.org/10.1111/j.1467-8551.2011.00762.x (archived at https://perma.cc/Q735-RSKT)

PART THREE
Systems complexity

In this part of the book we explore system complexity in greater detail. In Chapter 8 we use the En-ROADS Climate Solutions Simulator as the backbone to introduce systems dynamics as a method for modelling and understanding complex systems. It focuses on highlighting the behavioural dynamics within a system including unintended consequences of decisions and interventions. In the penultimate section, using the knowledge from previous sections, you are guided to use the En-ROADS simulator to understand the climate change problem and develop your own solution. In Chapter 9 we explore the ever-changing nature of complex systems by exploring the levers or leverage points in complex systems that can influence and change the behaviour of the entire system. We introduce different types of levers, specifically structural levers, temporal levers, conceptual levers and boundary levers, and give examples of how they can be used in practice.

Understanding the behaviour of complex systems 8

This chapter has been developed with help and assistance from Dr Merve Er, an assistant professor at the Marmara University in Istanbul.

In the previous chapters we have discussed different methods used in modelling soft systems and the complexity associated with them. In particular, we introduced causal loop diagrams in Chapter 6 and causal mapping in Chapter 7 as structured approaches for exploring causalities between different elements of the system interacting with each other. In this chapter, we will take these methods one step further and demonstrate how you can build on qualitative understanding of such systems and construct a quantitative model based on the descriptive qualitative conceptualization of the system, which can then be simulated to explore the system's behaviour in the future.

The purpose of this chapter is to demonstrate how systems can be modelled and how this modelling to study their future behaviour can help managers learn about the systems as the new systems emerge. It is important to note that when we create these models we make assumptions about how various autonomous parts (organizations/people) would behave in a given circumstance. Over time, as things unfold and we keep on comparing the model to how things are unfolding in reality, we can learn from this experience and refine the model. Therefore, the core value of modelling is not about developing a high-fidelity model. Instead, it is the PROCESS of MODELLING that enables the modellers to learn more about the system as it emerges, thus making it more predictable.

The objective of this chapter is to introduce systems dynamics as a method for modelling and understanding complex systems. It will focus on highlighting the behavioural dynamics within a system, including unintended consequences of decisions and interventions. In the penultimate section, using the knowledge from previous sections, the reader will be guided to use the En-ROADS simulator, developed by the MIT Sloan School of Management, to understand the climate change problem and an example of a complex and wicked problem, and develop their own solution to solving the climate challenge.

LEARNING OUTCOMES

- Understand
  - the value of modelling future behaviour of systems
  - purpose of system dynamics
  - stocks and flows
  - approaches to and challenges of quantifying relationships in a stock and flow model
  - Basics of analysing stock and flow model simulation
- Learn how to study the system through the process of modelling its future behaviour
- Learn about behavioural dynamics of complex systems

8.1 Systems dynamics: an approach to modelling and simulating complex systems

In Chapter 6 we talked about causal loop diagrams as one of the methods used in Soft Systems Methodology. They can be very useful when we try to capture soft aspects of a system. They show us the forces in the system and how they impact various aspects of the system. Although they can give us an idea of how the whole system will behave, they predominantly capture the system's present behaviour. Although by looking at the interactions between different forces we can deduce what the system's behaviour may look like in the future, it is much more difficult to predict how the system's behaviour will change over time as the forces upon the system change.

This is where system dynamics proves useful as the next development in causal loop diagrams. The method was developed by Jay W Forrester (Forrester, 1958). He proposed using causal loop diagrams as a foundation where you can then apply mathematical/statistical equations to model relationships between different elements of the systems. Then the model can be used to simulate how the system will behave over time in the future. In such simulations, the behaviour that the system exhibits over time is called a dynamic. Systems tend to be dynamic, which means that the behaviour of the system will change over time. If you understand the relationship between different elements in the system, and how they impact each other, you can model the behaviour of the system and then simulate it and see what it will turn into in the next 1, 5, 10, 20 years. Such models can also help 'play out' different scenarios, by doing what-if analysis where variables are changed. By changing one or more variables we can further learn how the behaviour of the whole system may change in the future.

The purpose of this chapter is to introduce the foundations of the method and help you understand how to interpret and use system dynamics models. If you would like to learn more about the method and build models of your own, we recommend that you read specialized textbooks dedicated to this method, for instance starting with Donella Meadows, *Thinking in Systems* (2008).

8.2 Building on soft systems thinking

When trying to build a system dynamics model of a system, the first step is usually conducting a review of what is already known about the system and about the internal and external forces that may impact it. The review will reveal current trends that might lead to the changes in the system, variables that might determine these changes, and relationships between variables. With this understanding you can then begin to represent a system with a causal loop diagram as discussed in Chapter 6. The diagram will give a static representation of the system, in which the future changes cannot be observed, but rather speculated about based on the links between different forces. However, it can help capture all the forces affecting the system.

When a causal loop diagram is built, you will normally need to reduce it to the most significant trends and forces that should be captured and quantified in a system dynamics model. This will require redefining the boundaries of the system as the first step to decide what is indeed important in the simulated system and what should be left outside the boundaries. Although it might be tempting to try and capture all the forces identified, it might lead to an overly complicated model with a lot of noise that might not necessarily be more accurate than a less-complicated version. Quantified relationships are often at least partly based on assumptions. Each assumption would have errors, and thus incorporating too many assumptions in the model might lead to high accumulated errors in the simulation results, particularly over the longer simulation horizon.

Depending on your area and breadth of expertise, it might be necessary to involve a group of people or external experts in focusing on what are the most essential elements of a causal loop diagram that need to be considered in the simulation model. This might be facilitated with focus groups or using more structured approaches, such as the Delphi method.

Having developed the causal loop diagram and simplified it to focus on the pertinent forces, you can build the simulation model for further analysis of the future of the system in three steps: modelling stocks and flows, quantifying the relationships, and running the simulation and analysing the results. Each of these steps is described below.

Modelling stocks and flows

In Chapter 3 we introduced the concepts of stocks and flows. They are two of the foundation elements of system dynamics. A **stock** is a variable that is measured at a specific period in time, for example on a specific day. It represents a quantity or a value that exists at that particular point in time. The stock might accumulate or get depleted over time. But at each given period in time, we can measure it. A **flow** is measured over an interval of time, for example per day, week or month. The flow changes the amount of stock, i.e. the inflow leads to the accumulation of a stock (is added to the stock), while the outflow leads to its depletion (is subtracted from the stock). The **flow rate** is related to the flow over time and shows the speed with which the flow flows into the stock or flows out of the stock. The flow that originates from outside the boundaries of the system will originate from a **cloud** on a system dynamics diagram, and conversely a flow that leaves the system's boundaries will terminate at a cloud on a systems dynamic diagram. It is assumed that clouds have an infinite capacity that does not constrain the system. And finally, a **link** is used to indicate dependencies between different variables that determine the rates of the flow. Figure 8.1 illustrates the commonly used symbols and a simple stock and flow diagram for population change.

Let us look at the simple stock and flow diagram in Figure 8.1. In the centre of the diagram you have a population, which is a stock represented as a rectangle. To define the starting point, you need to put an initial value for

Figure 8.1 Stock and flow diagrams: symbols and an example

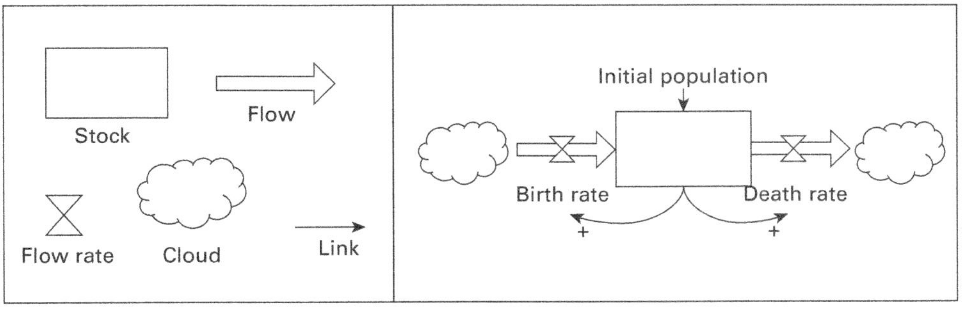

the population, that is what the population was like at a particular point in time from which the model will start simulating the change in the population. The population is increased by an inflow, which is defined by the birth rate, and reduced by an outflow, which is defined by the death rate. Both are positive values.

The inflow represents a reinforcing loop – the more population is born, the more of the population will give birth in the future, and therefore the more the population will increase in a country. The death rate represents a balancing loop – the more population there is, the more of the population will die, and therefore with this reduction the population will be balanced out. In this simple example we define quite narrow boundaries in the form of clouds, as they do not examine what external factors might define the birth rate and the death rate in this particular system.

In this example, the only two variables that change the behaviour of the system are the birth and death rates, which are assumed as constant. Depending on how they compare to each other, the population will grow, decline or remain stable. If the birth rate is higher than the death rate, then the population will glow, and if its growth is simulated and plotted, the relationship will be non-linear. If the birth rate is lower than the death rate, the population will decline, and again, the simulation will reveal a non-linear relationship. If the birth and death rate are the same the population balances out and remains stable.

Using this model as a basis, we can build a more complex system of population change by expanding the boundaries and adding more variables to create a more nuanced representation of relationships. In Figure 8.2, instead of looking at the population as a whole, we can examine stocks of population by different groups. New-born people flow into the stock of young people whose volume might reduce as defined by the young mortality rate, or an average rate of how many people will die at a young age. The remaining young will mature to adulthood and inflow into the stock of reproductive adults. Some of them will also get ill or die in accidents at a defined adult death rate. The rest are likely to have children, defined by an adult fertility rate and contributing to the stock of young people. They will also age and move to the stock of non-reproducing adults, which will decrease at a death rate.

If you know these parameters, you can predict more accurately how the population will change over time. For example, if you want to increase the population of a country, but there is a worrying trend observed in this country, you can see where the levers or pressure points discussed in the next chapter can be introduced. If you want to further analyse at-risk groups of populations, such as adults that define the reproduction rates in the population, you can further break it down into female and male adults. Such a breakdown might help you further understand the impact of various trends on how the society will reproduce and what the population will be in, let's say, 20 years' time. The two examples above show that you can start with a very simple model that describes the behaviour of a system. And then you can add layers of complexity by introducing new variables and expanding the boundaries by considering additional factors that help explain the variables, such as social policies or practices that might influence birth rates. Once you start unravelling all these parameters, the system can become really complex.

Quantifying relationships

Although there are general principles for building system dynamics models (Bala et al, 2017; Forrester, 1994), when it comes to quantifying relationships,

Figure 8.2 A more complex stock and flow diagram for the population change

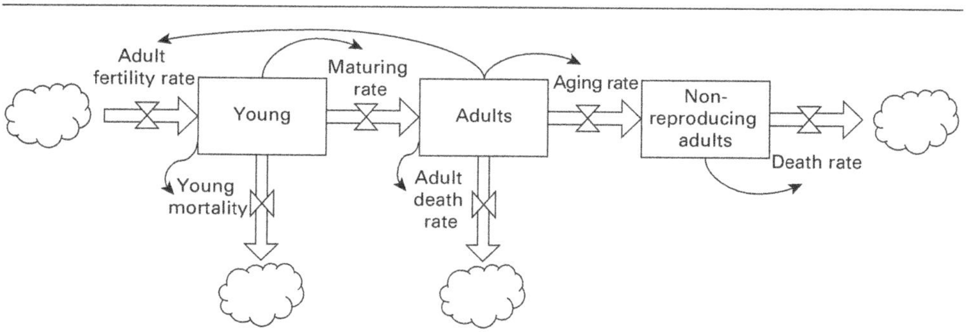

there are no strict rules to follow. Quantification of relationships usually relies on mathematical/statistical equations that define the relationships between different parameters in the model. The equations may be developed using data from a number of sources:

- prior studies that have investigated and validated the relationships between these parameters
- studies set up specifically to collect data on the relationships
- focus groups or Delphi studies with experts in the specific area to help develop assumptions and define the relationships

This presents **the first challenge** in quantifying the relationships. Complex systems include multiple variables and feedback loops. The number of variables that might need to be considered in a complex system might quickly overwhelm the data available and pose a challenge to choosing from alternative explanations and theories to interpret the behaviour of the system. The assumptions that aim at filling in the gaps in the model and interpretation of its behaviour can vary in degree of accuracy, adding multiple errors in the model. The longer the simulation horizon of the model, the greater the cumulative errors from these assumptions will be. This is particularly true about the assumptions and inferences about the consequences of external events that have not happened before, and thus we do not have reliable evidence of anticipated consequences. Making such assumptions is inevitably distorted with biases due to various cognitive prejudices, such as worldviews, that we all are prone to.

Furthermore, multiple feedback loops might cause many variables to correlate with each other, but human ability to unpack these relationships is quite limited, as people are poor judges of correlations due to cognitive biases. Engaging with multiple experts to cross-examine the assumptions will help to reduce the errors in the model.

The second challenge is related to the data and information being fed into the model. For example, if we build a model that simulates the impact of climate change on a system, the data on climate change will come from existing predictions that are publicly available. Quite often the developers of such models have to rely on what is available. However, what is available is not always accurate. Even if data we have is perceived as reliable, we should always be mindful that it is based on delayed measurement, approximations and averages, which in themselves introduce distortions and biases. Other times the data might not be available at all. Similar to quantifying the relationships, the model developers would need to surface the data either through data collection studies or engaging with experts. For example, in the context of climate change, this might mean exploring different scenarios of what trajectory climate change might follow, and then formulating what the effects of each trajectory might be.

The third challenge is related to the complexity of the dynamic system due to non-linearity in causal relationships as well as the time and space dependency of causes and effects.

All these challenges increase the difficulty of developing a model both mathematically and intuitively. Modellers can utilize different techniques and approaches to deal with these challenges, which we will refrain from covering in more detail in this book. If you would like to read more about this topic, please refer to the book by John Sterman, *System Dynamics: Systems thinking and modelling for a complex world* (2000).

Stakeholder, expert and client collaboration is an important leverage to enrich the systems thinking and modelling methodology. System dynamics is frequently used for policy analysis and design and deriving policy recommendations based on a series of simulation experiments. Modellers may prefer to model with stakeholders and update the simulation model based on stakeholders' feedback at each iteration, i.e. learning from stakeholders. *Participatory system dynamics* modelling is a methodology in which stakeholders participate in different stages of the model-building process such as structuring the problem and its scope, definition of the system, identification of the scenarios, dynamics causalities and policy levers, etc. Further information about participatory system dynamics may be found in Bala et al (2017).

System dynamics models often employ uncertain parameters; hence, parameter estimation and parameter sensitivity analysis are crucial steps for the reliability of simulation results. Model parameters may be identified based on empirical data or expert judgement and assumptions (survey results, etc.). Parameter sensitivity analysis is used to systematically analyse the impact of changes in parameter values on behavioural dynamics. Sensitivity analysis is usually performed by assigning different values to the selected parameter (e.g., ±10 %, ±10 %) and observing the changes in model outputs. Parameter sensitivity analysis may be used to find key parameters that affect the model significantly, evaluate robustness of the developed model and identify critical areas that need further data collection efforts to improve the model.

A system dynamics model is a simplification of a real-world problem, therefore the model we developed needs to be tested and validated for building confidence in the model. Different qualitative and quantitative tests exist for evaluating system dynamics models. We refer to Sterman (2000) for detailed information about model testing. Typical tests include:

- structural validity test, which measures the consistency of the model with knowledge about the real-life system being modelled;
- boundary adequacy test, which evaluates the appropriateness of the model boundary for the aim of the model;
- dimensional consistency, which tracks that each term on each side of a given equation has the same units of measurement;
- parameter evaluation, which includes a qualitative assessment that each parameter has a real-life example;
- extreme condition testing, which means that the model behaves consistently and returns reasonable outputs even when extreme inputs are given.

Simulating and analysing systems behaviour

When a system dynamics model is developed, what it allows us to do is simulate different scenarios by varying the values of certain parameters to conduct sensitivity analysis and thus examine the vulnerability of a system to particular risks. To illustrate the type of analysis that system dynamics models can produce, we are going to look at a case study examining the impact of climate change on supply chain performance (Er Kara et al, 2021).

The authors conducted a literature review to determine various aspects of climate change and the impact they will have on different elements of the supply chain. The review was aggregated into a causal loop diagram (Figure 8.3). The resulting diagram was quite detailed, but included too many parameters to model in a simulation.

To focus the model on the most important factors, the authors applied a survey that helped to reveal the most prominent variables interlinking climate change and supply chain performance dimensions. Based on the responses of managers from multiple industries, extreme weather events and temperature increase were incorporated into a more focused causal loop diagram (Figure 8.4) as the most influential factors impacting the overall performance of supply chains; availability of raw materials and delivery performance were selected as the significant vulnerable points for the climate change threat.

Figure 8.3 Causal loop diagram of the impact of climate change on supply chains

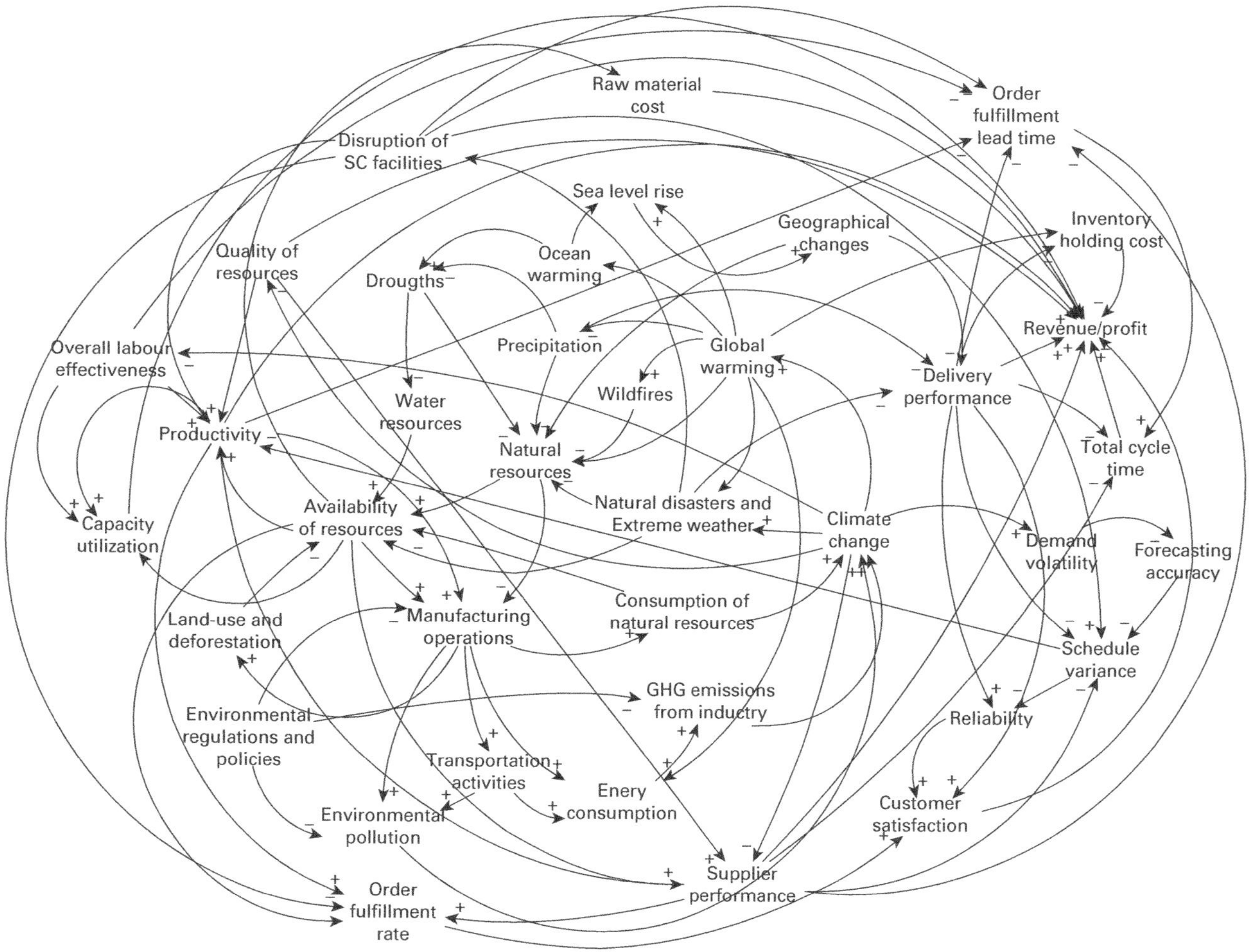

Figure 8.4 Causal loop diagram of the most important climate change factors impacting supply chains

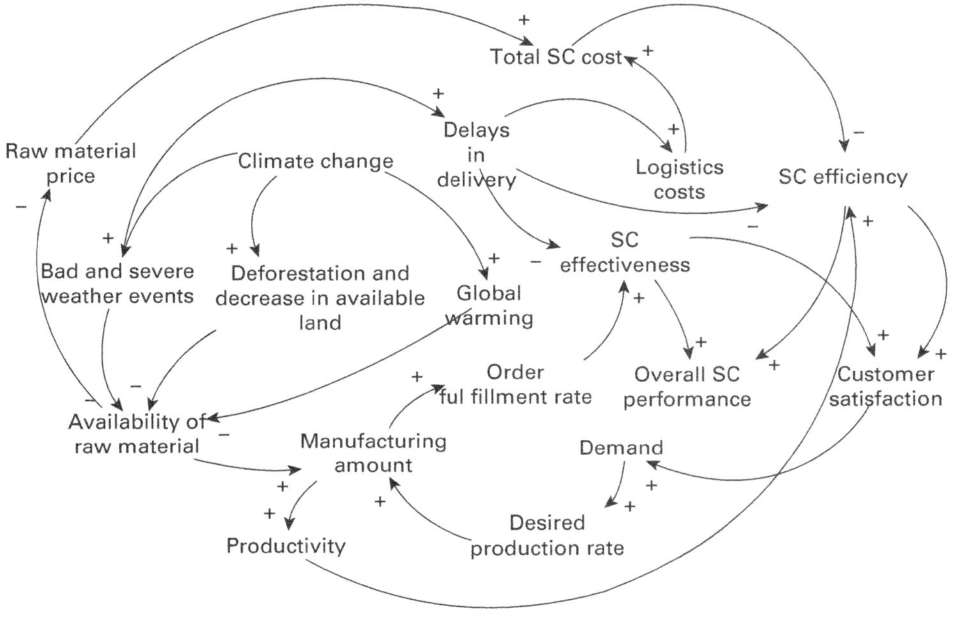

As the next step, a stock and flow diagram was developed by incorporating these climatic impacts into a traditional supply chain model (Figure 8.5). Model parameters and mathematical equations representing model variables were identified with the help of previous academic literature and full participation of supply chain management experts in the modelling phase. The diagram was developed around two stocks, supplier's inventory and manufacturer inventory, represented on the causal loop diagram as manufacturing amount. Supplier's inventory is changed by the supply inflow determined by the supply rate and inventory outflow determined by the supplier shipment rate. Manufacturer inventory is changed by the production inflow determined by the production rate and product delivery rate, which was represented on the causal loop diagram as order fulfilment rate.

All the other parameters were modelled using mathematical/statistical equations. For instance, climate change parameters, including temperature increase, decrease in available land, and bad weather conditions and extreme weather events were combined into a combined climate effect parameter that would affect the availability of raw materials. Once the system dynamics model was designed, a series of scenarios was developed based on availability

Figure 8.5 Stock and flow diagram of the impact of climate change on supply chains

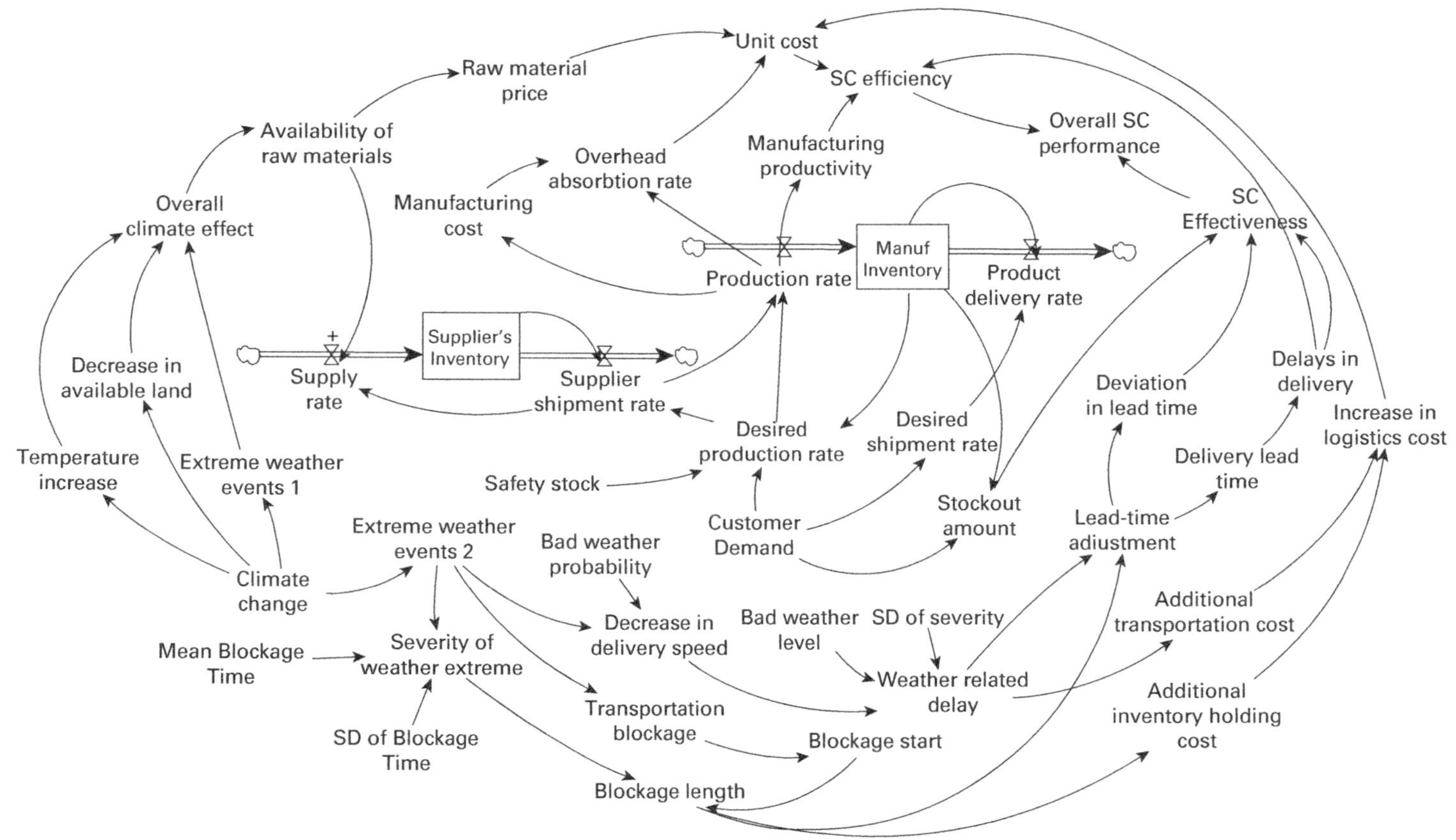

of raw materials and the capacity of logistics operations, both rated at low, medium and high. The subsequent model was then simulated for a horizon of 40 years. The output from the simulation is illustrated in two graphs shown in Figure 8.6.

The top graph shows the changes in the availability of raw materials as low, medium and high, with the observed drop between 40 per cent and 78 per cent between three scenarios. The bottom graph shows the increase in

Figure 8.6 Changes in the availability of raw materials and raw material prices impacted by climate change

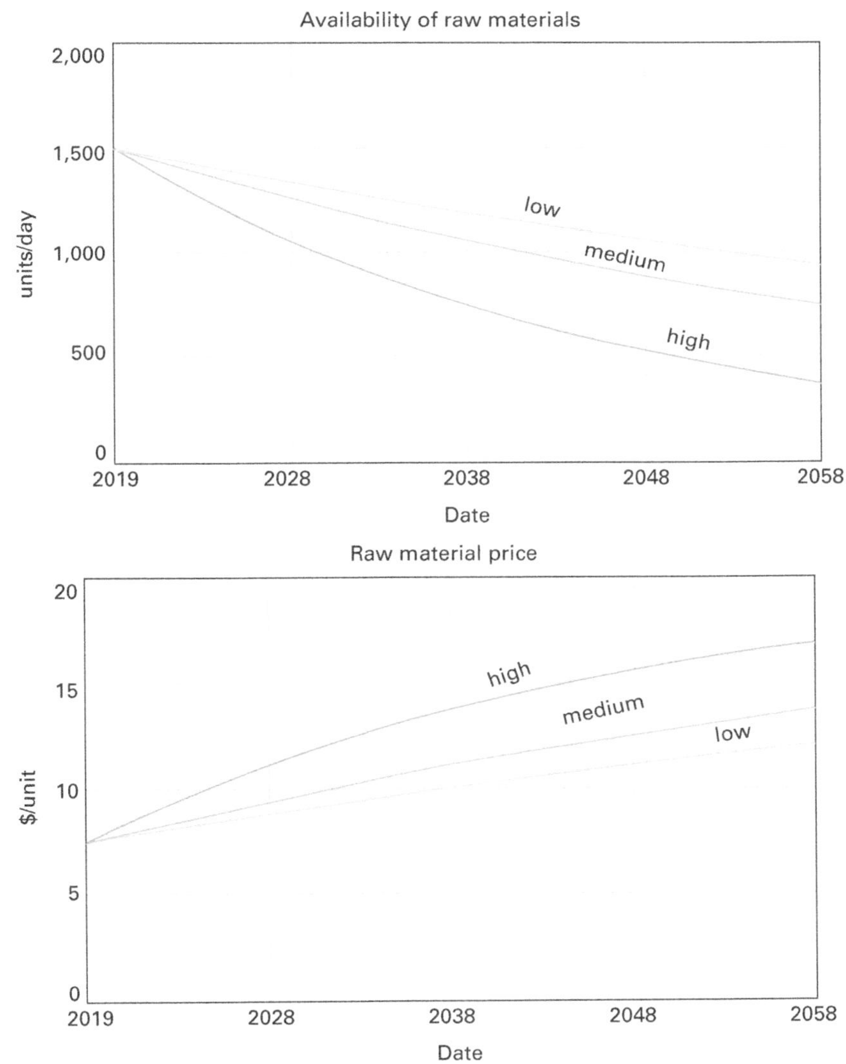

prices in absolute terms. If converted to percentages, even in the low impact scenario the price is projected to increase by 66 per cent, while in the impact scenario it demonstrates a much steeper increase of 130 per cent.

This visualization puts into context the impact of climate change on a specific system. While we all understand that the impact will occur, the simulation is able to show a projection of how detrimental the impact might be depending on the severity of the scenario. Depending on the type of supply chain this might have far-reaching implications. If we consider critical materials, the price and availability of raw materials will put significant pressure on productivity and manufacturing costs, which will then be reflected in the product costs. This might prompt a particular company to start looking for alternatives to mitigate the risks.

The model can demonstrate the changes in various other parameters too. For example, Figure 8.7 shows the potential changes in the production rate and stockouts depending on the scenario. From the top graph, we can see that the production rate in the worst-case scenario starts dropping much earlier than in the other scenarios. Similarly, the supply shortages leading to stockouts starts to rapidly increase much earlier for the worst-case scenario.

Such graphs can be plotted for various other parameters representing different aspects of the supply chain performance such as delivery performance and logistics costs. They can provide contextual information about the risks associated with the impact of climate change on supply chain performance and can be used as evidence in making strategic decisions about mitigating strategies for making the supply chain more resilient to anticipated disruptions. A disruption may create a snowball effect and propagate to the entire network. Hence, a system dynamics approach provides the opportunity to analyse the ripple effects of risks and evaluate the efficiency and effectiveness of the entire supply chain network.

8.3 Understanding and revisiting complex wicked problems

In Chapter 2 we talked about different types of problems that you might observe in systems and addressed these using a systems thinking approach. In complex systems, problems that have the most significant impact, or in other words problems that matter, tend to be wicked problems. Understanding these problems and quite often trying to revisit them requires understanding

Figure 8.7 Changes in the production rates and stockout amounts impacted by climate change

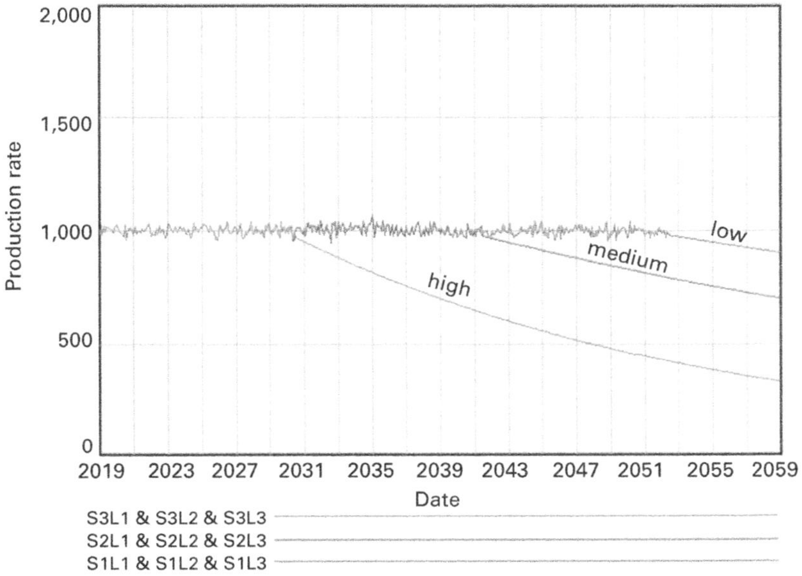

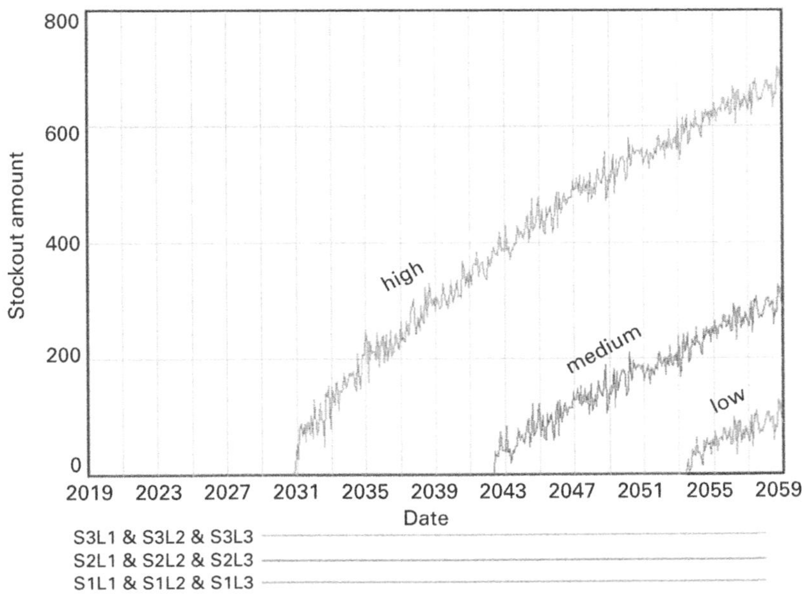

different systems and their interconnectedness. Therefore, taking a systems approach to understanding whole systems is absolutely essential in trying to manage these problems.

Climate change is one such problem. It is one of the most complex and wicked problems humanity has ever faced. Understanding the patterns of climate change requires understanding the interconnections between multiple natural and human-made systems, such as atmosphere, water systems, land biomass and its eco-systems, industry, agriculture, etc. These interconnections might for example help explain the changing weather patterns and the subsequent impact on other systems, like the supply chain, discussed in the previous section of this chapter. They might also help identify the primary causes of the observed changes, such as the increased greenhouse gas (GHG) emissions that produce global warming.

Understanding how the causes of the problem can be addressed includes adding more systems into the mix and examining how they are interconnected. Solutions in one system will most certainly have an impact on other systems, which might be both negative and positive, and failure to anticipate such impact will lead to unintended emergent behaviour in different systems.

For example, you can find lots of different types of 'clean' technology developed in the past decades aimed at reducing GHG emissions: renewable energy sources, carbon capture, energy storage, electric vehicles, to name a few. If you decide to promote electric vehicles as the solution to achieving net zero, simply putting more electric vehicles on the roads will not achieve the goal. You would need to also consider adjacent systems such as power generation, as well as charging and grid infrastructure. The electricity powering electric vehicles would need to come from clean sources for them to claim the reduction in carbon emissions. Otherwise, if the electricity is supplied from coal or oil, the effect might be the opposite. At the same time, the grid should be able to support the increased electricity demand and the charging infrastructure should be developed to make electric vehicles a viable alternative. Then you need to look at how this system interacts with the policy system, e.g. to incentivize citizens to switch to electric vehicles, as well as favourable conditions for industry to invest in supporting infrastructure such as charging stations.

All these systems interact with each other and add to the complexity of finding a solution to climate change, and in this example we have only looked at one of the myriad net zero solutions. In this and many other solutions we can look at benefits and drawbacks, but the information alone is not enough.

We need a way for stakeholders and interested parties to understand the interrelations between different systems and test implications of these solutions, and this is where system dynamics and systems thinking more broadly can play a role. An example of such solutions for exploring the issue of climate change in particular was developed by MIT Sloan School of Management. The En-ROADS Climate Solutions Simulator (www.climateinteractive.org/en-roads/) is based on a complex system dynamics model and simulates the impact of different policies and applications of net zero solutions on global temperature change. Solutions like this can help interested parties not only to be better informed about the issue, but to actively experiment with potential solutions and understand how they are interconnected. In particular, such simulations help to observe different emergent behaviours in complex systems, the most typical of which are discussed in the next section.

8.4 Behavioural dynamics in complex systems

In complex systems, multiple elements interacting with each other create emergent properties and behaviours. These behaviours are sometimes counterintuitive, and this is what makes models of complex systems so valuable, because they can demonstrate and visualize these behaviours. To demonstrate each of the most typical behavioural dynamics, we are going to use the En-ROADS simulator. For each of the dynamics you will be asked to try a solution (i.e. a combination of policies) and observe the changes in the system.

Economies of scale

For the first demonstration you will need to go to the En-ROADS Climate Solutions Simulator (www.climateinteractive.org/en-roads/) and then go through the following steps:

- On the top left graph, click on the title bar and choose Primary Energy Demand Totals → Global Sources of Primary Energy.
- On the top right graph, click on the title bar and choose Greenhouse Gas Emissions → Greenhouse Gas Net Emissions.
- To simulate the scenario of offering increased subsidy to renewable energy supply, slide the Renewables slider further right.

Observe what happens with the green curve on the left that shows renewables as the global source of primary energy. You can see that part of the curve will exhibit a significant growth in renewable energy supplies. The more you subsidize renewables the steeper and more visible the growth will be.

This demonstration illustrates a reinforcing feedback loop that is very positive in the context of climate change. It is often referred to as the economies of scale feedback loop. The feedback loop in Figure 8.8 helps to explain this behaviour. With the reduced price of renewables, we can see an increase in attractiveness of renewables, which will then lead to the increase in the amount of renewables in the overall energy portfolio of a country, and the subsequent increase in the installations of renewables. As this happens, the industry accumulates knowledge about the technology and brings technology improvements, which further reduces the price.

You can observe similar dynamics in many systems. However, it is always important to scrutinize whether the observed loop has positive implications for the system, leading to the economy of scale, or if it is an example of a vicious cycle that you would want to break.

Bathtub dynamics

Follow these steps for the second demonstration:

1 Reset all the values to original values.

2 In the top left graph, choose CO_2 Removals → CO_2 Emissions and Removals.

Figure 8.8 Renewable energy reinforcing feedback loop

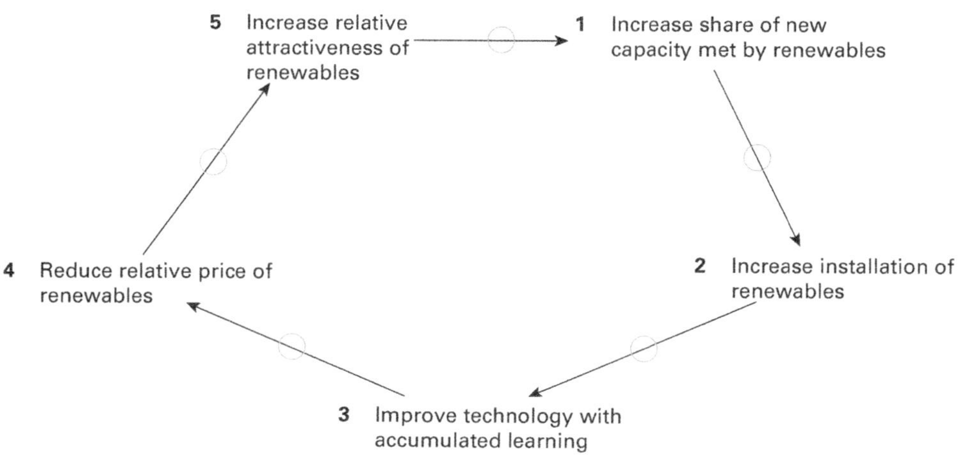

3 In the top right graph, choose Impacts → CO_2 Concentration.

4 Now we will change some policies and simulate their impact over time. Let's increase Energy Efficiency of Buildings and Industry.

Here you will observe that the CO_2 emissions are plateauing to become more or less flat on the top left graph. This change might give you the impression that if the CO_2 emissions are flat, it means that the concentration of CO_2 in the atmosphere should be flat too. But instead, you can see on the top right graph, that the concentration is actually rising. The observed dynamic is called the bathtub dynamic (Figure 8.9).

In system dynamics terms, the amount of carbon dioxide in the atmosphere is a stock. The amount of CO_2 emissions is the inflow of the stock, the amount of CO_2 removals is the outflow of the stock. If the rate of inflow is larger than the rate of outflows, and in this example it is, then the stock is constantly increasing. In this case, what we need to do to change this dynamic is to increase the outflow rate. For example, you can try to increase carbon removal through technological solutions (e.g. carbon capture) and afforestation, and then you will observe that the rate of CO_2 concentration will start to level off. It is important to understand this dynamic because it helps to address a common misconception that if we stop the rate of growth of CO_2 emissions, it will also reduce CO_2 emissions accumulated in the atmosphere. Similar misconceptions can be found in other systems too.

Figure 8.9 Illustration of the bathtub dynamic

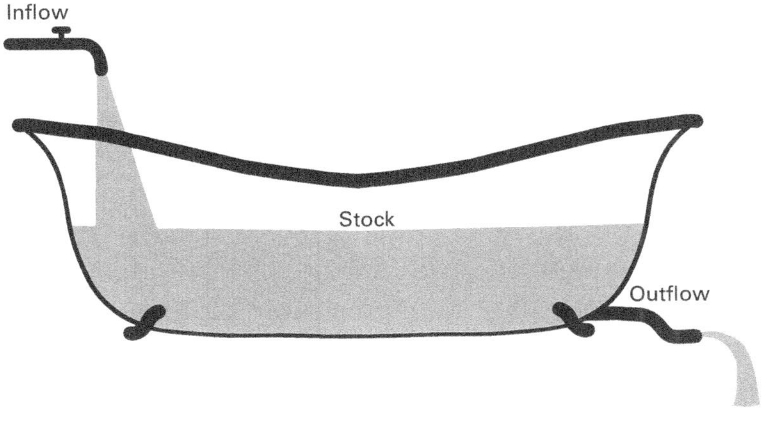

Squeezing the balloon

For the third demonstration follow these steps:

1. Reset all the values to original values.
2. In the top left graph, choose Primary Energy Demand Totals → Global Sources of Primary Energy.
3. In the top right graph, choose Greenhouse Gas Emissions → Greenhouse Gas Net Emissions.
4. Let's try to simulate the impact of policy of increase the taxes on fossil fuels by reducing the energy supply through oil.

In this case you can see that the lines change on the left graph representing different types of sources of primary energy. You will see that the lines for coal and natural gas, coal in particular, will grow more steeply. While the change in temperature will be insignificant (by 0.2°C, if the use of oil is changed to the minimum). The observed dynamic is called the Squeeze the Balloon dynamics.

In system dynamics terms it means that reducing the flow rate in one part of the system (e.g. squeezing down on the use of oil) could lead to the increase in flow rate in another part of the system (the balloon inflates in other parts of the system). In this example, we can observe that the use of other fossil fuels grows and the expected change in temperature does not happen. If you repeat the experiment with other types of fossil fuel and try to tax natural gas or coal, you will see that the consumption of oil will increase. In other words, pushing down on one fossil fuel alone does not necessarily produce the kind of effect that you would hope for. For example, with the Russian invasion of the Ukraine, Europe faced an energy crisis, as it imports 40 per cent of its natural gas from Russia. One would see this as an opportunity to boost renewable energy development, and indeed the European Commission committed to increasing energy coming from new renewable sources by 30 per cent. But at the same time, reliance on natural gas led to an increase in the use of coal-fired power plants in countries that previously pledged to achieve ambitious net zero targets, such as Germany.

What is required to combat this dynamic is to use a combination of policies. For example, increasing carbon price will lead to the reduction of the use of all fossil fuels and a more significant change in temperature (by 1°C, if the carbon price is maximized).

Time lag

For the fourth demonstration follow these steps:

1. Reset all the values to original values.
2. In the top left graph, choose Primary Energy Demand Totals → Global Sources of Primary Energy.
3. In the top right graph, choose Greenhouse Gas Emissions → Greenhouse Gas Net Emissions.
4. Highly incentivize electrification of transport. Observe what happens with Greenhouse Gas Net Emissions. You will see that there is very little change.
5. Then introduce a tax on coal. Now you can see a noticeable change in Greenhouse Gas Net Emissions when the two policies are combined. This means that the use of electric vehicles increased, and they are not being powered by coal. However, if you look at the timeline of Greenhouse Gas Net Emissions, the observed effect does not happen immediately. It starts deviating from the baseline much further down the line.

This demonstration shows the time lag dynamic. When it is caused by infrastructural change delays, it can also be referred to as **capital stock turnover dynamic**. It means that it takes a while after new policies have been implemented for new infrastructure to be developed, and for the system to reconfigure. In this particular case this happens because it can take coal power plants and coal mines some time to be decommissioned. Therefore, we observe a lag between the new policy and the effect that it intends to create.

You can open additional settings for coal by clicking on the three dots next to the coal policy, and there you can try to introduce additional supporting policies, e.g. the coal plant accelerated retirement. If you increase it up to 10 per cent, you will observe the change happening sooner; however, it did not eliminate the time lag in the system.

It is important to have awareness about this type of behaviour dynamics, because it demonstrates the vital importance of introducing changes in the system at the right time. For instance, in the context of climate change, if the countries want to meet their net zero targets, the policies incentivizing investment in green technologies need to be introduced very soon, as it will take time for the new technology to make a noticeable change in the system. This approach is quite different to short-term thinking and prioritizing immediate issues that traditional management logic tends to favour. This approach also demonstrates the need for a more holistic approach to developing interventions in the system. For instance, introducing electric cars alone will not change the Greenhouse Gas Net Emissions dramatically, as there will still be a lot of internal combustion engine cars waiting to reach end of life. Many governments combine this policy with various incentives, e.g. providing additional funding to buy back old fossil fuel cars and replace them with electric vehicles. If we add coal tax to them and invest in renewable energy, then we will see a cumulative effect of various policies leading to the reduction in Greenhouse Gas Net Emissions and lower temperature rise.

Rebound Effect

For the fifth demonstration follow these steps:

1 Reset all the values to original values.
2 In the top left graph, choose Financial → Cost of Energy.
3 In the top right graph, choose Final Energy Consumption Totals → Final Energy Consumption.
4 Subsidize renewables.

What you can see from the Cost of Energy graph is that it reduces, as expected. However, you can also notice that the amount of energy consumption increases.

This effect is called the rebound effect dynamic. As the energy becomes cheaper, people start using more of it. Therefore, you do not necessarily get the benefit that you would have hoped for when investing in renewables as a single source of energy. This example also demonstrates a balancing feedback loop in action (Figure 8.10). The subsidies in renewables lead to the reduced relative prices of renewables, which might ease consumers and industries into consuming more energy rather than only substituting fossil fuel energy with renewables. As a result, the impact on GHG emissions is not as significant as one would expect from subsidizing renewables. Just like in the example above, in this example decision makers might also need to think about the need for combining policies that would mitigate for this balancing effect.

Figure 8.10 Renewable energy consumption balancing feedback loop

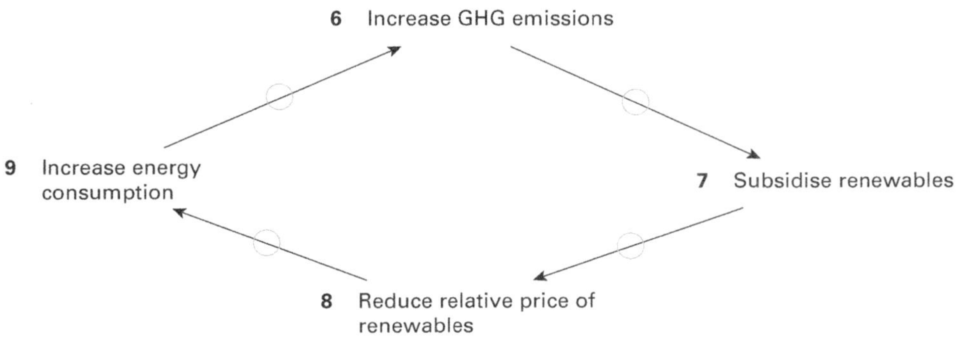

Crowding out

For the last demonstration:

1. Reset all the values to original values.
2. In the top left graph, choose Final Energy Consumption Types → Renewables Final Energy Consumption.
3. In the top right graph, choose Greenhouse Gas Emissions → Greenhouse Gas Net Emissions.
4. Now subsidize renewables.

You can observe how the energy consumption from renewables increases. Then try to add a New Zero-Carbon energy source, which might be a new breakthrough technology that we know nothing about yet, but it might come in the future. You can see how the energy consumption from renewables has dropped on the graph.

What you have observed in this demonstration is a crowding out dynamic. The two sources of energy start competing with each other. You might expect that with the new technology developed the consumption from clean energy sources might double, but this does not necessarily happen. The cumulative consumption from these sources will still be higher than renewables alone, but less than the sum of the two due to the competition element of the crowding out dynamic. This is the overlapping effect that you need to be aware of and that is opposite to the economies of scale that we have observed in the first demonstration.

CASE STUDY A systems thinking case study

As we have seen in this section, systems described using SSM methods can then be modelled using system dynamics and their future behaviour can be simulated. This method is particularly useful when thinking about complex systems, especially those spanning beyond the boundaries of one organization, such as the behaviour of an industry.

This case study is based around lithium and its utilization in products that rely on lithium batteries. Lithium batteries have traditionally been used in electronics as a fairly compact and well-performing source of energy storage. Recently there has been an increase in lithium demand, with growing demand from electric vehicles (EVs). Transport electrification is often seen as the most logical solution to the transport decarbonization challenge. However, this solution has one constraint. Most EVs rely on lithium batteries, and lithium is a non-renewable resource. Lithium can be partially recycled but a fraction of it will always be lost in the process. Currently there still are large deposits of unexploited lithium, but ultimately they will also be depleted.

We can try to understand how the system of lithium exploitation will behave and change over time by building a model of its system and simulating its behaviour over time. Figure 8.11 presents a simplified version of the lithium exploitation system. The demand for lithium is formed by two systems: electronics and EV markets (two stocks). While the electronics market is quite mature and has its natural growth rate, the EV market is still quite dynamic and shaped by numerous forces. On the one hand, in many countries, switching from conventional vehicles to EVs is incentivized and mandated through regulations. On the other hand, conventional vehicles have a lifespan, and so their replacement with EVs happens gradually. Here we might be able to observe capital stock turnover dynamic.

The required amount of lithium comes from mined lithium and recycled lithium. It is then processed, used in products and recycled. In Figure 8.11 we can observe these phases in a loop. However, part of lithium is never recycled, and part of recycled lithium is lost as non-recyclable in each cycle, which is determined by an average lifetime of lithium batteries. As a result, we always have a smaller amount of lithium going back to processing than in the previous cycle.

If we simulate the model, the graphs will look something like those in Figure 8.12. Exploration of lithium will be increasing until it peaks and starts rapidly declining when lithium reserves are depleted and lithium becomes increasingly difficult to mine. Processing of lithium in products will be trailing this dynamic. Unexploited reserves will be declining until they are fully depleted. Lithium in products will continue increasing until the total amount of lithium available starts decreasing.

Figure 8.11 Lithium exploitation system

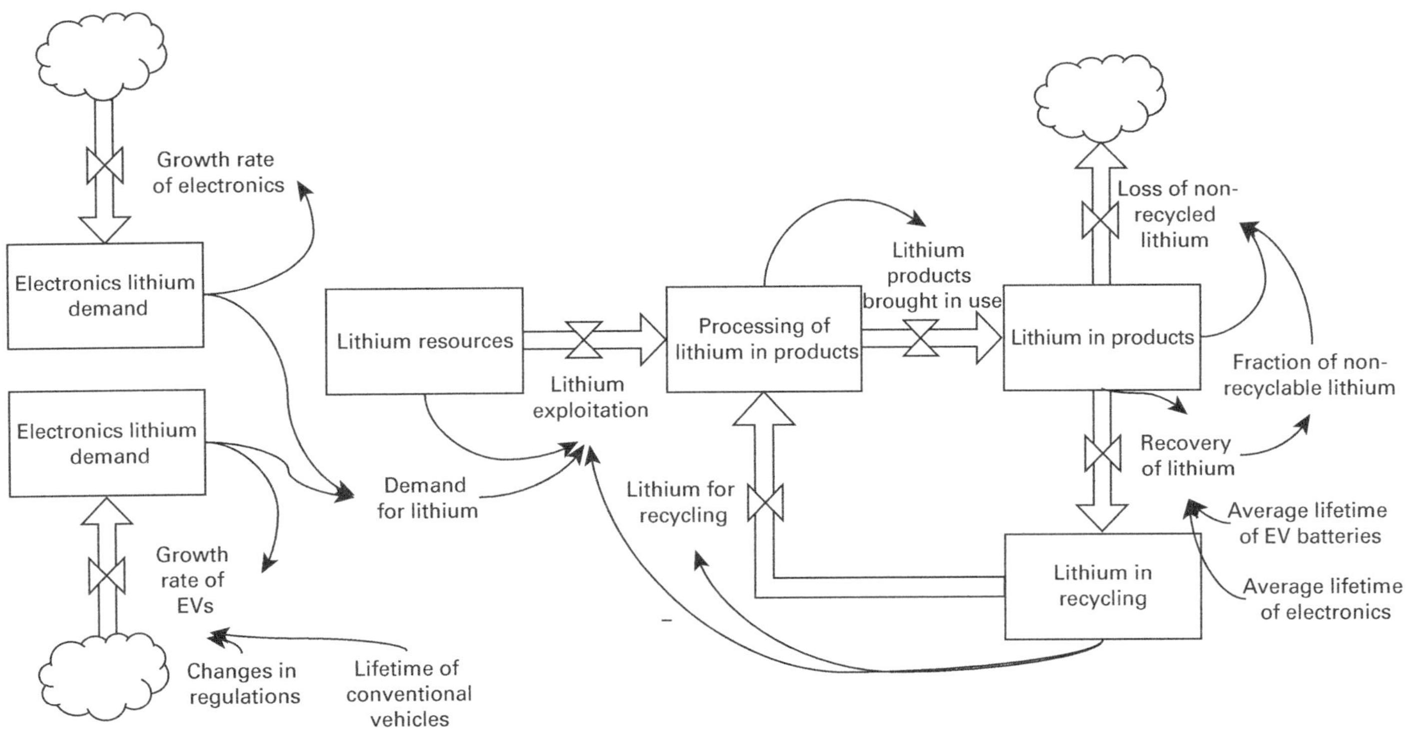

Figure 8.12 Simulation of the lithium exploitation system

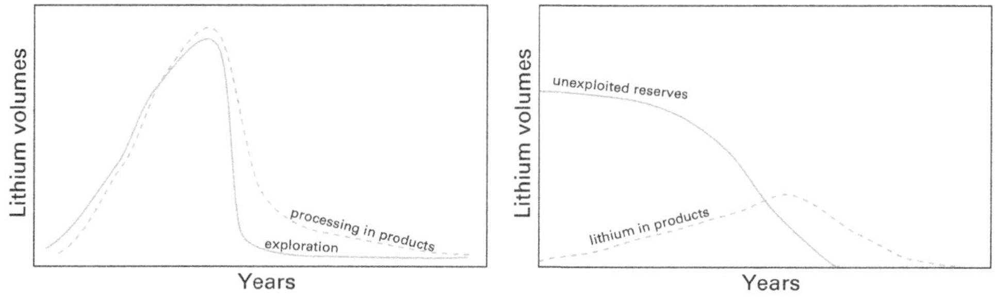

Reflective questions

- In the above case study, we have discussed how different systems (markets) shape another system (lithium exploitation) and how simulating the behaviour of this system demonstrates how the system will change in the future. Imagine that you are managing an electronics manufacturing company. How would the analysis of this system influence strategic decisions that you make?
- Think about the transportation system. If you are to make a decision about renewing the road fleet in your company, how would this analysis influence your choices?

8.5 Summary

In this chapter we have introduced system dynamics as an approach to simulate the future behaviour of a system, and discussed the basic building blocks of a stock and flow diagram as the foundation for system dynamics models and how this method builds on system modelling methods we discussed earlier. We have looked at the challenges associated with quantifying relationships in the model and analysis of the simulation results. Finally, we have discussed how system dynamics can help understand the behaviour of complex models and explore solutions to complex and wicked problems using the example of a climate change simulator. With the help of the simulator we have observed different types of behaviour that complex systems might exhibit.

REFLECTIVE EXERCISE

In the previous section, you have learnt to use the En-ROADS climate change simulator, which helps us understand how different policies and policy combinations can help address the climate change problem. For the purpose of this exercise, try to build your own scenario that would limit the temperature growth to 2°C. Be mindful of different behavioural dynamics that a complex system like this one might exhibit, when combining policies. When you have completed the challenge, reflect on how realistic this solution might be from the perspective of different stakeholders, such as governments of higher-income countries and lower-income countries, the oil and gas sector, the renewable energy sector, the manufacturing industry, agriculture, civil society and activist groups.

TEAM EXERCISE

Within your organization, select a system, e.g. supply chain or manufacturing, and think about an external challenge that might create disruptions in the future. Climate change is the most obvious one, but you can think of other disruptions, e.g. a disruptive technology, new entrant, another pandemic, regional military conflicts, etc. Then draw a simple causal loop diagram capturing forces and trends, and their relationships. Finally, think about how a stock and flow diagram might fit in the causal loop diagram – what would be the stocks and what would be the flows? How would you quantify these?

References

Bala, BK, Arshad, FM and Noh, KM (2017) *System Dynamics: Modelling and simulation*, Springer

Er Kara, M, Ghadge, A and Bititci, US (2021) Modelling the impact of climate change risk on supply chain performance, *International Journal of Production Research*, **59** (24), pp. 7317–35

Forrester, JW (1958) Industrial dynamics: a major breakthrough for decision makers, *Harvard Business Review*, **36** (4), pp. 37–66

Forrester, JW (1994) System dynamics, systems thinking, and soft OR, *System Dynamics Review*, **10** (2–3), pp. 245–56

Meadows, DH (2008) *Thinking in Systems: A primer*, Chelsea Green Publishing

Sterman, J (2000) *System Dynamics: Systems thinking and modeling for a complex world*, McGraw Hill

Changing complex systems 9

In the previous chapters we have gradually built understanding of complex systems, how they can be studied to describe them and understand their behaviour, and how their behaviour can be simulated to anticipate the performance of a system in the future. Ultimately, we analyse the systems to figure out how they can be improved. The objective of this chapter is to discuss the levers or leverage points in complex systems that can influence the behaviour of the systems. We will then take you through different types of levers, specifically structural levers, temporal levers, conceptual levers and boundary levers, and give examples of how they can be used in practice. It is important to note that the levers we describe in this book in a way refer to how people respond to change. In previous chapters we already emphasized that people's worldviews are shaped by their previous experiences, education, upbringing and so on, which in turn shape their beliefs, values and attitudes. Thus, a system's behaviour and how it responds to change is a reflection of evolution and interaction of these world views.

LEARNING OUTCOMES

- Understand
  - the essence of leverage points or levers
  - structural levers
  - temporal levers
  - boundary levers
  - conceptual levers
- Explore the concepts of robust and resilient systems

9.1 The levers for changing complex systems

The levers in systems are sometimes referred to as leverage points, the trim-tab introduced in Chapter 6, or places in the system where a small change can lead to large changes in the system's behaviour. For example, it might be an attempt to reduce undesirable behaviour or perhaps sometimes amplify a desirable one. In this chapter we are going to give a brief introduction to the types of levers that you might encounter in the system, and discuss where they can be found and how to make use of them to make changes in the system. In lower-complexity systems such levers and changes that need to happen in the system might be more obvious, but in more complex systems it is essential to understand what types of levers exist so as to understand where to look for them. Apart from that, simply identifying them is not sufficient. A more nuanced understanding of the nature of these levers and unintended consequences of applying pressure to them will also help you to avoid the mistake of moving them in the wrong direction and achieving the opposite of the intended result. The more complex the system is, the more unpredictable the consequences of interventions might be.

When we introduce the En-ROADS simulator, discussed in the previous chapter, to students, one particular policy always comes as a revelation to the vast majority of them. When they are asked to propose policies that would help to limit temperature growth, somebody always proposes to invest in economic growth. If you open the simulator and try to move the toggle of the economic growth policy to the right, you will see that the temperature rise goes up. It takes most people by surprise, but if you think about it, growth of established economic systems is based on consumption and its growth. In other words, we need to produce, distribute, consume and dispose of more goods to keep the economy growing. This paradigm is taken for granted and rarely challenged in mainstream discussions. However, from an environmental point of view, it achieves the opposite of reducing GHG emissions and curbing the temperature rise. In each step, we increase emissions to support the increase in consumption and positive externalities that it brings.

The levers can be broadly grouped into four categories: structural, temporal, conceptual and boundary levers. Most of the levers fall under the *structural* category. They are typically the easiest to identify and understand, but the impact of applying pressure to them tends to be less significant. The other types include the *temporal* levers that have to do with delays, the *boundary* levers that deal with the rules of the system, and the *conceptual* levers that are related to the goals and underlying assumptions. The latter are more difficult to recognize and then change, but they are the ones that would have the most profound impact on the system's behaviour. Let us look at each of these categories in more detail.

9.2 Structural levers

Structural levers can be defined as pressure points that engage with changing the rules of a system. They are associated with structural components of the system and include stocks and flows as well as reinforcing and balancing feedback loops. Structural levers are the most abundant type of levers and the easiest to recognize; however, applying pressure to these levers might not always be easy or even possible. The most obvious type of structural lever is the values of parameters that determine the dynamics, e.g. the rate of inflow and outflow that defines what happens to the stock over time. If we look at the bathtub dynamic discussed in the previous chapter, the rates of GHG emissions and absorption define the accumulation of GHG in the atmosphere. If the government decides to increase subsidies to renewable energy, introduce carbon tax or change regulations through standards to improve efficiency of energy use, all these measures will impact the flow of GHG emissions and subsequently slow down their accumulation in the atmosphere. Similarly, the government might decide to subsidize carbon capture technology or introduce stricter standards and regulations for the industry that would oblige them to implement carbon capture in the manufacturing processes. All these measures will increase the outflow of GHG emissions, which will also slow down the accumulation of GHG in the atmosphere.

The suggestions above are an example of how we can influence systems behaviour by changing the numerical values of the system parameters. Another example of structural levers is a buffer. When we talked about the theory of constraints in Chapter 4, you were introduced to the concept of a buffer as an intervention to minimize the flow disruptions in a bottleneck in case a disruption occurs at the other parts of the system. This intervention allowed us to maximize and stabilize performance of the system. In other words, we introduced the structural change in the system to make it more resilient.

In the organizational context, the availability of safety stocks in inventory management safeguards the ability of the system to satisfy demand without interruption while there might be delays or disruptions in supply. However, if you rely on this structural element too much, it might also make the system inflexible. If too large a buffer is absorbing the changes in the system in response to the changes outside the boundaries of the system, it reduces the system's ability to send such signals to feedback loops. Therefore, maintaining such buffers can be costly.

This brings us to the next structural lever: feedback loops. We have discussed the two types of feedback loops and their critical role in systems thinking and analysis throughout this book. Reinforcing feedback loops lead to growth and ultimately might collapse the system. In the previous chapter, we introduced a simple stock and flow diagram for the example of population change. That example contains a powerful feedback loop: the more babies are born, the more population will grow, the more babies will be born. However, this reinforcing loop is corrected with a balancing feedback loop: the more people are born, the more people will die, which limits the exponential growth of the reinforcing loop. Quite often, when reinforcing feedback loops emerge, sooner or later, balancing loops kick in. For example, if renewable energy technology gets progressively cheaper, and the technology more effective due to economies of scale, ultimately, all the energy will be replaced with renewable energy and the growth of the share of renewable energy in the energy portfolio will stop. However, such balancing loops are not always strong or effective. And thus, reinforcing loops should always be scrutinized in the system.

Balancing feedback loops, on the contrary, are a system's self-correcting mechanism, registering a deviation from a target value and enacting corrective measures to bring the actual value of the system's parameter back to its target. The basic example is a thermostat. When we think of a balancing loop as a lever, it might be a matter of introducing one or ensuring that the existing one works properly. In a free market economy, where price, demand and supply interact to naturally find the balance, price is the only lever governments can use to intervene in the system. Governments go to great lengths to protect such loops, specifically the price, from being artificially manipulated. Monopoly laws are one such example of protection. Other times governments introduce artificial manipulation themselves, for example, to change the target value (cost of renewable energy) by subsidizing renewable energy and taxing fossil fuels, thus making generated renewable energy cheaper and more competitive when compared to conventional methods.

Examining the mechanisms underpinning feedback loops can be one approach to identifying these levers. Let us take nuclear energy as an example. Putting aside the issue of nuclear waste, nuclear energy is perceived as a lower-carbon energy source when compared with coal, oil and gas. Furthermore, it is also cheaper than renewable energy. However, what the price does not include is the cost of decommissioning a nuclear plant. In the UK, one-third of the cost is met by the Nuclear Decommissioning Authority and two-thirds is borne by the government, the taxpayers to be precise, rather than included in the running cost of the operating company. This cost can be up to five times as high as the cost of building and maintaining a nuclear power plant during its operational lifecycle (NDA, 2019). Had the whole cost of nuclear energy been reflected in its price, the feedback loop would have led to a very different energy profile to what we see today (Figure 9.1).

In some cases, the balancing feedback loops might be missing naturally, or are too weak to generate desired changes in systems behaviour. Quite often, they have to do with the lack of information flow that might create a corrective action. For example, the depletion of ground waters used for irrigation might become visible to farmers too late to change agricultural practices, and will lead to catastrophic consequences for the agricultural system in the area.

Figure 9.1 Feedback loop in the energy portfolio

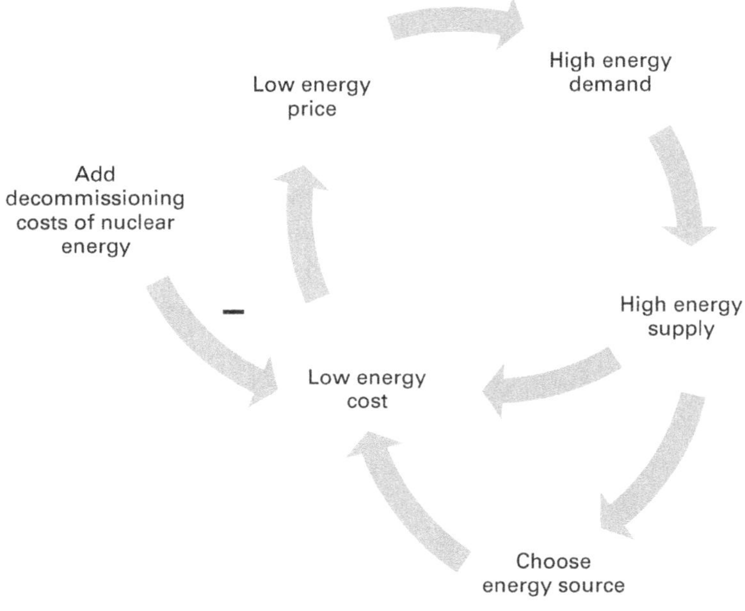

Even when it becomes obvious, the shortage of produce might lead to an increase in prices, prompting farmers to use what is left of the water to reap higher rewards. Introducing a corrective loop containing information flow might help to correct for external disturbance.

In the organizational context, analysing feedback loops can always provide opportunities for identifying levers in the system. The loop shown in Figure 9.2 provides an illustration of how the cycle of learning works in project management in an organization. In this loop we can identify several issues that can be addressed. For instance, the reports containing lessons learnt from a project are sanitized, which might make them less relevant for others to learn from. With reports just stored in a repository there is no visibility of work. This contributes to an already poor practice of checking for redundant projects. Addressing any of these issues would help improve project management in this organization.

9.3 Temporal levers

While structure levers have to do with the location of the lever in the system and its composition, temporal levers are focused on the temporal aspects of the system. They can be defined as pressure points that engage with changing

Figure 9.2 Example of looking for levers in a feedback loop

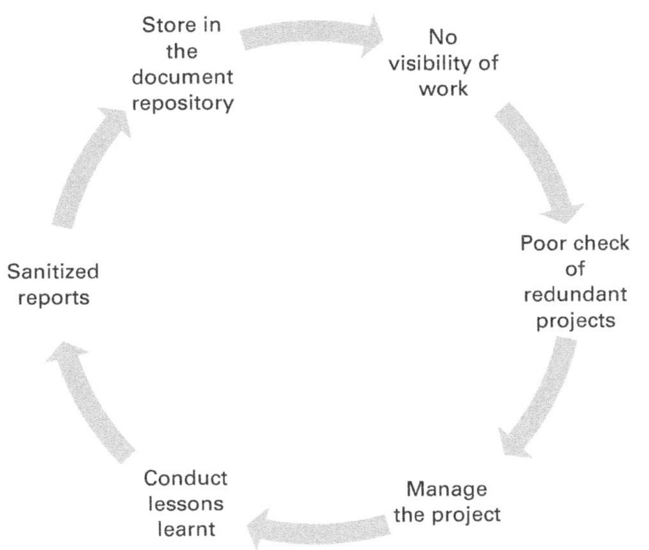

delays in a system. Specifically, they are delays in the system between a change in the system and its impact becoming apparent. Using the vocabulary of stock and flow diagrams, delays are the time lag between the input and output. In the previous chapter, we discussed time lag/capital stock turnover dynamic, which demonstrated a delay between incentivizing investment in carbon-neutral infrastructure or technology and the reduction in GHG emissions becoming noticeable. As was evident from the GHG emissions graph, it takes time to decommission old infrastructure and build a new one or replace old technology with new.

Some delays might occur in the form of adjustments in response to the information flow to the system. This type of delay is usually the easiest to address. Other delays are tightly bound with the structure and might be compensated for using buffers, as discussed in the previous section. The types of delays illustrated in the example of capital stock turnover dynamic are also tightly bound with the structure, but such levers are often not easy to change, even impossible. For example, the delays in infrastructural systems might be slightly shortened, accelerating the retirement of fossil fuel plants, but the delay cannot be completely eliminated. However, the impact of such changes on systems behaviour can be profound.

In the organizational context delays can occur or be embedded in the structure of many systems. For example, information about the performance of a process or organizational unit can flow in the form of key performance indicators. The frequency of updates of these indicators determines the delays in the system. It can be instantaneous, hourly, daily, weekly, monthly, etc., and more frequent updates are not always better for optimizing performance. For instance, if a sales manager receives updates about reaching their targets only once a month, they might lose an opportunity to work on their strategies to reach their targets. At the same time, they would not want to receive hourly updates on how they are doing. Delays might also need to be different for different groups. For instance, production managers might need to receive instantaneous information about any breakdowns on the production line. However, it might be beneficial for everyone if their managers receive this information with a delay, so that the production managers have time to resolve minor issues and their managers intervene only if a serious problem occurs that has not been resolved quickly.

9.4 Boundary levers

Boundary levers can be defined as pressure points that engage with changing the rules of a system. They can be applied to a system by changing the rules of the system, which is likely to redraw the boundaries of the system. The most obvious examples of such levers are policies, rules, regulations and laws. For example, when the UK introduced new regulations on disclosure of non-financial information in 2017, obliging companies to include in their annual reports information on environmental matters, their employees, social matters, respect for human rights, and anti-corruption and anti-bribery matters, it forced companies to create information flow, which was not necessarily present before then. Prior to the introduction of the regulations, disclosing any of this information would be a sign of goodwill, or a mechanism for companies to prove their claims for accountability to external stakeholders. With the introduction of the regulations, companies that did not necessarily make claims to incorporate business ethics and social responsibility into their strategy would also have to expand their boundaries and give more consideration to a broader range of stakeholders, such as local communities and local governments.

Boundary levers are very powerful and for that reason some companies spend millions every year lobbying their interests among policymakers. For example, Big Tech companies have become one of the largest lobbying industries. In the EU alone they spend over €97 million annually trying to water down regulations of the digital economy.

The extreme example of how powerful the boundary levers might be are the rules that enable self-organizing systems to self-organize. Here a set of rules can create systems that can adapt to changes in the surrounding environment or repair themselves. This is the ultimate form of systems resilience in nature. The best example of such systems is evolution itself, which is based on a set of rules directing how genes combine and mutate, creating new patterns and enabling species to adapt to change. Such systems are always decentralized in their organizational environment. In a business and management context, the network-based organizational structures such as holacracies, discussed in Chapter 2, are examples of such systems. In flat organizations, the hierarchy is dismantled and decision making is decentralized. The premise is that these organizations are more flexible, adaptable and resilient to dynamic environments. However, this approach is far from entering the mainstream. It is a scary thought for organizations to give away centralized or bureaucratic control.

In the organizational context, analysing the rules can lead to somewhat surprising insights about why certain behaviours persist and some initiatives fail. For example, when an organization wants to better manage their knowledge, they quite often run into a problem of people not being willing to share their knowledge and help others learn; this is rooted in what regulations govern people's work and what behaviours are rewarded. If experts are only paid for billable hours, they will not want to spend their time helping others by sharing their expertise, so making time spent on knowledge sharing billable might help to overcome this barrier. If only novel ideas are rewarded, people will not want to reuse what has already been done and learn from others, thus rewarding knowledge reuse and sharing mistakes might help address this problem.

9.5 Conceptual levers

Finally, the most powerful levers require engaging with a system at the conceptual level. They can be defined as pressure points that question the goals and the underlying assumptions/beliefs in a system. One such level is the purpose of the system. Re-evaluating the purpose of the system or its goals and changing them can set in motion the reconfiguration within the system structure and create new patterns of systems behaviour. In the simple example of a thermostat, changing the target temperature will trigger the corrective mechanisms in the balancing feedback loop to activate at different points in time. In more complex systems and subsystems interacting with each other, their goals might differ and even conflict with each other.

The conflict of goals is where problems can arise. For example, everybody would agree that keeping global temperature rise below 2°C to reduce the detrimental impact of climate change on the surrounding environment is a good goal. However, it requires a lot of different systems working together. It requires governments to introduce stricter environmental legislation, corporations to embed sustainability in strategy and business processes, consumers to change their habits and behaviours, etc. In this complex web of systems, corporations have their own goals, such as gaining a dominant position in the market or expanding to new markets. To achieve this goal, they might need to withstand fierce price competition, and therefore reduce their costs in any way possible. Shifting towards more environmentally sustainable processes can be costly and requires investment, which will not support their main corporate goal. For the government, the primary goal is to get re-elected. Achieving this goal, however, relies on a system of conflicting and competing goals of their stakeholders. Citizens, who are the ones electing the government, might have expectations that the government will commit to climate action and introduce stricter environmental regulations. However, they also expect the government to support economic stability and prosperity and, for example, create new jobs. This generates reliance of the government on businesses to support these goals and provide favourable business conditions. The government might even find itself competing with other governments to attract businesses to create new jobs, and they might do so by making more lenient environmental regulations. Furthermore, individual politicians and political parties might rely on businesses to help finance their campaigns in return for policy favours in the future, which might also have a negative impact on the environmental regulations.

In this example, you can see an emergent system of competing goals. Depending on which goals are more enforceable, and which systems have more power to prioritize their goals with the wider system, the whole system might steer in very different directions.

The other conceptual lever has to do with a paradigm, or in other words, the underlying assumptions, a set of unwritten rules or a system of beliefs or values that shape a system's behaviour. For example, one of the dominant beliefs in our society is that distribution of rewards by merit is justified, whereby we use qualifiers such as university degree and the reputation of the university as proxies for measuring merit and comparing individuals. Following this approach, graduates from the universities of Oxford and Cambridge are justified to be more professionally successful than those graduating from lower-ranked universities or those who do not have a university degree at all, because they're smarter, more hardworking, etc. However, if we think about how success is shaped at the beginning of a career path, when we do not have much professional experience, university ranking is particularly important and shapes opportunities that are opened to us. These opportunities define our professional growth that shapes further professional opportunities. The beliefs in merit persist despite overwhelming evidence, pointing towards other factors that could contribute to success, for example, luck, or family affluence that allows the parents to invest in better-quality education for their children (Sandel, 2020). As a result, inequalities in society keep reproducing, making social mobility less and less possible. Changing the paradigm can be hard, but it is not impossible. A carefully crafted narrative of a new paradigm can lead to profound changes in the system.

In the organizational context, different systems have different goals. These goals can be conflicting, which becomes more evident when different departments have to work with each other. For example, making a sales forecast of a product might require the involvement of different departments, such as sales, marketing, market planning and finance. Within this process different functions will pursue different interests. Marketing might want to show higher potential sales to gain higher budget for their campaigns. Sales might want the forecast to be lower, because then they can earn bonuses for achieving higher sales than planned. Market planning and finance might want the forecast to be as accurate as possible, because it will help them achieve better operational efficiency and higher precision in financial calculations. Such conflicting goals might help to balance the system as long as none of the functions dominate the discussion. However, giving higher powers to one of the functions might create an imbalance and ultimately lower the performance of the whole system.

9.6 Robust and resilient systems

So far in this chapter we have talked about the concept of levers or small changes that can lead to profound changes in the whole system's behaviour. It is important to mention the opposite of this phenomenon in systems thinking terms, namely **robust** or even stubborn systems, which are difficult to change even in response to a major change. In engineering systems robustness is usually perceived as a positive characteristic and is broadly defined as an ability of a system to maintain its performance in response to changes in the external environment or variations in internal parameters. In other words, robust systems are less sensitive to such variations or disturbances.

The other side of such a characteristic is that the system becomes less sensitive to change and less flexible in its ability to adapt. It might be no coincidence that most robust systems tend to be the most hierarchical ones, and hierarchical systems tend to exhibit lower levels of flexibility. In such systems, finding pressure points or levers can be very difficult and even large-scale changes might fail to produce desirable results.

Robustness in systems can be achieved through various mechanisms, such as controls, discussed extensively in this book, redundancies as a fail-safe mechanism, modularity and decoupling. If a system exhibits robust behaviour to the extent that it does not evolve in response to change, these are the mechanisms that can be identified to introduce change to the system and change its behaviour.

Robustness is quite often confused with resilience; however, the two terms describe systems with different characteristics. Although resilience is a much-debated term, in systems thinking **resilient systems** are defined as those systems that can return to a stable state in response to a disturbance. Unlike robustness, resilience is somewhat more reactive. While robust systems actively resist the disturbance to maintain performance, resilient systems can temporarily be disrupted but are able to recover or bounce back to their stable state after the disturbance has occurred. One quality is not necessarily better than the other, and each of them will find its own area of application.

CASE STUDY A systems thinking case study

In this case study we will look at how the levers covered in this chapter can be applied to a system to change its behaviour. We will continue with the case study of lithium exploitation described in the previous chapter and use the model to try to identify pressure points in the system.

The types of changes we are looking for in the system will depend on the goals we are trying to achieve. In this case study we are dealing with three interconnected systems that might have conflicting goals. For instance, we might want to extend the exploitation of lithium over a longer period of time, but this might have to be achieved at the cost of growth rates of electronics and electronic vehicles (EVs). Or we might want to increase decarbonization of transportation, in which case we might want to achieve the opposite – increase the growth rate of EVs.

If we focus on lithium exploitation as the main system, its objective will be to keep exploiting lithium in products for as long as possible. The most obvious **structural levers** are the rates of flow. For instance, we might want to decrease the amount of lithium that does not get recycled. This might be achieved by measures like implementing regulations that would increase the responsibility of producers or consumers for disposal of used products or incentivizing recycling of electronics. The other area that impacts the system is the demand created by the markets that consume lithium batteries, i.e. electronics and EVs. Thus, stretching available lithium might be possible by limiting the growth of these two markets. We have already seen attempts in legislation to limit the growth of electronics, such as the right to repair in the UK. Attempts to limit the growth of EVs might be somewhat more controversial, as EVs are seen as one of the main solutions for decarbonizing transportation.

If we look for **temporal levers**, two systems contain parameters related to the average lifetime. The average lifetime of batteries might be extended if they are properly taken care of during their exploitation. This is a behavioural challenge and would require behavioural interventions. The other temporal parameter is the average lifetime of conventional vehicles. Extending it will slow down the growth rate of EVs, and thus reduce the demand for lithium; however, such a solution would conflict with the goal of the decarbonization of transportation. It is highly likely that policy makers will introduce regulations and incentives to stimulate the opposite – switch faster from conventional vehicles to EVs.

If we look for **boundary levers**, in essence, they have been partly covered as approaches to influence temporal or structural levers. In this system, these are the regulations that governments can use to influence structural or temporal components of the system. They might also be the rules in adjacent systems. For instance, instead of simply incentivizing car owners to replace their conventional cars with electric ones, governments could consider alternative transportation models, such as different models of vehicle sharing. This will reduce the total number of vehicles required to transport the same amount of people, and reduce the amount of lithium required to support EVs in the future.

Finally, if we look at **conceptual levels**, we might want to consider underlying assumptions and beliefs in this and adjacent systems. For instance, in the system where we might want to limit the number of EVs to stretch lithium reserves, we might want to change the dominant paradigm of car ownership, where alternatives are available and convenient. This is a behavioural problem that might require a behavioural intervention.

Reflective questions

- In the above case study we have discussed different levers or pressure points in the system of lithium exploitation. Can you think of any other pressure points in the system or other approaches to influence these pressure points?
- Think about the transportation system. If you are to make a decision about renewing the road fleet in your company, how would each of the proposed changes in the system influence your choices?

9.7 Summary

In this chapter we have discussed the levers or pressure points in systems, and how engaging with them can help create changes in a system's behaviour. We have discussed the concept of levers and the reasons for paying close attention to them, particularly in complex systems. Then we looked at structural, temporal, boundary and conceptual levers, how they can be identified, and how you can work with them to create change.

REFLECTIVE EXERCISE

Take the example of population growth from the previous chapter, try to apply the model to your country and think about the levers in the system that might be used to change the dynamic of the system. To engage with the model at this level, you might need to think about the factor contributing to different rates within the system as well as the overall goal of the system. For example, a country might want to stimulate population growth or, on the contrary, slow it down.

Let us assume that we are analysing population growth in a country that has a trend for an ageing population. This trend indicates that the proportion of older population in the distribution of age groups keeps increasing, and the country might want to change this dynamic and increase the proportion of younger population.

If we look at the *structural* levers, the first example of what could be considered in the system is the numerical values of the parameters in the system, such as the amount of child support that each family receives. If this value is increased, the higher financial support might make it easier for families to have more kids. Similarly, other forms of child support might be revised, such as government provisions for childcare in nurseries and kindergartens. The other type of structural lever relevant in this example is feedback loops. In the diagram in Chapter 8 (Figure 8.2) we can identify several balancing loops involving mortality rates. You might want to examine the mortality rates of young adults in the system and the key reasons causing potentially high mortality rates in this age group. For example, if you discover that many young adults die in traffic accidents due to reckless driving, then an intervention aimed at increasing road safety might help reduce this factor. You might also consider other mortality rate factors, such as rates of outmigration. If young adults find few employment opportunities, they will be looking for opportunities elsewhere and the increase in reproduction rates or other interventions will at the end be balanced out by this feedback loop.

With regard to the *temporal* levers, the key factor to consider is the delay between the increase in reproduction rates and the surplus of new-born babies reaching young adulthood. This delay cannot be changed, as babies' growth cannot be accelerated. Therefore, you might want to consider complementary temporary interventions to see the changes in the system earlier, such as changing immigration policies for certain age groups.

If we look at the *boundary* levers, you might want to consider why an ageing population is a concern. In many countries the primary concern has to do with taxpayer burden, specifically that the decreased proportion of the population has to support the pensions of the increased proportion of the population. In many high-income countries that have observed the ageing population trend for the past few decades, this has led to changes in the rules of the system with regard to how the retirement age is defined as well as how pensions are being financed. As a result, the retirement age was decreased, while pensions are at least partially funded through private savings, making it a duty of each individual to think about their retirement (through mandatory pension contributions into a private pension fund).

Finally, at the *conceptual* level, you might want to look at the underlying assumptions and beliefs underpinning the system. For example, in many countries it is still common to see motherhood as getting in the way of professional growth. With more opportunities to fulfil themselves, women might see children as a distraction or a potential cause for discrimination in the workplace, e.g. being passed on promotion because they have a young child and therefore being perceived as not able to commit themselves fully to work. Changing the dominating narrative and normalizing balancing family and professional duties, as well as creating expectations for companies to support young parents, might have a profound impact on the system in terms of changing the underlying assumptions and beliefs that determine success.

TEAM EXERCISE

In the previous chapter, you were asked to take a system within your organization and analyse the impact of external environments, such as climate change, on this system. Based on this analysis you were asked to build a causal loop diagram and then convert it into a stock and flow diagram. Using the results of the exercise from the previous chapter, try to identify potential levers in the system. Start with structural and temporal levers, as they tend to be the easiest to identify. Then look for boundary levers and finally scrutinize whether the system might have conceptual levers based on the underlying assumptions and dominating paradigm within which the system exists.

References

Meadows, D. H. (2008). Thinking in systems: A primer. Chelsea Green Publishing.

NDA (2019) Nuclear provision: the cost of cleaning up Britain's historic nuclear sites, https://www.gov.uk/government/publications/nuclear-provision-explaining-the-cost-of-cleaning-up-britains-nuclear-legacy/nuclear-provision-explaining-the-cost-of-cleaning-up-britains-nuclear-legacy (archived at https://perma.cc/DYX8-N5MY)

Sandel, MJ (2020) *The Tyranny of Merit: What's become of the common good?* Penguin UK

Further reading

Meadows, D H (2008), *Thinking in Systems: A primer*, Chelsea Green Publishing

PART FOUR
The future

In this final part of the book we will look into the future and consider systems that do not yet exist. In Chapter 10 we discuss creativity and innovation, and barriers to thinking about the future creatively and innovatively. We then discuss why thinking about alternative futures is more useful than trying to predict the future and guide you through various aspects of trying to imagine systems that do not yet exist, specifically by identifying signals and drivers, and then creating alternative scenarios of a future system. In this chapter we also discuss how ideas about the future systems can be elicited using roleplay or alternate reality games.

Future systems thinking 10

We started discussing futures thinking in Chapter 8, looking at how we can think of a future system's behaviour. Specifically, we explored what the behaviour of the existing system might be in the future and how we can anticipate the ways in which the system will evolve. We looked at system dynamics as a method that can be used in order to simulate the behaviour of an existing system. In this chapter we will explore different ways to imagine systems.

In particular, we will focus on thinking about the systems that do not yet exist but might emerge in the future. We will start by discussing creativity and innovation and barriers to thinking about the future creatively and innovatively. We will then discuss why thinking about alternative futures is more useful than trying to predict the future and guide the reader through various aspects of trying to imagine systems that do not yet exist, specifically by identifying signals and drivers, and then creating alternative scenarios of a future system. The penultimate section will discuss how ideas about future systems can be elicited using alternate reality games.

LEARNING OUTCOMES

- Distinguish between creativity and innovation
- Recognize barriers to innovation
- Understand
  - future thinking
  - trends
  - signals
  - scenarios

  - scenario thinking
  - roleplay
  - alternate reality games
- Able to build scenarios of alternative futures

10.1 Creativity and innovation

It is often the case that a simple change can make a big difference to our lives, organizations and societies; however, this simple change can also be difficult to identify. In Chapter 6 we outlined how Soft Systems Methodology, together with some related techniques such as storytelling, rich pictures and causal loop diagrams, can engage people in a conversation about the system we are concerned with. And usually it is these conversations that lead to identifying the simple unexpected change we can make to change the behaviour of a large, complex system. However, often we look back and wonder in amazement at the simplicity of the change and why we did not think of it ourselves.

In Chapter 9 we discussed some of the types of changes in the system that might lead to significant changes in its behaviour. In practice, coming up with simple ideas that result in changes to complex systems is not easy; it requires a degree of creativity and innovation, which in turn requires us to come up with ideas, evaluate these ideas, select potential ideas, develop the ideas, implement them, learn about how they work and refine them.

The word/term creativity is quite often used in conjunction with innovation. Creativity is about ideas, not necessarily about new, unique or groundbreaking ideas – it is just about ideas. Innovation can be defined as a process of taking those ideas and putting them together in new ways, or making something useful from them. For example, in the business context, we would want to make those ideas marketable. It is not enough to have an idea; the idea needs to be turned it into a product or service that would be beneficial for the business and interesting for the customers.

The interrelationship between creativity and innovation can be well illustrated with the help of the innovation funnel, illustrated in Figure 10.1. You might have seen it before; it is not new and it exists in different variations. For example, you might find a different version of it for opening innovation.

All of them will have the same basic principle. We have lots of ideas coming in and then there is an iterative innovation process that sorts those ideas and filters some of them out. In most cases those ideas that are the most viable are combined or integrated through iterations within the innovation process and transformed into the final output. There can be different types of innovation, such as product innovation, process innovation, service innovation, business model innovation, etc. In all of these cases, lots of ideas get funnelled through and filtered out. In the process, some ideas might be combined, other ideas might come from the outside. And then these ideas are transformed into something useful.

10.2 Barriers to creativity and innovation

We have somewhat demonstrated this journey in the example above. However, throughout our practice we have also observed a number of factors that constrain the emergence of these ideas. In this section our aim is to summarize five of the common constraints that prevent us from innovating the system.

The first constraint is **how we define innovation**. When we ask people what innovation is, the definition is usually something as follows: *Innovation is about coming up with new/novel/wacky/different ideas and developing something useful from them*. The problem with this definition of innovation is the qualifications we put in front of the 'idea'. Such as *new* idea, *novel* idea, *wacky* idea and so on. These qualifications place conditions that prevent people from sharing their ideas just in case they are not new, novel or wacky. So, if we want to innovate the system, we need to encourage people just to come up with ideas – they do not need to be new, novel, wacky or different.

Figure 10.1 Innovation funnel

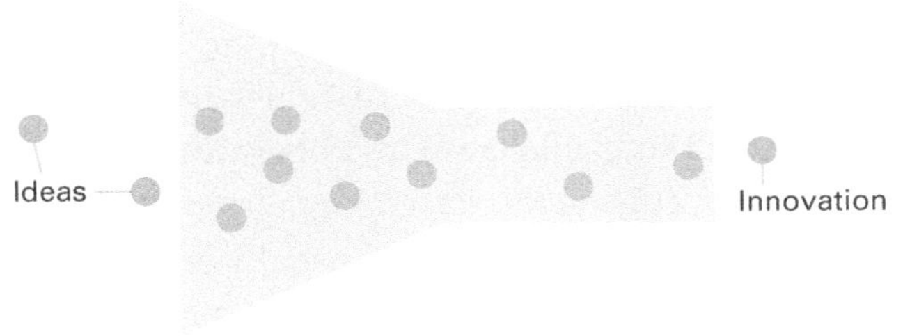

The second constraint is **psychological safety**. That is the permission individuals give to themselves to come up with ideas, no matter how silly. Naturally the individual is not likely to share any ideas if the group they are working within does not give them the permission to come up with ideas. Ridiculing ideas, or labelling them as silly or stupid, will just prevent people from coming up with ideas. If people feel psychologically safe, they are more likely to come up with ideas, even silly ones. How often have you experienced a situation where someone's silly idea or even a joke sparked something really useful in someone else's mind? We certainly have, more than once.

This brings us to the third constraint. Many of us do not appreciate that **innovation is a group process**. People are faced with a situation; different people see the problem or situation from different perspectives and they start throwing some ideas; their ideas spark other ideas in other people's minds; ideas are combined and developed in people's minds and eventually someone comes up with the game-changing idea. If we can tap into the power of this network and exploit it, we are more likely to be innovative about the system we are trying to influence.

The fourth constraint is **lack of diversity**. If you have worked with the same group of people for a long time you may know them well, you may know how they think and sometimes when something happens at a meeting, you may even know what is going through their heads. This is because you are like them and you think like them. Such a group is less likely to be innovative as they will come with the same or similar ideas, thinking like one brain and failing to think out of the box. If this is the case, it is often worthwhile bringing in some diversity into the team in terms of education, experience, gender, culture, etc. One of the most interesting system innovation exercises we have been involved in was with an engineering company that comprised engineers that had worked with each other for over 20 years. To mix the group, we brought in customers' marketing people, people from a local enterprise support agency, a few art school students and a couple of social sciences graduates. This disrupted the 'one brain' thinking and resulted in ideas that were developed into the solutions that resolved a number of issues with the way the company delivered their products and services to customers.

The fifth and final constraint to innovating the system is the **subconscious assumptions** that we fail to challenge. This is best illustrated by a couple of examples. I often put six dots on the screen, organized like a domino, and ask the audience to write down what they see. I usually get back answers like six dots, two groups of three dots, a domino and so on. I get this response despite the fact that I have not asked them what they see on the screen. They could have easily said they see a person standing in front of them presenting something (i.e. me). If they are sitting at the very back of the lecture room, they could have even said that they see a bunch of heads in front of them. But they rarely do. In the second part of the exercise, I ask them to draw a single straight line to join the six dots together. People struggle with pen and paper, they draw curves, squiggly lines etc., but they rarely think about folding the paper or even just getting a big fat pen or brush to join the six dots by a single straight line. This is even after just having been told, during the first part of the exercise, that our subconscious assumptions constrain our ability to innovate. Often, surfacing these unwritten, uncommunicated subconscious assumptions and then challenging them leads to ideas emerging that result in some game-changing solutions.

10.3 Imagining systems that do not yet exist

The above discussion provides grounds for the mindset required for thinking about future systems. Imagining future systems is usually the job of futurists, those people who try to imagine how the future might look and what the alternatives might be. When trying to imagine future systems, we are not trying to predict the future. Rather, we are trying to imagine different futures and then analyse which future is more desirable or what conditions are required for a particular future to happen, what future we might not want and what could be done for that future not to happen. Therefore, do not seek statistical accuracy in the forecast. Instead, we are interested in alternative views of the future in order to become more proactive in shaping the future the way we want it to happen.

Signals and drivers are key aspects that inform futurologists' work (Howard, 2021). For them, signals are a glimpse of the future. Then they try to think about what is behind these signals, i.e. the drivers. In essence, the signals become a tool in the dark that shows what the way might look like, while the drivers are the driving force behind these signals.

Signals

Everything that we see around us might potentially be a signal. There are certain characteristics of the strong signals that are worth considering. Firstly, they can be observed and they are quite concrete. You can experience them, you can look around them, and see them happening. Secondly, they are not evenly distributed, and this is another important feature of the signal. The signals are interesting because they show us what might happen in the future that is already here. However, they cannot be found everywhere yet. Once they become commonplace, the change has already happened and the whole system has started to change. So it is important to see the signals at an early stage. There will be many such signals and most of these signals may not come to anything, but some will gain traction and will start shaping the future. It is the job of the futurologists to try to think about what the future systems might look like if the identified signal becomes widespread and more evenly distributed. In other words, you can think of them as early signs that change might be coming.

For example, for a while we have seen interesting developments in chatbots. Most of the commercially viable chatbots were limited to automated answering of questions in customer service. Anything more sophisticated was limited to (not always successful) experiments with introducing chatbots that try to mimic human interactions, or personal assistants like Amazon's Alexa, which are still largely toys. However, these were signals that conversational AI will soon revolutionize the way we interact with technology. The introduction of ChatGPT, which was integrated into Microsoft's search engine, might be one such step that will change how we search for information and make AI more widespread and mainstream.

Signals indicate to us that things might become different, for better or worse. They are showing some change, a shift or a disruption that is underway, and it's up to us to understand what that change or disruption might look like. Of course, some signals might indicate a promising future but then something else happens and they come to nothing, but that is an essential part of futures thinking.

Examples of signals include new technology, a scientific breakthrough that changes the way we understand our world, new business models that become possible, perhaps because of new technology, new government policies or projects, demographic changes, new laws, etc. Let us look at a specific example.

Here is an example of a signal. In April 2022 the French government banned short-haul flights where a train or bus alternative of two-and-a-half hours or less exists. Although the environmental impact of different types of transport has been discussed for a while, with calls for making more environmentally friendly choices, this is the first time a government has taken a more radical step in outlawing a more polluting type. Take a moment and think what it might mean for the transportation and adjacent systems and what the future might look like if this kind of law becomes more widespread.

Perhaps this law indicates a new trend that environmental parameters of different modes of transport, specifically their contribution to GHG emissions per passenger, will become a more dominant characteristic in the regulations of transport. It might become a prevailing practice for governments to encourage certain behaviours among passengers through a more nuanced system of regulations, from heavy taxation, to outlawing dirtier options, to incentivizing cleaner ones. Maybe private jets will be among the other options to be targeted for heavy regulations next. This might have a severe impact on the industry of private jet hire. It might also make the development of new types of individual air transport, like quadcopters, less attractive for investment, as they certainly will not be among the cleanest options of individual transportation available, unless of course they are powered by clean energy. What happens if aeroplanes powered by clean energy become commercially available? Would they be exempt from strict regulations? Perhaps vehicle occupancy will become one of the new characteristics to be considered in taxing or even allowing operations. Would flights with the number of passengers below a threshold not be allowed to run? In January 2022 Lufthansa admitted that they might fly 18,000 empty planes to keep airport slots. Would this type of behaviour potentially be banned under new regulations? And how would it impact airport operations if flights are subject to occupancy regulations? Perhaps similar regulations might be imposed on private vehicles to encourage car sharing. How would these regulations be enforced? They might also accelerate the development of new services, like demand-responsive transport. This is just an example of how you might work with a signal you have identified. You start unpacking it and asking what it would mean in different systems, and what the concerns and possibilities are that we haven't thought of yet.

One way to practise your skill in identifying and working with signals is to think about something that you are sure will not change in the next 10 years. Then you can try to disprove yourself and imagine how this thing might change, as well as starting to look for signals that might indicate a change. For example, you might say that we will still have to work. This is a valid point, but we can find examples of cities and countries that started experimenting with universal basic income, where every citizen of a city is guaranteed an income, which in essence replaces the social benefits system.

This means, in principle, they do not have to work if they do not want to. What would this mean, if you do not have to work to meet your basic needs? Would the meaning of work change? What would you do with your freed time? Many people find meaning in the work that they do. How would they then construct a new meaning in life? Would the available jobs become more competitive? And would compensation no longer be the primary motivation? How would the country find workers for the jobs that are unappealing, but essential for the public benefit, like waste collection? In fact, we can look for potential answers to these questions in science fiction, like Star Trek. In the Star Trek universe money has become obsolete and instead people are working to better themselves or to provide service for the common good. Although work is not mandatory, as all the basic needs of the citizens are met, everybody is always busy doing something.

When you have identified an interesting signal, it is useful to think about what kind of change it represents, from what to what, and what the driver of change is behind this signal as well as what might give the signal momentum. This is when we start to define drivers behind the signals and discuss what might make these signals more widespread in the future. With these considerations you can then start imagining what the world will look like in the future if the signal gets amplified and more evenly distributed.

Drivers

The next important aspect of the work of futurists is the **drivers**. Signals might be concrete examples of what might change in the future; drivers are the driving force behind signals. It is very important to identify those powerful drivers as they make us think about what might happen in the future, how the world might change and in what direction. For example, if we have encountered a new significant scientific discovery or technology development, we might think about the powerful drivers that might make this technology more widespread. It might be a change in public opinion, a political trend, etc.

The questions that might help you work with drivers include what might become much more or less common in the next decade or so as a result of this driver, what might become possible in the future that is not possible today, what new problems might it lead to that we do not have today?

The pandemic is an example of a recent driver that has created a significant shift in how we do things in everyday life, how we work. A significant proportion of people moved to remote working, at least for a period of time. As we gradually shift back to 'normal', hybrid working is becoming more common. Perhaps in the future, when hybrid/remote working becomes more normalized and well-established, it will be much more common for people to live in a place or even a country different from where they work. Physical location of offices will become much less important for companies when attracting new talent, while countries might start competing with each other to attract working adults and their spending power. This shift will also have an impact on the commercial real estate market, particularly in the cities with the most expensive properties, like New York or London. Already now these places are seeing a drop in demand, and this trend might continue. Imagine being able to live on a Mediterranean or Caribbean island but work from home for a company based in New York, Tokyo, Shanghai or London.

Another example of a powerful driver is climate change. We can already observe the changes driven by this trend, such as more frequent and extreme weather events. The degree of change climate change will bring is still in question, but it will change how the system will work in the future. In Chapter 8 we discussed how climate change might impact existing supply chains. If we apply principles of thinking about future systems, we might try to imagine how new supply chains might look. For instance, supply chains might become more localized, as international shipments might be more frequently disrupted by increasingly unpredictable weather. Hence, production might need to become more localized. Already now there is a trend to consume food that has been grown locally, in an attempt to minimize carbon footprint. This trend might continue to grow, driven by the instability of global supply chains. Other systems, for example energy, will also be significantly impacted by climate change. We often look at energy systems as a mitigating strategy to reduce carbon emissions; with intensified extreme weather events, the energy grid will become more vulnerable, and already now developers have started thinking about not only mitigating for extreme weather, but also harnessing it. For instance, in tropical areas that are prone to typhoons, countries have started experimenting with vertical turbines that can harvest energy from typhoons and work during times when wind turbines become non-operational. Energy generation might also become increasingly more distributed and stability and predictability of energy generation might become a more significant factor in assigning value to different generation points. This, for example, might reshape the way manufacturing facilities are distributed, away from the existing manufacturing clusters and closer to the sources of energy generation, such as large offshore wind farms.

Sometimes the signals can be there for a long time, and you might start thinking about what drivers could potentially make these signals more widespread. For example, we have observed signals for electric cars for a long time. The first electric vehicle was developed by Robert Anderson in 1932. The first practical models appeared in the 1980s, e.g. the Sinclair C5. But it was increasing concern for the environment and cleaner energy (the driver) that accelerated the development and adoption of electric vehicles.

Working with drivers and trying to unpack how systems might look in the future will help to imagine new system configurations. It might be useful to look at bundles of drivers and try to develop different scenarios of what the future might look like. For instance, we can try to combine the climate change trend with another powerful trend – the shift in demographic distribution around the world. Many countries, traditionally higher-income countries, are experiencing ageing populations. Increasingly the proportion of working populations is shifting to other geographic regions, first and foremost Africa. What would it mean for energy systems and manufacturing systems? If in the future finding a workforce is much easier in Africa, would this lead to moving manufacturing clusters to African countries? How would energy systems need to be reconfigured to support this shift and how would the impact of climate change need to be accounted for? For example, if areas of land become no longer suitable for agriculture because of frequent droughts, perhaps they might be turned into large solar farms. And how would the regulatory frameworks of specific countries need to change to support new opportunities? Answering these and other questions will help you imagine how new systems might look and what scenarios might be possible in the future.

10.4 Scenario thinking

Building scenarios is at the heart of futures thinking as it helps to better prepare for the future. However, it is common to encounter more conventional thinking about the future that is based on extrapolation of the past. In other words, we tend to assume that in the future we will see more of the past. However, if we think about it, we approach a more immediate future in everyday life more diligently and apply scenario planning to important situations concerning us. For example, when preparing for a sales meeting, in our mind we might play out different developments, prepare different responses and think about alternative solutions depending on the response of the potential customer. This helps us to make a better impression.

Thinking in terms of scenarios is particularly important because we cannot ignore the possibility of improbable events occurring. In business in particular, this might cost the future of an organization. In his book *The Black Swan* (2007), Nassim Nicholas Taleb coined the eponymous term to describe such events. They are improbable, but might have a devastating impact on a system if no provisions are made to prepare for what we might do in case it happens. Among recent events the Covid-19 pandemic was a major black swan. In retrospect we can see that the occurrence of such an event was not entirely improbable. We have seen local and regional outbreaks of different viruses, such as the Ebola outbreak in Western Africa in 2014 and the SARS outbreak in 2003 which affected 29 countries, and epidemiologists have been warning about the risk of a larger-scale event occurring. However, if we looked at the risk analysis of your company pre-pandemic, it is unlikely that you would see the risk of disruptions caused by an epidemic in the document.

It is important to reiterate that we cannot predict the future, and this is not the purpose of futures thinking. Instead, we can consider different alternatives and our responses to these alternatives, which can help organizations be better prepared for the future. Scenario planning has been actively practised in organizations over the past 50 years and has experienced a new wave of interest in the past decade (Courtney et al, 2013; Wilkinson and Kupers, 2013).

Cairns and Wright (2017) suggest a term, *Scenario Thinking*, and propose an eight-stage approach to applying it in organizations, which overlaps with and builds on other approaches to scenario building. They emphasize the importance of working with a broad range of stakeholders, particularly key stakeholders, and the need to consider power relationships between different stakeholders and their interests in the system (the purpose of the system for different actors and the conflict of goals, discussed in Chapters 8 and 9). This helps to make inferences about the impact of different drivers more realistic. If we take the viewpoint of the key stakeholders in the system, who are, however, on the receiving end and have no decision power over shaping the system, the discussion about what a system might look like in the future is then more likely to be fantasizing about the future than thinking about what is possible. Furthermore, because futures thinking can be a time- and resource-consuming process, developing different scenarios with stakeholders can also be iterative, whereby you might develop initial narratives and then validate them with the stakeholders and explore causality with them. Opposite to causal mapping, discussed in Chapter 7, the purpose of engaging with stakeholders is not to develop shared understanding and reach consensus, but rather to explore differences in views of the future.

Drivers and signals can provide evidence as to why a particular scenario is plausible. Cairns and Wright propose clustering the drivers – or the driving forces, as they refer to them – and evaluating them based on uncertainty and impact. In this book we are not going into details of their methodology; you can read more about it in their book, *Scenario Thinking*. One step in their methodology that is consistent with systems thinking is related to exploring causality. Before moving to building scenarios, it is worth considering how different drivers might relate to each other using the causal mapping method discussed earlier in this book.

For example, Figure 10.2 presents causal links between some of the trends that can shape how artisan fisheries in the Choco region of Colombia might look in the future. We can see that there is an increasing realization of the need to protect biodiversity, and a growing engagement of the local communities to commit to environmental stewardship, such as good fishing practices. But at the same time there are multiple other trends that have a negative impact on this trend, such as climate change, plans to start large infrastructural projects such as building a new port in Tribuga and a road network in the region, and risk of overfishing, if this is the sole livelihood for fishermen.

Figure 10.2 Causal links between different trends shaping the future of artisan fisheries in the Choco region of Colombia

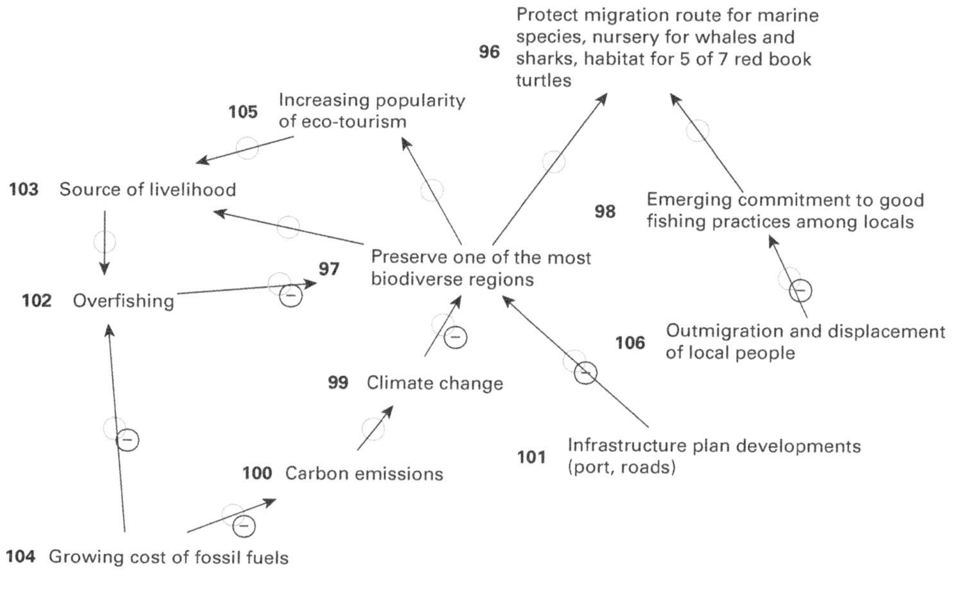

Looking at trends through a causal map helps to build more specific scenarios of what the future might look like and understand the conditions that make cause one trend to prevail over other trends, or how they may work in synergy.

10.5 Building scenarios

One of the approaches to looking at future scenarios frequently used in futures thinking was developed in the Hawaii Research Center for Futures Studies (Dator, 2009). The proposed framework describes four future archetypes: Growth, Limits and Discipline, Decline and Collapse, and Transformation.

The *Growth* scenario assumes that the identified drivers or trends will continue on the current trajectory and therefore the behaviour of the systems will continue in a predictable pattern. Such thinking is dominant in large bureaucratic organizations that do not foresee that any radical change might happen in the future. Instead, the future will be an amplified version of the present. In a way, it is a baseline scenario.

The *Limits and Discipline* scenario assumes that there are limits to growth and current drivers or trends will reach a plateau in the future, or certain drivers (e.g. new government regulations or changes in societal values) will constrain the system's growth. In systems thinking terms, systems reach their equilibrium.

The *Decline and Collapse* scenario considers disruptive events in the future or a change that will lead to the stagnation or collapse of the system. Quite often it is considered as the worst-case scenario although that is not always the case. However, it is important to consider this future and the conditions for it to happen in order to think about how it can be prevented if it is an undesirable scenario.

The *Transformation* scenario assumes that a significant change in the future, such as a disruptive technology or event, will take the development in a new direction or lead to growth in an unexpected direction. This might lead to a whole reorganization of a system, or the creation of new systems. Examples of such disruptive events in the past include the invention of internet, which among others led to the development of new markets, new working practices, new ways for people to communicate with each other, etc. If tomorrow a new source of energy is developed that is clean, abundant and cheap, this will transform the energy and other systems and help solve many of the climate change issues.

Let us look at how such scenarios might look in the context of electric heavy-duty vehicles within logistics systems. The case study below will demonstrate how the scenario archetypes described above can be applied in practice. Drivers and signals discussed in the previous section are useful indicators of what different scenarios and adjacent systems might look like.

CASE STUDY A systems thinking case study

Decarbonization of road freight is a much-debated topic, with competing solutions yet to determine the future of the current logistics systems. The most well-developed competing solutions include electric trucks with batteries, electric trucks with electric overhead lines and hydrogen trucks.

In the **growth** scenario for electric vehicles, the current technologies will continue to be developed to make vehicles as well as renewable energy cheaper to lower the energy tipping point for delivery businesses to make the necessary investments and renew their fleets. In some countries, governments have already passed laws to stop the production and distribution of fossil fuel engine vehicles by a set date, and if this trend continues, new infrastructure will be developed to support a more widespread adoption of electric vehicles. In 2022 we observed a major disruption in the oil and gas market, making gas more expensive. Since hydrogen is predominantly produced from natural gas, it makes the operating costs of hydrogen vehicles much higher. If this trend continues, it will limit the potential growth of the competing technology, hydrogen trucks and the necessary infrastructure, for example refuelling stations. Therefore, the electrification of road freight will continue to grow.

In the **limits and discipline** scenario, the growth of electric vehicles in road freight might be constrained by the adverse effects of climate change. In particular, if the weather becomes more unpredictable, and frequent extreme weather events disrupt local renewable power generation and the grid, this will create disruptions in the operations of electric trucks, making fuel-powered trucks, such as hydrogen trucks, look more reliable.

Decline and collapse can be driven by various trends. In particular, the exponential increase in demand for lithium might lead to tensions between the countries rich in this resource and those producing electric vehicles, as well as competition between producers over the supply of the scarce resource. This might create local and international conflicts, with countries holding the largest deposits at the heart of it, similar to the conflicts we observe over oil and gas resources and infrastructure. Currently we can observe the trend towards more conscientious consumers demanding transparency from the supply chain and favouring products that are ethically produced. With this trend growing, an increasing number of consciously concerned customers might organize large campaigns to boycott companies that use electric trucks with batteries made using the conflict metal. With the reputation of electric vehicles tainted, many companies may revert to hydrogen or even back to combustion engine trucks. Electric trucks with overhead electric lines might still withstand the competition, but as their use is limited to highways and they require large additional investment in infrastructure, they alone might not be sufficient and the system of electrification of road freight might collapse.

In the **transformation** scenario, rapid reconfiguration of the system is likely to happen with the development of a new technology. For example, if new technology for battery storage is created and developed to a point of successful commercialization, reduced need for expensive and toxic lithium batteries will make electric trucks and electric vehicles more broadly significantly more attractive. Another aspect of this system that might lead to a transformational impact has to do with energy generation. If a more reliable source of green energy is developed that is cheap and reliable, e.g. fusion energy, this will also lead to a rapid electrification of road freight.

Reflective questions

Once you have developed future scenarios, you can start analysing: which future seems more likely, which future seems most desirable, who is likely to benefit from each of the scenarios, who is likely to suffer in each of these futures? You might want to use the CATWOE framework discussed in Chapter 6 to help answer some of these questions. Then you might want to analyse what disruptions each of the scenarios might cause and how you can prepare for them. And from there, you will be able to start designing a system using the methods that we have covered in the previous chapters in order to design how a future system might look.

10.6 Gaming the future

In this section we would like to introduce a more creative way of thinking about the future. You can play games as a way to elicit thoughts about the future from different stakeholders or as a tool playing out different scenarios using games. If you think about it, when a gamer plays a game, they repeatedly fail and try new approaches to succeed next time. In essence, they repeatedly develop hypotheses and try them out, and this is how they get better at the game. In multiplayer games, the multiplayer component creates complexity, as it is not only our decisions but also the decisions that other players make that have an impact on the outcome. In a way, the future is like a game and play is the highest form of learning.

There are two dominant approaches to thinking about the future: **roleplay** and **alternate reality games**, both of which have been used in innovation (Shpakova et al, 2019).

Roleplay emphasizes different types of stakeholders. In these games the players assume different roles (of different stakeholders) and try to play them out through a scenario or within a system bound by rules and with an end purpose, e.g. to come to a consensus. This approach helps us to empathize with stakeholders other than ourselves by stepping in their shoes within the boundaries of the game. For that reason it has been widely used in innovation as an approach to understanding different types of customers when designing a new offering (Agogué et al, 2015) and is proposed for use in scenario planning for interrogating scenarios (Cairns and Wright, 2017).

Without a doubt, it can prove very useful to understand the perspective of others and can even initiate a discussion between different stakeholders. For instance, this approach has successfully been used to help policy makers in European countries start designing a Marine Spatial Plan (Abspoel et al, 2021). Through the structured roleplay facilitated by a large gameboard, they were able to understand competing marine interests of not only different sectors, but also different countries that might be reliant on some sectors more than others. For instance, the En-ROADS simulator covered in the previous chapter can be used as part of the roleplaying game, whereby the players assume the roles of different governments, industries and associations. Each of them wants to lobby their interests; they can propose policies but also veto the proposals of others. They are offered the opportunity to negotiate with each other and explore different trade-offs to reach the common goal of curbing climate change. From our experience of playing it with students, we observed that they were able to gain a more balanced perspective on the issue and understand better the worldviews and interests of different stakeholders, particularly those negatively associated with climate change, such as the oil and gas sector.

Roleplay can yield useful results in terms of understanding how actors might respond to the changes. Research has shown that even though players might not have personal experience of the stakeholder they play, through interactions they manage to reach a good approximation. However, from this perspective, roleplay still has limits. Although we might approximate what others might think if we have had an encounter with them, like those in our cultural environment, we might arrive at naïve conclusions when playing out those we know nothing about. For example, if we have never encountered an indigenous person, it will be much more difficult for us to step in their shoes, even if we are given a detailed script. This is what makes the second type of game more compelling.

Alternate reality games suggest that the players assume the role of themselves, but instead the reality around them changes through the gameplay and they are invited to share how they might respond to these changes and how they think the immediate environment around them will change. This approach is different from the roleplay discussed in Chapter 6, because while in Chapter 6 people are asked to play out what has happened and usually happens, in alternate reality games people play themselves in an imaginary future based on prompts of what it might look like. In futures thinking this approach allows us to gather ideas based on progressive scenarios that use signals as triggers of change. We can learn two things by employing this approach.

Firstly, we can learn about new interconnections between different systems and how a change in one system might affect and change other systems in unpredictable ways. When such games gather a diverse group of people, they will give different dimensions to the problem, perspectives and ideas you would not have thought of before. These opinions and discussions can then be clustered and analysed as future potential signals and trends.

One of the big advocates of this approach is a futurist and game designer, Jane McGonigal. She refers to them as social simulations and organizes them as massive multiplayer games. One of the first games she organized was called World Without Oil, which simulated how the world would change if oil demand exceeded supply and this trend continued over a period of eight months (McGonigal, 2011). The participants were invited to register on a dedicated social network and each day they receive an update, e.g. that fuel prices rose or a certain region started experiencing fuel shortages. The players posted all sorts of ideas and discussed with each other how different situations would play out. For instance, someone suggested that public transport will become more popular and others started discussing that in those places where it is particularly underdeveloped, such as Denver and Atlanta, the public transport network will be overwhelmed. Interestingly, when fuel prices spiked one year later, this is exactly what happened. Even though some people claimed that nobody could have predicted such an impact, this impact was predicted through McGonigal's game.

Secondly, such games can help us learn about the behaviour of people or organizations, and what they might do as opposed to what we think would be logical for them to do. These insights might then be fed back into the models of systems, increasing their fidelity. Additionally, we can build gamified simulations to help stakeholders play out different futures (Glenn and Gordon, 2009) and expose them to different experiences that they cannot obtain in real life, because that would require living different futures. If real stakeholders play within the same simulation, their actions will create an emergent behaviour and lead to an alternative future from which they can learn.

10.7 Summary

In this chapter we have discussed creativity and innovation, and summarized the five constraints that prevent us from being innovative about the systems we are concerned with and that might also hinder thinking about possible futures. We then discussed futures thinking as a way to imagine how systems might look in the future and key components of the work of futurists, signals and drivers. Then we looked at scenario thinking and discussed different scenario archetypes and how they can help us think about alternative futures. Finally, we discussed how games can be used to elicit thoughts about alternative futures from different stakeholders.

REFLECTIVE EXERCISE

This exercise consists of two parts. For the first part of this exercise, take a look at Figure 10.3 and describe what you see.

The purpose of the first part of this exercise is to reflect on different perspectives and underlying assumptions. If you do this exercise in a group, you will see that everybody has a slightly different view of the same picture. It is fairly common that the participants will describe six dots, a die or even a domino. Much less frequently people will comment on the title of the figure or its font, the page it is printed on or even the fact that the figure is in a book.

One lesson from this reflective exercise is that people look at the same thing, but they can describe it in different ways. There is another reflection from this

Figure 10.3 Six dots

exercise, and it is about underlying assumptions. If you look back at the question, it asks you to describe what you see. If you read this book from the screen, very rarely will you comment on the navigation or menu buttons on your screen. Most participants will subconsciously automatically focus on the dots and assume that the question was referring to the six dots.

Part of learning about systems thinking is to get people to look at the whole system. And one of the reasons that prevents us from looking at the whole system is that we have some underlying assumptions about systems. We tend to focus on certain things without questioning our assumptions. And depending on the perspective these assumptions might be different for different people. One of the objectives of this book is to help you develop a habit of taking a step back and asking yourself if what you are looking at and seeing is the right thing to focus on, e.g. the dots, the page, the book and so on. Perhaps you should be looking at a bigger picture.

For the second part we would like to ask you to come up with a solution for how to join the dots with a single straight line. Please take a moment and try to complete this exercise.

For example, you might take a very big, thick line and draw them together. This is a perfectly valid solution, because we did not tell you what the thickness of the line should be. Or perhaps you might suggest folding the paper to bring the dots together, and then drawing a line. That is also right, because we did not say that you cannot fold the paper. We also did not say that you cannot move the dots.

If you try to do this exercise with your friends while at a restaurant, it takes a few minutes before somebody says, can I use a thick line? Or somebody starts folding the paper. But it is interesting that the majority of people will sit there for quite a while, trying to join the dots using a single line. Based on what they have heard, they automatically assume that they are not allowed to fold the paper, because that will be cheating. Or they are not allowed to move the dots, that's also cheating. They also assume that the point of the pen they are using is the only pen they can use.

The key message behind this exercise is that we do certain things and there are underlying, unwritten assumptions we make about systems. This exercise is a very simple problem – joining six dots together in a single straight line. That is the only constraint you have. But very quickly, we start putting other assumptions around it.

What can we learn from this about trials and barriers to innovation, thinking innovatively about the system? A lot of the barriers and drivers to innovation are in our minds. For example, if you ask yourself to come up with a new idea, you are fixated on the novelty. Instead you can ask yourself to come up with an idea.

TEAM EXERCISE: REFLECTIONS ON AN ORGANIZATION

In Chapter 8 you were asked to take a system within your organization and analyse the impact of the external environment, such as climate change, on this system. Based on this analysis you were asked to build a causal loop diagram. Using your improved understanding of this system, try to think about signals and trends that might impact it. Perhaps you have read something interesting in a magazine that might be a signal of change. Then try to think about the driving force behind this signal. Then think about other trends you have observed in your industry or adjacent industries. Engage with the questions proposed for analysing the trends and signals. Using the identified trends, compose four scenarios for the system. Engage with the questions proposed to analyse the scenarios. Now, look at the causal loop diagram that you designed and think about how it might change in each of the scenarios.

References

Abspoel, L, Mayer, I, Keijser, X, Warmelink, H, Fairgrieve, R, Ripken, M, Abramic, A, Kannen, A, Cormier, R and Kidd, S (2021) Communicating maritime spatial planning: the MSP challenge approach, *Marine Policy*, **132**, 103486

Agogué, M, Levillain, K and Hooge, S (2015) Gamification of creativity: exploring the usefulness of serious games for ideation, *Creativity & Innovation Management*, **24** (3), pp. 415–29

Cairns, G and Wright, G (2017) *Scenario Thinking: Preparing your organization for the future in an unpredictable world*, Springer.

Courtney, H, Lovallo, D and Clarke, C (2013) Deciding how to decide, *Harvard Business Review*, **91** (11), p. 62

Dator, J (2009) Alternative futures at the Manoa School, *Journal of Futures Studies*, **14** (2), www.futures.hawaii.edu (archived at https://perma.cc/DM2M-9DRQ)

Glenn, JC and Gordon, TJ (2009) *Futures Research Methodology 3.0*, The Millennium Project

Howard, S (2021) *Drivers and Signals: How are they different?* Institute for the Future, https://legacy.iftf.org/future-now/article-detail/drivers-and-signals-how-are-they-different/?p=future-now/article-detail/drivers-and-signals-how-are-they-different/ (archived at https://perma.cc/6M7R-YK4F)

McGonigal, J (2011) *Reality is Broken: Why games make us better and how they can change the world*, The Penguin Press

Shpakova, A, Dörfler, V and MacBryde, J (2019) Gamifying the process of innovating, *Innovation: Organization & Management*, **22** (4), pp. 488–502

Taleb, NN (2007) *The Black Swan: The impact of the highly improbable* (Vol. 2), Random House

Wilkinson, A and Kupers, R (2013) Living in the futures, *Harvard Business Review*, **91** (5), pp. 118–27

Summary and key takeaways 11

This book has introduced you to the foundations of systems thinking. We started by discussing why systems thinking is important and a life skill that will be useful to people from all walks of life. It is essential because in our world systems do not exist in isolation but are rather connected with each other in ways we do not always understand. Such connections can produce emergent behaviours, and if we ignore this interconnectedness, making changes in one system might produce unintended consequences in other systems. Life is full of such examples, and we demonstrated this interconnectedness with examples from the financial crisis in 2008 and the attempt to control malaria-carrying mosquitos in Borneo with the DDT pesticide that led to unintended consequences of rooftops collapsing, destruction of grain stores and outbreaks of plague.

Systems thinking can help us to at least partially understand this complexity and anticipate such consequences, because it teaches us to look at issues as part of a larger system and examine how different parts of a system might affect each other. Once we understand how things are connected within one system and between the systems, we can attempt to change the system by introducing controlled interventions. We can also anticipate how such interventions will impact the system.

In this book we have focused mostly on the business and management context, because regardless of your position, your work contributes to the wider goal of your organization. Organizations are complex social systems consisting of individuals and groups of people interacting with each other and with material and informational assets to produce flows that result in emergent behaviours. Furthermore, you and your organization exist as part of wider systems, e.g. industry, regulatory, societal and economic systems, and thinking in systems will help you understand why organizations reproduce certain behaviours and how you can attempt to change them. In this book, in covering systems thinking from a business and management perspective, we placed emphasis on soft systems, i.e. human-centred systems, where people and their unpredictable emergent behaviours influence virtually all systems we are interested in.

To demonstrate the applicability of systems thinking in a business context, we introduced a case study on the supply system between an international chemical manufacturing company producing dynamite and quarries that use dynamite to mine rocks for gravel. In this case, we showed that if a problem is seen in isolation, e.g. how to improve the efficiency of transporting dynamite, the solution will be different from looking at the chemical manufacturer as part of a wider system of their customers' operations. The former would result in incremental improvements to the process of producing and transporting dynamite. The latter resulted in changing the business model of the company from producing a product (a dynamite) to delivering a service of blowing up rock using significantly more efficient mobile manufacturing units.

11.1 Part One: Fundamentals of systems thinking

In the first part of the book, we introduced the fundamental concepts and definitions that underpin systems thinking, starting from a system itself. **A system is a collection of interacting parts/components/actors, in which the interactions result in system-level properties and behaviours not attributable to the sum of individual parts**. In other words, the whole is 'bigger' than the sum of its parts. If we apply this logic to the collections of things around us, we will see that not everything is a system. For example, sand scattered on the side of the road is not a system, because it does not lead to emergent properties as a result of different pieces of sand interacting with each other. As such, interactions are important and interactions between systems can lead to emergent behaviour as much as the interactions of different parts within the system.

Systems can be characterized in a variety of ways. For example, we can look at systems as open and closed. **Open systems** interact with the surrounding environment, **closed systems** do not; however, it is very difficult to find closed systems outside of lab experiments, as most systems will interact with the environment at least to a degree.

Systems can be hard or soft. **Hard systems** have high-integrity components that interact through well-understood patterns and reproduce predictable behaviours. Deviations from expected behaviour can be compensated through feedback loops using technical controls. **Soft systems** are composed of autonomous agents that are characterized by high variety of change and unpredictable behaviours. Social systems are an example of soft systems, and many hard systems are embedded into soft systems.

In this part we introduced the concept of complexity that we continued to explore throughout the book. Complex systems cannot be understood by simply studying separate parts individually, as their interactions can be influenced by the whole range of external factors, producing unpredictable behaviour. They tend to be hierarchical, but we can find examples of **self-organizing systems** that, through a set of simple rules, can produce complex behaviours.

All systems have a **function** (how it does things); however, not all systems have a **purpose** (what it does), or at least it might not be obvious to us. A system interacts with its environment through **inputs** and **outputs**. Inputs **flow** through the system and are transformed into outputs. Some of the specific inputs include **resources** that are consumed by the function, and **controls** that define the parameters within which the system needs to function. The flows that come into the system originate from **stocks**, which either exist within the system or come from outside the system. Their relation to the system is defined by the boundary of the system. Apart from flows, the connections between different parts of the system as well as between different systems can be understood through **causal relationships**, which sometimes form **feedback loops**.

Finally, systems without an intrinsic or extrinsic control system tend to move from order to disorder. This phenomenon is known as **entropy**. An example of this phenomenon is a neat garden that is left unattended and gradually falls into disarray. The opposite of entropy is a phenomenon called **homeostasis**, which describes an ability of a system to maintain its steady state and performance.

11.2 Part Two: Models and methods

In the second part of the book, we introduced the theories and frameworks that can help to conceptualize and understand a system, and different methods that can be used to model a system. Different theories and frameworks approach conceptualization of a system from different perspectives. For example, **Miller's Living Systems Theory** positions a system within a hierarchy of other systems, starting from a cell and organ and going up to the society and supernational level.

Beer's Viable Systems Model focuses on the mechanism through which systems self-produce. Beer devised a generic structure of a viable system that comprises five subsystems (referred to as systems). Different parts of the system form System 1s and they communicate with each other through System 2. Systems 3, 4 and 5 form the management of the system, wherein System 3 provides controls, System 4 monitors the surrounding environment and System 5 sets out the direction of the whole system. Similarly, **Hitchens' Systems Architecture** focuses on a system's viability and defines how a system's architecture, i.e. how various parts of the system are organized within the system, supports its purpose and function and ensures its viability through maintenance and evolution (self-production/creation).

Deming's System of Profound Knowledge helps us to understand and predict the behaviour of a system. What makes this framework different from others is that it emphasizes variations in behaviour of different parts of a system as essential components of the system. It is these variations and the interactions between them that make the behaviour of the system difficult to predict.

In line with the distinction between the hard and soft systems, we can approach the modelling of the same system using a **hard systems thinking** mindset, i.e. assuming that the behaviour of the system is predictable, or a **soft systems thinking** mindset, i.e. assuming that the system has unpredictable behaviour and consists of autonomous agents that are connected through a loosely defined dynamic web of relationships.

In the organizational context, hard systems thinking is often applied to organizational processes, and depending on the objective of modelling, different methods may be suitable. For instance, **flowcharts** are the most generic method that can be utilized in many different contexts and are often used to map out different steps in the process. Other methods resemble flowcharts. For example, **swim lane process maps** have an added emphasis on which functions are responsible for which steps in the process. **Data flow diagrams** have a more standardized choice of symbols and are used specifically to map out the flow of data through the process.

The **structured systems analysis and design method** is a further development from data flow diagrams. It exists in different variations, and the most relevant type for the organizational context is IDEF0, or the functional modelling approach. It uses inputs, controls, outputs and mechanisms (ICOM) to model the relationships between entities, where an output from an entity can be an input, control or a mechanism for another entity. Depending on the needs of the system's analyst, each entity can be modelled further in greater detail in the next level of analysis.

Similar to other methods, **value stream mapping** is used to map out the process, but the focus of this method is on determining which steps add value and which do not, with the subsequent purpose to reduce non-value-adding activities. As such, this method does not have a standardized way of representing process elements. Instead, it is a thinking approach to minimizing waste (of resources) that stems from lean manufacturing.

If we approach modelling of a system using soft systems thinking, the overarching approach is referred to as **Soft Systems Methodology**. It consists of a set of iterative steps that form an interplay between real-world thinking and systems thinking. It starts with exploring the real world and the problem that exists. It then focuses on applying systems thinking methods to conceptualize the world and the problem to gain better understanding of the problem. It then finishes with exploring potential solutions based on the newly gained understanding of the problem, and taking action to address the problem.

Some of the methods that can be useful in this process include rich pictures, storytelling and roleplay, and causal loop diagrams. **Rich pictures** are a free-form way of conceptualizing a complex system and are often used in the early stages to help creators to engage more deeply with the system, as well as explore the differences in the worldviews of different creators. **Storytelling** and **roleplay** are in essence a narrative of what is really happening in the system, and are used to explore different perspectives to reveal soft aspects of the system that are not captured by hard systems thinking approaches.

Causal loop diagrams are a more structured method that illustrates the causal relationships between the entities within a system. In a diagram, entities are described in words as statements and are linked with each other using arrows that represent causal relationships between them. The causal relationships can form reinforcing and balancing feedback loops. These feedback loops help to conceptualize the system and understand why certain behaviours in the system persist and how they can potentially be changed.

A development of causal loop diagrams is the **causal mapping** method, which uses a more structured approach to organizing entities into hierarchies. It starts from the problem to be addressed or key objectives in the middle, and then helps explore higher-level goals or the consequences of problems if left unaddressed on the top, and alternative approaches to addressing problems or achieving goals at the bottom. Such a structured method is particularly useful in problem structuring and exploring solutions to a problem when working within groups, as it helps negotiate the meanings, explore different viewpoints and build consensus.

The objective of this book is not to provide you with an exhaustive list of methods, but rather to suggest those methods that are commonly used in addressing issues in the organizational context. These are the methods that we find most useful based on our experience.

11.3 Part Three: Systems complexity

In the third part of the book, we explored systems complexity in greater detail. Most methods introduced in Part Two help us understand a system in its present state, and although they can infer future behavioural patterns from the relationships between different parts and emergent properties, in more complex systems this can be increasingly difficult. Future behaviour of such systems can be studied by building a model, the behaviour of which can be simulated over time. One of the most commonly used methods for simulating behaviour of complex systems is called **system dynamics**.

System dynamics builds on causal loop diagrams. In this method, we take as a basis conceptualization of the system in the form of a causal loop. We can then add stocks and flows in the model, and quantify relationships between different entities through mathematical/statistical equations. The model can then be simulated over time, and the behaviour that the system exhibits over time is called a dynamic. Stocks and flows are the basic building blocks of a system dynamics model. A **stock** is a variable that is measured at a specific period in time, while a **flow** is a measurement of an entity over time.

In a model of a complex system with multiple stocks and flows, and non-linear relationships determining the rates of different flows, the behaviour of the system can change over time. However, there are common behavioural patterns (dynamics) observed in such systems. The system can exhibit the **economy of scale dynamic**, a behaviour that is powered by a reinforcing loop. For instance, improvements in renewable technology might lead to reduced costs of renewable energy, which will stimulate investments that will further improve the technology.

Many systems that can be modelled through stocks and flows will exhibit a **bathtub dynamic**, whereby the difference between the inflow and outflow of an entity will lead to its constant accumulation or depletion. Systems can exhibit a **squeezing the balloon dynamic**, whereby an attempt to reduce the use of one entity leads to an increase in the use of substitute entities instead of an overall reduction in the use of similar entities. Systems might be affected by a **time lag**, that is the time it takes for an intervention to have an effect. In some systems we can observe a **rebound effect**, whereby the changes in one part of the system might lead to unintended changes in the flow elsewhere. For example, reducing the cost of renewable energy might lead to an increase in energy consumption, which will lessen the impact of renewables on GHG emissions. Finally, a system can demonstrate a **crowding out dynamic**, whereby the cumulative impact of two interventions is smaller than the sum of the individual impacts of each intervention separately.

When we understand how a complex system behaves over time, we might start thinking about how to change the system's behaviour, and to do that, we can identify levers or pressure points, affecting what may produce the desired effect. We have introduced four categories of levers that you might be looking for. The easiest to identify are the **structural levers**. They are the structural components of the system and include stocks, flows as well as reinforcing and balancing feedback loops. We can change them by either changing the numerical values of the parameters that determine the rates of flows, introducing a buffer, or intervening into feedback loops. Similar to structural levers are **temporal levers**. They are pressure points that engage with changing delays in a system. Most often we would like to reduce delays in the system; however, sometimes introducing a delay might be desirable.

The most difficult to change are **boundary levers**. They determine the rules of the system, but changing them will have a more significant effect on a system's behaviour. Finally, the most powerful are **conceptual levers**. They determine the goals of the system or subsystems or the underlying assumptions that influence the behaviour of the system. They will have the most profound impact on a system's behaviour.

11.4 Part Four: The future

In the fourth part of the book, we discuss how you can think about future systems or the systems that do not exist yet. Imagining the future is linked to creativity and innovation, the two terms complementary to each other. While **creativity is about coming up with ideas, innovation is about turning them into something useful**. One aspect that is particularly relevant to systems thinking is barriers and constraints to creativity and innovation. We might be constrained with how we **define innovation**, that is whether we have to come up with new ideas or just ideas. We might need **psychological safety**, or permission, to create ideas. We have to recognize that **innovation is a group process**, whereby people build ideas on those of others. **Lack of diversity** in a group can constrain creativity. And finally, our **subconscious assumptions** and worldviews can also limit the ideas we create.

When thinking about the future or trying to imagine a system that does not yet exist, identifying signals and drivers can help give directions. Signals are observable examples of a change that might happen, but are not commonplace yet, while drivers are the trends or the force that power the signals and help explain what kind of change might happen in the future.

When we combine signals and trends together, we can start thinking about the future in terms of scenarios. When thinking about the future, it is more useful to try to imagine alternative futures rather than predict the future that will happen. Then we can start proactively thinking about how to make the more desirable future happen, and how to safeguard from the undesirable future. Thus it is important to imagine different types of future, no matter how unlikely they are.

A useful classification of scenarios includes four future archetypes: Growth, Limits and Discipline, Decline and Collapse, and Transformation. The **Growth** scenario assumes that the current trends will continue. **Limits and Discipline** assumes that the current trends will be constrained by something in the future. **Decline and Collapse** suggests that a significant disruption will lead to stagnation or collapse of the system. **Transformation** suggests that a significant disruption will develop a system in a new direction.

When thinking about the future, you can adopt a more creative approach. You can play games as a way to elicit thoughts about the future from different stakeholders or as a tool playing out different scenarios using games. In **roleplay**, the players assume different roles (of different stakeholders) and try to play them out through a scenario or within a system bound by rules and with an end purpose, e.g. to come to a consensus. This approach helps us to understand the perspective of 'others'. In contrast, in **alternate reality games** the players stay themselves, but instead the reality around them changes through the gameplay and they are invited to share how they might respond to these changes and how they think the immediate environment around them will change. This approach helps to gather ideas about how the future might change.

11.5 Limitations of systems thinking

From a business and management perspective, we have extensively discussed complex social systems, organizations being one of them, that consist of individuals and groups of people interacting with each other and non-human elements of the systems, resulting in emergent behaviour. In this book, we emphasized people's perspectives, and it is important to note that, from a business and management perspective, people and their emergent behaviours influence virtually all systems, while the behaviour of a system is shaped by people's behaviour. And this extends to how systems thinking is applied.

Humans decide on the system's boundaries, i.e. what is inside and what is outside the system, and what the system's key factors and interactions are. If different people have different views, they might see different systems. It would be reasonable to ask then to what extent human behaviour undermines the outcome of applying the principles of systems thinking. Some might even suggest that the systems thinking approach is inappropriate for human organizations, because individuals attempt to understand social systems that are of a higher level of complexity than them.

It might appear that systems thinking takes an 'outside-in' (the observer) view, and thus it does not accommodate the flexible agency associated with human action and interactions. However, when engaging with the process of understanding the system, we can rarely claim to be a complete outsider. Furthermore, a single person's view is almost certainly biased. By bringing together more views, we attempt to develop a more complete understanding of the system.

11.6 Conclusion

This book has provided the foundations of systems thinking and introduced you to various theories, frameworks and methods that will help you to look at things more holistically, within a wider system. Thinking in systems is an essential skill in the complex modern world, and the context of business and management is no exception. Seeing connections within and between systems can help you understand better the complexity of the world around you and address problems more effectively. After having read the book, you are equipped with the basic skills of thinking in systems.

The tools provided in the book are by no means an exhaustive list of theories, methods and frameworks; however, now you are equipped with the knowledge to continue exploring this discipline yourself. For instance, there is a new systems thinking movement called Awareness-based Systems Thinking (Koenig et al, 2021) created by Peter Senge and Otto Scharmer (Koenig having made a considerable contribution to popularizing the field) and embraced by the United Nations Development Programme (Blanchard and Mukerjee, 2022). This approach combines mindfulness with systems thinking in order to 'sense the future that wants to emerge' by tapping into our attention and intention. As systems collapse, we do not yet recognize the new systems that will replace them because they will be so radically different. You cannot fix current problems with the thinking that created them. This and other approaches can enrich your understanding of the surrounding complexity and help make our world a better place to be.

To conclude, systems thinking is an essential life skill.

References

Blanchard, V and Mukerjee, D (2022) Awareness-based system change as the basis for transforming systems and social norms, UNDP Global Policy Network Brief, 1–6

Koenig, O, Seneque, M, Pomeroy, E and Scharmer, O (2021) Journal of Awareness-Based Systems Change: The Birth of a Journal, *Journal of Awareness-Based Systems Change*, **1** (1), pp. 1–8

GLOSSARY

actuality what the system is able to do now with existing resources and under existing constraints.

algedonic signal a pre-emptive message concerning pleasure or pain that provides an important survival mechanism to a system by alerting it to an imminent threat.

alternate reality games the type of games whereby the players assume the role of themselves, while the reality around them changes through the gameplay and they are invited to share how they might respond to these changes and how they think the immediate environment around them will change.

assets what an organization has.

autocracy a governance structure based around centralized command and control of organizations.

autopoiesis the ability of systems to reproduce certain behaviours by repeating their own operations.

balancing loop in a system is a feedback loop that reduces or eliminates the effect of the reinforcing loop.

bathtub dynamic the effect of accumulated change in the stock, if the rates of inflow and outflow are constant, but different in absolute values.

boundary levers pressure points that engage with changing the rules of a system.

buffer additional stock in a system that compensates for the disruptions in the flow.

bureaucracy a governance structure based around the well-established hierarchical control of organizations.

capability what the system is able to do now with existing resources and constraints, if it really worked at it.

capital stock turnover dynamic the effect of impact delay of the intervention on the system, e.g. due to the lifecycle of existing infrastructure.

CATWOE acronym that stands for Customers, Actors, Transformation, Worldview, Owners and Environmental Constraints, which defines the key parts we need to consider when analysing and modelling soft systems.

causality the influence of one part of a system on another part through the interconnections.

centrality entitles or statements that demonstrate the highest impact on a system through high degrees of connections.

closed system a system that does not interact with the environment.
cloud the source or sink of the flow.
competence outcomes what an organization achieves.
competences what an organization does.
complex system a system that can only be understood as a whole with different parts woven together.
complicated system a system that can be understood in parts with predictable behaviour that is based on the behaviour of each part.
conceptual levers pressure points that question the goals and the underlying assumptions/beliefs in a system.
constraint anything that prevents a system from achieving its goal.
control system a system that regulates the behaviour of other systems using a feedback signals system. A control system can be internal to the system it is managing, e.g. the blood sugar control systems in human bodies, or external to the system.
control(s) the internal or external rule(s) that order, limit or guide a system's actions. In terms of systems, controls are often seen as the levers managers and/or owners of a system could manipulate to change the behaviour of a system, e.g. increasing or lowering taxes is a control lever for managing the rate of inflation by controlling the spending power of individuals.
creativity the ability to create ideas.
crowding out dynamic the effect of partial substitution of one flow with another if the impact they produce is similar.
distinctive assets (DA) assets that can be exploited to achieve distinctive competences.
distinctive competence outcomes (DCO) competence outcomes that support business goals directly.
distinctive competences (DC) competences that develop through networks of relationships between competences and organizational purpose.
drivers the underlying trend behind the signals driving the change.
economy of scale dynamic the effect of accelerated growth of the flow when it gains a critical mass.
effectiveness the performance dimension that measures how well the system meets its expectations, standards or requirements.
efficiency the performance dimension that measures the number of resources a system consumes through its function in producing its useful outputs.
emergence the behavioural properties of the system that are caused by the interactions and relationships between elements rather than by the elements themselves.
entropy the natural tendency of systems to move towards disorder or disorganization.

escalating cycles reinforcing feedback loops.

feedback/reinforcing loops when a change in something ultimately comes back to cause a further change in the same thing.

flow the quantity that can be measured over a period of time.

flow rate the flow in or out of the stock per unit of time.

function of a system how the system carries out or delivers its purpose. Different systems may use different functions to deliver the same purpose.

hard system a system consisting of high-integrity components that are connected through well-understood interaction patterns producing predictable behaviours.

hard systems thinking a way of thinking about systems where the analyst/thinker assumes that systems behave as hard systems.

heads/higher-level goals the statements that do not have outgoing links and represent strategic goals.

holacracy a form of organization that distributes authority and decision making through a network of self-organized teams that are bound together with a shared purpose and common set of goals and rules.

homeostasis the state of a system that is in dynamic equilibrium or in a steady state condition.

human behaviour how people behave in a given context/circumstance, or how people respond to change.

innovation the process of turning ideas into something useful.

inputs tangible or intangible resources that are processed and transformed through the system.

interconnections a direct connection between two parts of a system for the purpose of enabling flows.

inventory the accumulation of work through the system.

laddering up and down building a causal map by asking why [this issue is important] and how [this issue can be addressed].

levers control points in a system, where small changes will lead to changes in the system's behaviour.

link dependency between different elements of the system.

living system a system that integrates divergent parts into a convergent whole in dynamic relationships internally and externally in an ongoing process of self-organization and self-creation.

messy problem a problem that is poorly defined and does not have a single correct solution, but rather a 'good enough' solution.

netocracy a governance structure based on a self-managing and self-organizing network.

open strategy a strategy built using a bottom-up approach involving managers at different levels in the organization.

open system a system that interacts with the environment.

operating expenses the resources the system consumes to turn inventory into throughput.

outputs produced by the system in line with its function and its purpose.

paradigm unwritten assumptions and beliefs underpinning a system.

perceived complexity the view of how stakeholders see a system and its complexity.

potentiality what the system should be achieving if it developed its resources and removed its constraints.

purpose of a system why a system exists or what it does.

rebound effect dynamic the effect of an unintended change in the flow in one part of the system as a consequence of changes in constraints in another part of the system cause by an intervention.

reinforcing loop a feedback loop in a system that reinforces its current behaviour.

resilient systems systems that are able to return to a stable state in response to a disturbance.

resources (also a form of input) tangible or intangible resources consumed by the function of the system.

robust systems systems that are able to maintain their performance in response to a disturbance.

roleplay the type of games whereby the players assume different roles and try to play them out through a scenario or within a system bound by rules and with an end purpose.

root definition the statement of purpose for a system that clearly identifies the transformation that is performed by the system to deliver its purpose.

scenarios possible alternative futures.

self-correcting cycles balancing feedback loops.

self-organization a phenomenon where some form of overall order arises from the interactions between apparently independent autonomous parts of an initially disordered system.

self-production the ability of a system to renew its parts, and in some cases create improved enhanced parts appropriate for the environment within which it operates.

signals concrete and observable examples of the changes that might happen and become widespread in the future.

soft system a system consisting of autonomous agents that are characterized by high variability in and unpredictability of behaviour, and connected through a loosely defined dynamic web of relationships, power structures, shared interests and values.

squeezing the balloon dynamic the effect of partial relocation of the flow to another stock with similar properties instead of the reduction intended by the intervention.

statement of strategic intent (SSI) a report written after a strategy-making workshop and defining goals, strategic issues and actions resulting from the workshop.

stock the quantity that is measured at a particular point in time.

strong emergence the behaviour of a system that is more difficult to explain, model or predict.

structural levers pressure points that are connected to the structural elements in a system.

system a collection of interacting parts/components/actors, in which the interactions result in system-level properties and behaviours not attributable to the sum of individual parts.

system boundary a conceptual and somewhat artificial line drawn by the manager or analyst that separates the system that we want to study from everything else.

system dynamics the behaviour that systems exhibit over time.

systems of systems higher-level systems that comprise several subsystems.

system performance the effectiveness and efficiency of a system.

system reference model an abstract framework consisting of an interlinked set of clearly defined concepts to encourage clear communication.

systems architecture the pattern made by all the subsystems and their interconnections to support the function, purpose and performance of the system.

systems within systems/subsystems systems that exist as parts of larger higher-level systems.

tails/actions the statements that do not have incoming links and represent strategic actions.

tame problem a problem that can be defined and solved.

technical complexity intrinsic properties of a system shaped by its composition, nature of relationships and interactions between the parts and predictability of responses.

temporal levers pressure points that engage with changing delays in a system.

throughput the rate at which the system processes work.

trim-tab the single small change we can make to the system that would change the behaviour of the whole system.

variation a change or difference in form, condition, position or amount.

viable system a system that can self-produce, i.e. renew its parts in order to adapt to changing environmental conditions.

waste anything that customers do not believe adds value and are not willing to pay for.

weak emergence the behaviour of the system that can be explained, modelled or predicted.

wicked problem a problem that cannot be solved but must nevertheless be managed.

worldview underlying assumptions about a system shaped by a person's background, culture, upbringing, education, profession and life experiences.

INDEX